Investing in Cannabis

by Steven R. Gormley

A Wiley Brand

Investing in Cannabis For Dummies®

Published by: **John Wiley & Sons, Inc.**, 111 River Street, Hoboken, NJ 07030-5774, www.wiley.com

Copyright © 2021 by John Wiley & Sons, Inc., Hoboken, New Jersey

Published simultaneously in Canada

For general information on our other products and services, please contact our Customer Care Department within the U.S. at 877-762-2974, outside the U.S. at 317-572-3993, or fax 317-572-4002. For technical support, please visit https://hub.wiley.com/community/support/dummies.

Wiley publishes in a variety of print and electronic formats and by print-on-demand. Some material included with standard print versions of this book may not be included in e-books or in print-on-demand. If this book refers to media such as a CD or DVD that is not included in the version you purchased, you may download this material at http://booksupport.wiley.com. For more information about Wiley products, visit www.wiley.com.

Library of Congress Control Number: 2020952057

ISBN 978-1-119-67476-4 (pbk); ISBN 978-1-119-67478-8 (ebk); ISBN 978-1-119-67474-0 (ebk)

Manufactured in the United States of America

SKY10023579_010421

3 9547 00471 0575

Contents at a Glance

Introduction 1

Part 1: Getting Started with Cannabis Investing 5
CHAPTER 1: Taking the Nickel Tour 7
CHAPTER 2: Exploring Cannabis Business Types 23
CHAPTER 3: Understanding the Political, Cultural, and Regulatory Landscape 39
CHAPTER 4: Sizing Up the Risks and Rewards of Cannabis Investing 57

Part 2: Doing Your Homework 71
CHAPTER 5: Exploring Your Investment Options 73
CHAPTER 6: Digging Up Cannabis Investment Opportunities 89
CHAPTER 7: Researching Cannabis Businesses and Stocks: Fundamental
Analysis 103
CHAPTER 8: Analyzing Market Trends: Technical Analysis 125

**Part 3: Buying and Selling Cannabis Stocks,
ETFs, or Mutual Funds** 147
CHAPTER 9: Choosing a Broker or Advisor 149
CHAPTER 10: Using Screening Tools 161
CHAPTER 11: Placing Buy and Sell Orders for Cannabis Stocks and ETFs 177
CHAPTER 12: Exploring Advanced Trading Techniques 191

Part 4: Exploring Cannabis Investment Strategies 201
CHAPTER 13: Following the Money: Momentum Investing (aka Speculating) 203
CHAPTER 14: Investing in Canadian Cannabis Companies 213
CHAPTER 15: Investing in Countries Where Marijuana Is Legal 221
CHAPTER 16: Minimizing Risks While Maximizing Gains 237

Part 5: The Part of Tens 247
CHAPTER 17: Ten Ways to Profit When the Market Drops 249
CHAPTER 18: Ten Reasons Not to Invest in Marijuana Stocks 255
CHAPTER 19: Ten (Plus One) Criteria for Choosing a Cannabis Investment 261
CHAPTER 20: Ten Mistakes to Avoid 267

Index 273

Table of Contents

INTRODUCTION 1
About This Book. 1
Foolish Assumptions. 2
Icons Used in This Book 3
Beyond the Book. 4
Where to Go from Here 4

PART 1: GETTING STARTED WITH CANNABIS INVESTING 5

CHAPTER 1: Taking the Nickel Tour. 7
Weighing the Pros and Cons of Investing in Cannabis. 8
Pros 8
Cons. 9
Deciding Whether to Invest in Businesses That Touch
the Plant or Those That Don't 11
Exploring Your Investment Options 12
Starting your own business 12
Investing in cannabis real estate. 13
Buying and selling stocks 14
Diversifying with exchange traded funds and mutual funds 15
Considering private investment opportunities. 15
Finding Investment Opportunities 16
Researching Investment Opportunities 17
Planning Your Investment Strategy 19
Investing in a Cannabis Business 20

CHAPTER 2: Exploring Cannabis Business Types 23
Choosing Sides: Medical or Adult-Use? 24
Investing in medical marijuana 24
Investing in adult-use marijuana. 25
Recognizing Different Cannabis Business Types 26
Cultivation. 27
Manufacturing 28
Processed product brand. 30
Retailers/dispensaries. 30
Device makers 31
Considering Ancillary Businesses 31
Breweries 32
Banking, payroll, and other cash management services. 32
Blockchain and other technologies. 34

Delivery services 34
Grow equipment manufacturers and suppliers 35
Marketing, public relations, and advertising firms 35
Professional employer organizations. 36
Pharmaceutical and biotech companies 36
Real estate 37
Security services and security equipment suppliers 38
Software companies 38

CHAPTER 3: **Understanding the Political, Cultural,**
and Regulatory Landscape. 39
Recognizing the Impact of Laws on the Industry 40
Getting up to speed on U.S. federal law and enforcement. 40
Brushing up on state cannabis laws. 44
Considering local laws, too. 45
Examining cannabis laws in other countries. 46
Riding the Waves of Politics and Culture 46
Checking the nation's pulse 47
Debunking misconceptions of cannabis and users 49
Examining activism 50
Tuning into cannabis culture 52
Accounting for the High Costs of Doing Business 53
Regulatory and compliance costs 53
Federal, state, and local taxes 54
Security costs 55

CHAPTER 4: **Sizing Up the Risks and Rewards**
of Cannabis Investing. 57
Weighing the Risks 58
Falling victim to con artists. 58
Investing in an overvalued company 60
Accounting for dilution risks 61
Weighing the risks of potential commoditization. 62
Recognizing the possibility of changes in how federal
marijuana laws are enforced. 63
Considering the impact of state and local regulation
and enforcement. 64
Evaluating risks associated with obtaining banking
and financial services 65
Anticipating the impact of possible supply and demand
imbalances 65
Considering the possibility of business failure 67
Assessing the Potential Rewards. 67
Deciding Whether Investing in Cannabis Is Right for You 68
Considering your investment goals 68
Assessing your own risk tolerance 69

PART 2: DOING YOUR HOMEWORK..........................71

CHAPTER 5: **Exploring Your Investment Options**..................73
  Comparing Public versus Private Investment Options 74
    Understanding how companies raise capital 74
    Investing in private companies 76
    Investing in public companies 78
  Investing Domestically or Abroad? 79
  Investing in Cannabis or Ancillary Businesses?..................81
  Buying and Selling Cannabis Stocks 83
    Going mainstream with listed stocks 83
    Bargain hunting with unlisted, over-the-counter stocks 84
    Diversifying with exchange traded funds....................84
    Betting on an index with exchange traded notes..............86
    What about mutual funds?...............................86
    Buying and selling shares of Canadian cannabis companies 87
  Investing as a Venture Capitalist..............................88

CHAPTER 6: **Digging Up Cannabis Investment Opportunities** ... 89
  Using Online Investment Tools and Apps 90
    Cannabis Stock Trades 91
    Yahoo! Finance..91
    Morningstar 92
    FINVIZ 92
    ETFdb.com 93
    FeeX 93
    FRED 93
    The Marijuana Index 94
    Marijuana Stocks 94
    Barchart 94
    Apps...95
  Staying Abreast of Cannabis Industry News 96
  Scoping Out Opportunities in Exchange Traded Funds...........100
  Finding Private Equity and Venture Capital Funds and Firms.......101
  Getting Investment Leads from a Broker.......................102

CHAPTER 7: **Researching Cannabis Businesses and Stocks: Fundamental Analysis**.................................103
  Grasping Fundamental Analysis Basics 104
  Researching Any Company You're Thinking of Investing in 106
    Assessing the management team........................106
    Evaluating the company's financial health.................109
    Evaluating startups and investments in licenses 111
    Looking at the company's business strategy.................112

Checking out the company's competitive position. 115
Checking any insider buying or selling. 116
Looking into warrants and convertible securities. 117
Following analyst coverage and conference calls. 119
Digging up dirt 120
Evaluating Cannabis Cultivation Businesses 121
Sizing up the grow master 121
Checking a grower's cost per gram. 122
Comparing cost per gram 123
Considering the cultivator's clientele .123

CHAPTER 8: **Analyzing Market Trends: Technical Analysis** 125
Comparing Technical and Fundamental Analysis. 126
Grasping the principles of technical analysis 126
Weighing the pros and cons of technical analysis 128
Combining the best of both worlds 129
Gathering your tools. 130
Spotting and Monitoring Trends. 131
Examining different trends 131
Gauging a trend's length. 134
Following trendlines 134
Looking for resistance and support 135
Referencing Technical Charts 136
Getting to know the different chart types 136
Identifying chart patterns. 138
Interpreting Technical Indicators 143
The Relative Strength Index. 143
The Money Flow Index 144
Moving averages 144
Moving average convergence divergence 144
Bollinger Bands 145

**PART 3: BUYING AND SELLING CANNABIS
STOCKS, ETFS, OR MUTUAL FUNDS**. .147

CHAPTER 9: **Choosing a Broker or Advisor** 149
Defining the Broker's Role 150
Distinguishing between Full-Service and Discount Brokers 150
At your disposal: Full-service brokers. 151
Just the basics: Discount brokers 153
Deciding Whether to Fly Solo or Consult a Broker or Advisor 154
Finding a Cannabis-Savvy Broker or Advisor. 155
Evaluating Brokers and Advisors. 155
Comparing costs 156

Comparing quality and service 156
Checking credentials. 157
Comparing online brokers 158

CHAPTER 10: **Using Screening Tools**. 161
Searching the Marijuana Stock Universe 162
Getting Up to Speed on the Different Exchanges and Markets 165
Browsing through the Daily Marijuana Observer's List
of OTC Cannabis Stocks 167
Checking Out Other Stock Screeners 168
Screening Cannabis Investment Funds 170
What to Screen for 172
First up: The major categories. 172
The main event: Specific filters 173
Valuation measures 175
Financial Highlights 176
A Few Final Points to Keep in Mind. 176

CHAPTER 11: **Placing Buy and Sell Orders for
Cannabis Stocks and ETFs**. 177
Understanding the Bid-Ask Spread. 178
Placing an Order to Buy or Sell Shares. 179
Choosing an Action 182
Buy. 182
Sell 182
Sell all shares 182
Understanding the Different Order Types. .183
Market orders 184
Limit orders 184
Stop orders. 185
Trailing stop orders. 186
Specifying a Timeframe 187
Day. 187
Good till canceled 188
Fill or kill 188
Immediate or cancel 188
Market on open 189
Market on close 189

CHAPTER 12: **Exploring Advanced Trading Techniques**. 191
Buying on Margin 191
Registering to buy on margin 192
Examining marginal outcomes 193
Striving for success on margin. 194

Shorting a Stock. 195
   Setting up a short sale 196
   Taking a hit when the stock price keeps rising 197
   Responding when you feel the squeeze .198
   Recognizing the ups and downs of shorting cannabis stocks. . . .198

PART 4: EXPLORING CANNABIS INVESTMENT STRATEGIES. 201

CHAPTER 13: Following the Money: Momentum Investing (aka Speculating) 203
Spotting Opportunities to Buy: Upward Momentum. 204
Watching for Signals to Sell: Downward Momentum. 207
Following the Smart Money. 208
Avoiding Some of the Risks Inherent in Momentum Investing. 209
   Watching out for the short squeeze. 209
   Steering clear of pump-and-dump scams 210
   Avoiding cannabis stock and industry bubbles. 211
   Knowing when momentum investing works and when
   it doesn't 211

CHAPTER 14: Investing in Canadian Cannabis Companies. 213
Deciding Whether to Invest in Canadian or U.S. Cannabis
Businesses 214
   The pros and cons of the Canadian cannabis market 214
   The pros and cons of the U.S. cannabis market 216
Scoping Out the Four Leading Canadian Cannabis Companies. 217
   Canopy Growth Corporation 217
   Cronos Group. 218
   Aurora Cannabis 218
   Aphria 219

CHAPTER 15: Investing in Countries Where Marijuana Is Legal. 221
Argentina 222
Australia 223
Brazil 224
Chile. 224
Colombia. 225
Czech Republic. 226
Ecuador. 226
Germany. 227
Greece. 227
Ireland. 228

Israel 228
Italy 229
Jamaica 230
The Netherlands 230
New Zealand 231
Norway 232
Peru 232
Poland 233
Portugal 233
Switzerland 233
Thailand 234
United Kingdom 234
Zambia 235

CHAPTER 16: Minimizing Risks While Maximizing Gains 237
Staying Plugged in to the Industry 238
Investing in the People, Not the Plant 239
Performing Your Due Diligence 239
Trading Cannabis Stocks on Private Markets 240
Investing in the Biggest Markets 241
Diversifying Inside and Outside the Industry 241
Investing in Multi-state Operators 242
Keep an Eye on the ETFs 243
Invest in Innovative Companies 244
Use Different Stock Order Types to Your Advantage 245
Don't Get Greedy 246

PART 5: THE PART OF TENS 247

CHAPTER 17: Ten Ways to Profit When the Market Drops 249
Be Patient, But Vigilant 250
Review Your Portfolio 250
Cut Your Losses 250
Buy More Shares 251
Focus on Value Stocks 251
Short Bad Stocks 251
Find Potential Treasures with Bond Ratings 252
Rotate Sectors 252
Buy a Call Option 252
Write a Covered Call Option 253

CHAPTER 18: Ten Reasons Not to Invest in Marijuana Stocks 255
Marijuana Is Still Federally Illegal in the U.S. 256

Marijuana Investment Scams Are Rampant 256
Earning a Profit as a Cannabis Business Is a Huge Challenge 257
Illegal Operations Undermine Demand for Legal Products 258
The Industry Is Very Fragmented 258
Oversupply Is More Likely Than Not. 258
Bad News Is Just Around the Corner 259
Marijuana Laws Are Slow to Change 259
Company Shares Are Being Diluted 260
Demand Is Unpredictable 260

CHAPTER 19: **Ten (Plus One) Criteria for Choosing
a Cannabis Investment** 261
Experienced and Successful Management Team 262
Steady Revenue Growth 262
Consistent Profit Growth 263
Comparatively Low Price-to-Earnings Ratio. 263
Positive Money Flow Indicator 264
Expanding Free Cash Flow 264
Operations in Other States or Countries 264
Growing Market. 265
Increasing Market Share. 265
Positive Reputation in the Industry. 266
Manageable Debt 266

CHAPTER 20: **Ten Mistakes to Avoid** 267
Failing to Diversify Sufficiently. 267
Relying Solely on Online Information 268
Not Performing Due Diligence. 268
Believing Federal Legalization Will Happen Soon 269
Failing to Account for Regulations 269
Failing to Consider the Possibility of Bad News 269
Buying or Selling Too Late or Too Early 270
Ignoring Business Fundamentals 270
Expecting All Marijuana Stocks to Be Winners 271
Buying a Stock Just Because It's Cheap 271

INDEX 273

Introduction

Based on a report published in 2020 by Grand View Research, the global legal marijuana market, valued at US$17.7 billion in 2019, is expected to expand at a Compound Annual Growth Rate (CAGR) of 18.1 percent, to be worth US$73.6 billion by 2027. That represents incredible growth and explains why the push by many entrepreneurs and investors to capitalize on this growing market is often referred to as the "Green Rush" (comparing it to the California Gold Rush, which lasted from about 1848 to 1855).

The trouble with any rush, whether green, gold, or no color at all, is that it's often accompanied by chaos, uncertainty, and failure — what former U.S. Federal Reserve Board Chairman Alan Greenspan called "irrational exuberance." Sure, some people got rich during the Gold Rush, as will some people during the Green Rush, but most prospectors during the Gold Rush went from boom to bust, many without experiencing the boom. Likewise, until the cannabis market stabilizes, many businesses will fail, many investors will lose their shirts, and many con artists will scam unsuspecting investors and business owners out of millions, if not billions, of dollars.

To profit from cannabis as an investor, you really need to know what you're doing. You need to know the industry, know how to find leads on potentially profitable investments, be able to size up a business's potential for earning a profit, and have the knowledge and skills necessary to reduce your exposure to risk.

About This Book

Welcome to *Cannabis Investing For Dummies,* your personal guide to investing in the cannabis industry profitably and without losing your shirt. Of course, I can't guarantee either of those outcomes (making gobs of money or not going broke), but as an expert in the legal marijuana sector, I can show you how to find and research cannabis investment opportunities in a way that increases your chances of earning a profit while reducing your chances of investing in a lousy business or getting scammed by savvy con artists.

To make the content more accessible, I divided it into five parts:

- » **Part 1, "Getting Started with Cannabis Investing,"** brings you up to speed on the basics of investing in cannabis, introduces you to the different types of businesses you can invest in, and discusses numerous factors that can impact a business's ability to turn a profit. Here, I also lead you through the process of weighing the pros and cons of investing in cannabis, so you know what you're getting into before getting into it.

- » **Part 2, "Doing Your Homework,"** provides guidance on how to find leads on potentially profitable cannabis companies, and then research those companies and their management teams before investing in them. Unless you're going to base your entire investment strategy on luck, this part is essential reading.

- » **Part 3, "Buying and Selling Cannabis Stocks, ETFs, or Mutual Funds,"** gets down to the basics of trading securities in cannabis businesses. If you're already an experienced investor who has bought and sold securities on the stock market or you're working with a qualified broker, this may be optional reading for you.

- » **Part 4, "Exploring Cannabis Investment Strategies,"** presents different strategies for earning a profit by investing in cannabis businesses. Buy low and sell high, right? Well, generally speaking, that's certainly the goal, but this part breaks down that overarching strategy into more practical steps.

- » **Part 5, "The Part of Tens,"** features four "top ten" lists: ten ways to profit when the market drops, ten reasons not to invest in cannabis, ten criteria for choosing a cannabis business to invest in, and ten common mistakes to avoid when you're just getting started.

In short, this book serves as your guide to investing in cannabis profitably without getting scammed by clever con artists or overhyped investment leads.

Foolish Assumptions

All assumptions are foolish, and I'm always reluctant to make them, but to keep this book focused on the right audience and ensure that it fulfills my purpose in writing it, I had to make the following foolish assumptions about you:

- » You're interested but a little hesitant to invest in the new and growing cannabis industry, knowing it's risky but wanting to profit from it in some way.

» You're willing to invest your time to properly research a cannabis business before investing in it. (If you're not, don't waste your time reading this book; just forge ahead, speculating in businesses you know little or nothing about.)

» You're looking for guidance on how to increase your chances of earning a profit by investing in cannabis while reducing your exposure to risk.

» You don't expect me to give you recommendations on specific companies or sectors of the industry to invest in. The cannabis industry has a high turnover rate in terms of new companies coming on the scene and old companies disappearing. Even if I did recommend a company to invest in, by the time you picked up this book and started reading it, I may have changed that recommendation.

Other than those four foolish assumptions, I can honestly say that I can't assume much more about you. The vast number of people who invest in cannabis or express some interest in doing so represent a diverse demographic. You may be 21 or 90 years old or somewhere in between, a white-collar or blue-collar worker, a housewife or househusband, a doctor, a lawyer, rich or poor. Regardless of the demographic, I applaud you for being open minded and willing to explore what I believe is a great opportunity for earning big returns in an exciting, new, and fast-growing industry.

Icons Used in This Book

Throughout this book, icons in the margins highlight certain types of valuable information that call out for your attention. Here are the icons you'll encounter and a brief description of each.

REMEMBER

I want you to remember everything you read in this book, but if you can't quite do that, then remember the important points flagged with this icon.

TIP

Tips provide savvy insight from an industry expert (me). When you're looking for a better, faster way to do something, check out these tips.

WARNING

"Whoa!" Before you take another step, read this warning. I provide this cautionary content to help you avoid the common pitfalls that are otherwise likely to trip you up (and lose you money).

Beyond the Book

In addition to the abundance of information and guidance related to cannabis investing that I provide in this book, you get access to even more help and information online at Dummies.com, including a Cheat Sheet that serves as a quick reference guide to this book. To access this book's online Cheat Sheet, go to www.dummies.com and search for "Investing in Cannabis For Dummies Cheat Sheet."

Where to Go from Here

You're certainly welcome to read this book from cover to cover, but I wrote it in a way that facilitates skipping around. For a quick tutorial on cannabis investing that touches on all the key topics, turn to Chapter 1. To get up to speed on the types of businesses that constitute the cannabis industry, check out Chapter 2. Turn to Chapter 3 to get to know the various factors outside the industry that can impact the industry (and your investments), and to Chapter 4 to figure out whether cannabis investing is even something you want to get into.

All the chapters in Part 2 are essential reading. Before you invest a single penny in a cannabis business, you should carefully vet that business. Otherwise, you're not investing, you're speculating, and you may not even be doing that very well. The chapters in Part 2 guide you through the process of digging up leads on potentially profitable businesses, researching a business and its management team, and conducting fundamental and technical analysis, so you have a pretty good idea of what you're getting in exchange for your investment.

If you're new to investing in general, head to Part 3, and if you're a seasoned investor looking for more advanced information on different investment strategies, turn to Part 4.

Consider the chapters in Part 5 bonus material. These chapters are all quick reads that are chock full of tips and guidance on how to invest profitably in cannabis . . . or decide not to invest in cannabis after you consider the risks.

1
Getting Started with Cannabis Investing

Getting a quick primer on cannabis investing — from identifying investment opportunities and researching them to buying and selling investment securities.

Distinguishing between cannabis business types — medical versus adult recreational, and plant-touching versus ancillary businesses.

Understanding how politics, laws, regulations, and the high costs of doing business in the cannabis industry can impact investments.

Weighing the pros and cons of cannabis investing to determine whether it's the right move for you.

> » Investing in businesses that touch the plant or those that don't

> » Scoping out different ways to invest in cannabis

> » Digging up leads on potential investments and researching them

> » Creating and executing your investment strategy

Chapter **1**

Taking the Nickel Tour

Whenever you're getting started on a new topic or trying to develop a new skill, you can benefit from having a general understanding of what's involved. It's sort of like reading the plot or synopsis of a movie or book before starting to watch or read it . . . or seeing the finished product before you start following the instructions to assemble it. You get the gist of what you're about to encounter, which serves as both a framework on which you can hang the details, and the context for more quickly and easily understanding those details.

The purpose of this chapter is to bring you quickly up to speed on the topic of investing in cannabis and to provide the framework and context for understanding topics covered in subsequent chapters.

REMEMBER

This book is structured in a way that facilitates skipping around, so feel free to skip this primer if you think you don't need it or if you're looking for more detailed information and guidance about a specific aspect of investing in cannabis. On the other hand, if you're a quick learner with an intuitive mind, you might read this primer and start investing right away based solely on the general directions it presents (not recommended, but it's certainly an option).

Weighing the Pros and Cons of Investing in Cannabis

I don't try to sell anyone on the idea of investing in cannabis, except, of course, prospective investors with lots of cash who want to invest in the cannabis company *I* run. Even then, I want them to invest with eyes wide open, knowing the potential for both profit and loss. In fact, I actually spend more time *discouraging* people from investing in cannabis, because I can usually tell quickly from talking with someone who's eager to invest in this industry whether they're too eager and ill-informed or simply won't perform the due diligence necessary to invest wisely.

I don't know you, so I'm not going to try to encourage or discourage you from investing in cannabis businesses. Instead, I present some of the most important pros and cons you should consider and leave the decision up to you.

Pros

The biggest motive people have for investing their money in any venture is profit. Chances are good that you, too, are curious about investing in cannabis because you want to profit from it. The industry is growing in leaps and bounds, and you want in on the action. Nothing wrong with that, but consider other benefits. Here's a complete list (or as complete as I can think of at the moment):

» Profit (which I already mentioned) is the biggie.

» Getting in at or near the bottom of a new and exciting industry is always a thrill. By investing in cannabis, you become a participant, not merely an observer, in the green rush.

» Being able to tell people you know that your investment portfolio or retirement account includes cannabis stock. This may sound silly, but being invested in cannabis says something about who you are and may help you engage in conversations you would otherwise be excluded from.

» If you consume marijuana, you get to invest in a product you enjoy and help to make it more available to others.

» If you invest in medical marijuana, you're investing in medical research and helping to bring those new medicines to market, potentially alleviating some of the world's physical and perhaps even mental suffering.

Life offers us few choices to invest in a new industry in its infancy. I like to think of investing in cannabis as what it would have been like to invest in alcohol three to five years before prohibition was repealed. How often do you get to participate in an industry at the dawn of legalization? Investing in cannabis also reminds me what investing in the dot-com era was like. I got into the technology boom shortly after graduating college and learned a great deal about new industries. Cannabis is a new industry. It presents an opportunity for an investor to be a pioneer.

Cons

As you may have guessed from my reluctance to encourage people to invest in cannabis, I can come up with more reasons *not* to invest in cannabis than *to* invest in it. Here's a list of reasons not to invest in cannabis that you should seriously consider before investing in this industry (see Chapter 4 for more details):

>> Cannabis attracts money, and money attracts thieves. In addition, many novices eager to invest in cannabis are easy marks because they're eager, naïve, and have money — just the combination of traits a con artist is looking for.

Many of the successful entrepreneurs in cannabis got their start in the black market, which attracts a very particular personality type. Leopards don't change their spots. Some savvy former black marketers have simply chosen a different crime — instead of dealing in illegal marijuana, they're now on the prowl for unsuspecting investors they can fleece. And they're not the only thieves that pose a threat to cannabis investors, as illustrated in the sidebar, "Crooks in law enforcement."

>> With lots of money flowing into the industry from eager investors, even legitimate cannabis stocks are overvalued. The more overvalued a stock is, the further the potential fall. Short sellers often target overvalued stocks just for this reason; then, when the stock price drops, they cash in and everyone else loses. (See Chapter 12 for more about short selling.)

>> Cannabis businesses struggle to be profitable due to numerous factors, including the high costs of complying with federal, state, and local marijuana laws; increased security costs; increased bank fees; and the cost of specialized software.

>> Cannabis stocks have an increased susceptibility to *dilution* because cannabis companies have a tougher time getting bank loans in the U.S. (due to federal laws that discourage banks from doing business with cannabis companies). Companies issue and sell more shares to raise money, but that dilutes the value of existing shares.

>> Companies that grow cannabis are at risk of cannabis becoming a commodity, and if (when) that happens, prices and profits drop.

>> Laws, and enforcement of those laws, are susceptible to change, and if they change in a direction that hurts cannabis businesses, their investors suffer as well.

>> Supply-and-demand imbalances are common in the cannabis industry. These imbalances not only disrupt the supply chain but also negatively impact profits by creating market gluts (which drive down prices) or shortages (which increase costs and reduce demand); either way, profits suffer.

>> Cannabis still has a healthy black market, even in states where it's legal, and black-market growers and dealers don't pay taxes, so they can afford to sell their product for less. If state and local authorities don't crack down on illegal production and sales, legal businesses have a tough time competing.

TIP

Don't rule out investing in cannabis just because of this long list of potential drawbacks. You can considerably reduce your exposure to risk by doing your homework and investing in well-run companies. See Part 2 for guidance on how to properly research businesses and their management teams, and keep up on what's happening in the industry.

CROOKS IN LAW ENFORCEMENT

Corrupt law enforcement officers pose a threat to both legitimate cannabis operations and their investors. These bad cops have been known to raid lawfully operating cannabis operations and take cash and product. Operators have little recourse. What are they going to do, call the cops? Likewise, operators get little sympathy and support at the judicial level.

An unjustified raid can be fatal to a business. I was a partner in a dispensary in Los Angeles that was raided by the police. They took cash and damaged the on-site cultivation facility, causing hundreds of thousands of dollars in losses, not to mention the loss of revenue that occurred as a result of the closure of the business. It took months to recover from the raid, and the city eventually dropped the charges.

Incidents like that still happen and likely will until federal prohibition of marijuana is repealed.

Deciding Whether to Invest in Businesses That Touch the Plant or Those That Don't

One of the first decisions to make before investing in cannabis is whether to invest in businesses that have contact with the plant or those that don't (often referred to as *ancillary* companies):

>> **Plant-touching:** These businesses come into contact with the plant at some point during the growth, manufacturing, distribution, or sale. They include grow operations, manufacturers of infused products (MIPs), shipping firms, dispensaries, and licensed delivery services. Plant-touching businesses stand to profit most from cannabis, and they're also at the greatest risk of suffering losses when the industry takes a hit.

TIP

If you decide to invest in a plant-touching business, consider a *vertically integrated company,* which means the business does its own cultivation, manufacturing, distribution, and sales. Vertically integrated companies are less susceptible to supply chain disruptions because they control their entire supply chain.

>> **Ancillary:** These businesses serve the plant-touching businesses in some way. Perhaps the best-known ancillary business is The Scotts Company, which provides fertilizer, pesticides, and disease control products, primarily for lawn care but also for agricultural operations, including cannabis cultivation companies. Other ancillary companies include manufacturers and dealers of equipment for cultivation operations; legal and accounting services that specialize in cannabis; software companies that develop point-of-sale and supply-chain managements systems; security equipment and service providers; and real estate groups that buy, sell, and rent land and buildings for cannabis businesses.

While plant–touching businesses carry the most potential for profit and risk, ancillary companies still stand to profit from the industry, but they have less exposure to risk. For example, if the U.S. federal government decided to crack down on cannabis businesses across the country, that revenue stream would be negatively impacted for The Scotts Company, but the company would still have value as a business selling lawn care products.

REMEMBER

According to a study published by Deloitte in 2016, ancillary businesses are estimated to be 2.5 times the size of the cannabis industry itself, so ancillary businesses stand to profit handsomely from the success of the cannabis industry.

Exploring Your Investment Options

You can profit from legal cannabis businesses in several ways, depending on how directly you want to be involved. The most direct approach is to start your own cannabis business. The least direct approach is to trade cannabis-related securities, such as stocks, bonds, or exchange traded funds (ETFs).

In the following sections, I present different ways to invest in the cannabis industry to make you aware of the wide variety of options.

Starting your own business

One approach to investing in the cannabis industry is to start your own business — either a plant-touching or an ancillary business. Here are some of the more popular opportunities cannabis entrepreneurs pursue.

>> **Cultivator:** Cultivators start and grow plants from seeds; harvest the plants; separate the useable portion of the plants and properly dispose of the green waste; dry, cure, and trim the harvested bud; arrange for third-party lab tests to ensure the safety and quality of the product; pack and ship product to manufacturers and dispensaries; and track and report all processes as required by law to government regulatory agencies. Note that cultivation operations are the lowest profit-margin segment of the industry.

TIP

Cultivation is a great choice if you have a passion for the plant and a green thumb.

>> **Manufacturer of infused products:** MIP is an industry term used to describe a company that makes marijuana-infused products, including concentrates such as wax and shatter; oils and tinctures; and lotions and edibles. This segment of the industry acts as a laboratory as well as a processing plant. It may be even more tightly regulated than other segments of the industry, with additional rules and regulations that extend to manufacturing and commercial kitchens.

TIP

MIP is a great choice for those who want to get more into the science of extracting active ingredients from the plant and using those extracts to create a wide variety of consumer products.

>> **Processed product brand:** A processed product brand could be an MIP or a combined grow/MIP business that makes products and sells them to numerous retail outlets. For example, you could set up your own grow/MIP business to produce a line of infused chocolates that you sell to a variety of medical and recreational dispensaries in Oregon. Another option is to create your own brand and develop unique products and then farm out the growing, manufacturing, and distribution operations to other businesses that specialize in those areas.

>> **Retailer/dispensary owner:** Cannabis retailers run the dispensaries and other retail outlets that sell products directly to consumers. Depending on the rules and regulations in your area, you may be permitted to run a medical dispensary, an adult recreational dispensary, or a dispensary that serves both medical and adult recreational clients. This is like owning a liquor store but with more rules and regulations to follow.

>> **Ancillary business:** Ancillary businesses you may want to consider include the following:

- Nursery owner

- Manufacturer or seller of grow lights

- Heating, ventilation, and air conditioning (HVAC) service provider specializing in ventilation and circulation for grow operations

- Packaging and labeling manufacturer/supplier

- Security service, or manufacturer or supplier of security systems and equipment

- Marketing, public relations, or advertising specialist

- Real estate sales, rentals, or management (for more details, see the next section)

- Legal, accounting, or consulting service provider

- Banking and cash management services

WARNING

If you're interested in starting a business that comes in contact with the cannabis plant in any way, don't go it alone, and do be prepared for a high cost of doing business. Especially be sure to consult with a lawyer who has knowledge and expertise in helping businesses comply with state cannabis laws.

Investing in cannabis real estate

An often overlooked way to invest in cannabis is to buy land zoned for cannabis businesses or to buy land and have it zoned for such businesses and then sell or lease the land to cannabis businesses. You can even erect buildings on the land (or buy land with buildings suitable for certain types of businesses) and sell or lease the commercially improved land to businesses.

If you've seen the movie *The Founder*, about Ray Kroc, the founder of McDonald's, you probably remember his lawyer/advisor telling him, "You don't seem to realize what business you're in. You're not in the burger business; you're in the real estate business. You build an empire by owning the land." Kroc followed that advice and made a fortune buying the land on which McDonald's franchises were built and then leasing that land to the franchise owners.

You can take a similar approach to profit off the cannabis industry. However, you really need to know not only the cannabis industry and the real estate market, but also the rules and regulations in place that govern where (and what type of) cannabis businesses can be conducted on differently zoned plots of land.

See Chapter 2 for additional details about investing in the cannabis real estate market.

Buying and selling stocks

The most common way people invest in cannabis is to buy and sell stock in privately or publicly owned cannabis companies. Stocks provide you with a share of the company without your having to get your hands dirty or deal with the complex legal and regulatory issues (and other matters) of starting and running your own cannabis business. Of course, buying shares in an existing business leaves you with less control over the business, leaving the value of your shares in the hands of others. If they're innovative, intelligent, and manage the company effectively, your shares are likely to increase in value, but if they drop the ball, you're likely to lose money on your investment.

REMEMBER

Investing in publicly traded companies has a couple advantages. First, to list their stocks on public stock exchanges, companies must be a certain size and comply with stringent financial reporting standards, which provides a greater level of transparency for investors. In other words, you have more data on which you can base your investment decisions. Second, stock in publicly traded companies is a very liquid investment. You can convert your shares to cash almost immediately by listing them for sale on the exchange, assuming, of course, that someone's willing to buy the shares at a price you're willing to sell them for.

For guidance on how to buy and sell stock in publicly traded companies, see Part 3.

REMEMBER

In this book, I assume you're investing in cannabis by buying and selling securities (stocks or bonds) in public or private companies and not by starting your own cannabis business or investing in real estate, which may be the focus of other books on investing in real estate. The goal of this book is to provide the information and guidance you need to research businesses and their management teams to determine whether they're likely to be profitable and good investments for you. You can then decide whether to invest in the company.

Diversifying with exchange traded funds and mutual funds

Most financial advisors recommend *diversification* as a way to reduce an investor's exposure to risk. A diversified investment portfolio contains both *stocks* (shares of ownership in a company) and *bonds* (like IOUs, short for "I owe you"); investments in numerous companies in a particular industry; and investments in various industries, such as cannabis, automobiles, pharmaceuticals, and energy.

One quick and easy way to diversify is to purchase shares of an exchange traded fund or mutual fund, both of which contain investments in a variety of businesses. The basic difference between the two is that shares of an ETF can be traded throughout the day like shares of stock, whereas shares of a mutual fund can be traded only after the markets close or before they open, because the share value is calculated a couple of hours after the markets close. You can find several cannabis-specific ETFs to invest in. Cannabis mutual funds are a rarer species.

WARNING

The main drawback of cannabis ETFs and mutual funds is that a fund manager chooses the businesses to invest in, and fund managers may not be experts in the cannabis industry, so they may not make the best choices. You're generally better off doing your own research and making your own choices.

Considering private investment opportunities

Investing in private companies (in contrast to publicly traded companies) carries significantly more risk but has more potential for a higher return on investment (ROI). You basically have four options for investing in private companies depending on the business's stage of development.

>> **Angel investing:** If you know someone who wants to start a cannabis business, you can bankroll the operation as an *angel investor*, usually in exchange for *ownership equity* (shares of stock) in the company or *convertible debt* (a loan that can later be converted to ownership equity). You can also join a group of angel investors, pooling your money to finance startup businesses.

>> **Venture capital investing:** One step up from angel investing is venture capital investing, which involves providing capital and expertise to take a promising startup to the next level. As with angel investing, you can join venture capital groups to pool money and expertise.

>> **Mezzanine investing:** One step up from venture capital investing is mezzanine investing, which involves private financing in the form of debt or preferred stock. (*Preferred stock* is a higher class of ownership than that provided by common stock. With preferred stock, you have first claim on any assets and earnings if the company struggles or folds.)

>> **Private equity:** Private equity is financing that doesn't appear on public exchanges. It usually comes from funds and investors that invest directly in companies or that engage in buyouts of public companies, which results in those companies being delisted.

REMEMBER

Private investing is usually the realm of high-net-worth individuals — and a perfect example of how the rich get richer.

Finding Investment Opportunities

Before you can invest in a cannabis business, you need to find a business to invest in. Sure, you can Google "cannabis companies to invest in" or head to an online discount brokerage such as Firstrade, Ally Invest, or E*TRADE, and use their tools to track down cannabis companies and ETFs, but those searches are likely to turn up only the biggest, publicly-traded cannabis companies. (And a Google search would be likely to turn up some of the biggest scams.) To get quality leads on cannabis businesses, you have a few options, including the following (see Chapter 6 for details).

>> **Word of mouth:** People talk, especially when they're planning something big like starting their own cannabis business. You may hear something from a friend, relative, or casual acquaintance about someone who's interested in starting a cannabis business and is looking for investors.

WARNING

Be especially careful in your research of word-of-mouth leads, especially if someone approaches you out of the blue about a great investment opportunity. Head to Part 2 for guidance on how to properly vet businesses and their owners and managers.

>> **Online resources:** Dozens of general and cannabis-specific investment websites are available to keep investors informed of opportunities. General sites include Yahoo! Finance (`finance.yahoo.com`) and Morningstar (`www.morningstar.com`). Cannabis-specific resources include The Marijuana Index (`marijuanaindex.com`), Marijuana Stocks (`marijuanastocks.com`), and Cannabis Stock Trades (`www.cannabisstocktrades.com`).

>> **Apps:** Several smartphone apps are available, including Investing in Weed Stocks, Marijuana Handbook, and Scutify. Search your smartphone's app store for cannabis or marijuana investment apps.

>> **Cannabis industry news:** You can find more sources for cannabis industry news than you have time to read. I provide a long list in Chapter 6. If you have time only for one, I recommend Marijuana Business Daily (mjbizdaily.com). Even if you don't use these sources to find leads on investment opportunities, they're valuable for getting up to speed on the industry and gaining the knowledge you need to make better-informed investment decisions.

>> **ETF sites:** If you're interested specifically in cannabis ETFs, check out ETFdb.com.

>> **Private investment groups:** If you're a high-net-worth individual, consider joining a group of private investors who focus on the cannabis industry. When choosing a group, decide where you want to enter the picture with new businesses — as an angel investor, venture capitalist, mezzanine investor, or member of a private equity firm. Then, look for a reputable group that fits with your investment strategy.

>> **A broker:** Many investors are drawn to online discount brokers because of the cheap (or free) trades, but paying extra for a broker who knows the cannabis industry may be the best long-term investment you'll ever make. See Chapter 9 for more information about the benefits and potential drawbacks of working with a broker and how to choose a broker with the right stuff.

Researching Investment Opportunities

You just got a lead on a new cannabis company looking for investors. Now what? First things first — watch your wallet. Don't invest any money until you thoroughly research the "opportunity." Then, do your research, which should include the following (see Chapter 7 for details):

>> A background check of all owners, managers, and operators. Hire a reputable private investigator to conduct the background checks, and make sure everyone on the team has experience in the industry.

>> An online search for the business and its owners, managers, and operators. Conduct a general Google search and check out some cannabis industry-specific news sites, such as mjbizdaily.com and www.cannabisbusinesstimes.com to find out more about the people starting and running the business.

>> An evaluation of the company's financial health, to ensure that it has the capital required to operate until it begins to turn a profit.

>> Verification of the business's license to operate in the state or states in which it plans to operate.

>> A careful evaluation of the business plan or business strategy to ensure that the owners and managers have a solid plan in place to turn a profit.

>> An evaluation of the company's competitive position relative to other companies in its space.

>> An evaluation of the company's existing *warrants* and *convertible securities* — essentially contracts with existing investors regarding their current or future equity ownership in the company. You want to know how ownership in the company by current investors could impact your equity ownership in the company and the share price.

>> A check with other investors and reputable analysts with expertise in the cannabis industry to find out whether they know anything about the company or its owners/managers/operators.

>> A conversation with the CEO or other leaders in the business to hear directly from them about their vision and plan for success.

>> A check with a reputable broker in Canada or the U.S. to verify that the prospect is real, compliant, and listed on a credible exchange. This is necessary only for publicly traded companies.

>> A conversation with your lawyer and your financial advisor to get their opinions about investing in the company. (In other words, get a second and third opinion.)

Additionally, if the business you're thinking of investing in is involved in cultivating cannabis, research the grow master (the person in charge of setting up and managing the operation), the grower's *cost per gram* (average cost to grow one gram of product) compared to competitors' cost per gram, and the cultivator's clientele (to be sure the cultivation operation has reliable customers). Turn to Chapter 7 for more details.

REMEMBER

Bet with your head, not with your heart. Three big market movers are greed, fear of loss (FOL), and fear of missing out (FOMO). Regardless of what you choose to invest in, make rational, data-based decisions.

Planning Your Investment Strategy

Prior to investing, give some thought to your investment strategy. Common investment strategies for any industry you choose to invest in include the following.

» **Value investing:** This strategy involves buying stocks in *undervalued companies* — companies that appear, based on their fundamentals (see Chapter 7 for details), to be worth more than their share price indicates. Value investors believe that the markets are driven, to a large part, by emotion, and that by investing in profitable companies, they'll do better in the long run.

» **Growth investing:** This strategy involves investing in small companies you think have the potential to increase their earnings faster than their competitors or other companies in the industry. Unlike value investors, growth investors may be willing to pay more than "book value" for shares in the company. (*Book value* is the total amount a company would be worth if it sold all its assets and paid back all its liabilities.)

» **Momentum investing:** This strategy involves following trends in the prices of securities to capitalize on a company as its share price is rising or to short-sell shares as the share price drops. (To sell short, you borrow a stock and sell it. When the price drops, you buy back the stock and return it to the lender. The difference between the sell price and the buy price is your profit. See Chapter 12 for more about short-selling stocks.)

» **Income investing:** This strategy focuses on earning a steady income from investments. It usually involves buying shares in companies that pay dividends, and buying bonds, which pay out interest on a consistent basis. Income investing is generally safer than value, growth, and momentum investment strategies, but the potential return may be lower.

» **Investing in what you know:** Many investors buy shares in only the companies they know or the companies that provide the products and services they like, believing that those products and services will likely become increasingly popular among consumers, thereby driving the company's success. For example, if you're an Amazon Prime member, you may think to yourself, "Wow, Amazon is great. This company really has the potential to make it big," and, based solely on your personal experience, you decide to invest in Amazon.

>> **Dollar-cost averaging:** With dollar-cost averaging, you buy shares regularly (for example, the same day each month) whether the share price is high or low, so you're not overpaying for a large quantity of shares at any one time. Of course, with this strategy, you're not getting a large quantity of shares at a low price, either.

>> **Diversification:** This strategy involves spreading your investment dollars across a number of industries or a number of companies in the same industry to reduce your exposure to risk if one particular industry or company you invest in goes south.

In the context of cannabis investing, other strategies may include the following:

>> Investing in ancillary businesses that serve the cannabis industry but don't touch the plant. Regardless of which cannabis businesses win or lose, ancillary businesses increase their earnings as the industry as a whole grows.

>> Investing only in vertically integrated companies, which control their entire supply line. These companies also tend to be larger than those that are not vertically integrated.

>> Investing exclusively in medical cannabis or exclusively in adult recreational cannabis, or investing a specific percentage in each.

>> Investing in strong brands that have a presence in multiple states and perhaps even multiple countries.

>> Investing in foreign markets such as Canada, Uruguay, and the European Union.

Investing in a Cannabis Business

Businesses have two options for raising capital to get started or to grow.

>> **Debt:** They may borrow money from a bank or issue bonds, which are sort of like IOUs, promising to pay back the debt with interest.

>> **Equity:** They may issue stock — selling shares in the business.

As a result, you have two ways to invest in a cannabis business: by lending the business money or purchasing shares in the business. Regardless of which approach you take, the process is pretty easy. For example, if you're lending some-one you know money to start a cannabis business, you have your attorney draw up a loan contract, and you and an authorized representative of the business sign the loan contract, after which you provide the agreed-upon capital. If the business issues bonds, you can buy bonds instead of using a loan contract. And if the business issues shares of stock, you simply buy shares at an agreed-upon price.

You can also buy stocks and bonds by purchasing shares of an ETF or mutual fund. These funds have a collection of investment securities (stocks and bonds) from different business and often different industries, which facilitates diversification; you're not putting all your eggs in one basket. (See the section, "Diversifying with exchange traded funds and mutual funds," for details.)

The actual process of buying stocks, bonds, ETFs, or mutual funds is easy. You set up an account with a *broker* — a person who's licensed to buy and sell stocks and bonds, or a company that enables you to place your own orders online. You can then contact your broker to place your order or log into your online brokerage account and place the order yourself.

Regardless of whether you place orders through a broker or an online system, you need to specify several details, including the following:

» The company name or ticker symbol

» Whether you want to buy or sell

» The number of shares you want to buy or sell (when selling, you usually have an option to sell all shares or a specified number of shares)

» The order type:

- **Market.** Buy or sell the security immediately at the going price.

- **Limit.** Buy or sell the security only at the specified price or better.

- **Stop loss.** Buy or sell the security as soon as its price reaches the price specified.

- **Stop limit.** Buy or sell the security as soon as its price reaches the price specified but only within the specified price range.

- **Trailing stop.** Buy or sell the security as soon as its price reaches a specified percentage or dollar amount above or below the current market price. With a trailing stop, as the price of the security moves in a favorable direction, the trailing stop price adjusts automatically, but as soon as the price turns in an unfavorable direction by the dollar amount or percentage specified, the trade is triggered. (Trailing stop orders can be trailing stop loss or trailing stop limit orders.)

>> The timeframe:

- **Good till cancelled.** Keep the order open until you choose to cancel it.

- **Fill or kill.** Execute the transaction immediately and completely or cancel it.

- **Immediate or cancel.** Fill as much of the order as possible in the next few seconds and then cancel anything that couldn't be filled.

- **On open.** Execute the order as soon as the market opens.

- **On close.** Execute the order after the market closes.

WARNING

Because many cannabis companies are not profitable (especially early on), be aware of the difference between investing and speculating. *Investing* involves generating a reasonable return from a profitable company. *Speculating* involves betting on a company's ability to become profitable or betting that other people will buy shares speculatively, driving up the share price. Buying shares of unprofitable companies is more about speculating than investing.

Chapter **2**

Exploring Cannabis Business Types

Before you invest in any company, you should have at least a general under-standing of the industry, starting with the different types of businesses and the products and services they offer. Cannabis businesses can be broken down into the following five categories:

» **Growers** are generally breeders or cultivators. Breeders develop new strains of cannabis. Cultivators grow cannabis to supply to manufacturers, dispensaries, and sometimes directly to consumers.

» **Manufacturers** use cannabis plant material, usually the flower/bud (the part of the plant that contains the highest concentration of active ingredients), to make various products for consumption, including pre-rolled joints, vape oils, edibles, beverages, concentrates, body lotions, and more.

» **Brands** are companies that create and market individually recognized products. A successful brand fosters a sense of ownership and belonging among consumers (brand loyalty) with each purchase. Brand identity also increases product visibility, simplifying the product selection process for consumers.

» **Dispensaries** are retail operations that obtain products from manufacturers and growers and sell them to consumers. They may sell medical or adult-use (recreational) products or both.

>> **Ancillary businesses** are traditional businesses that provide products and services that support the cannabis industry, such as fertilizer, delivery services, financial services, legal expertise, real estate, and software.

In this chapter, I bring you up to speed on different cannabis business types and the products and services they offer, so you have the foundational understanding to make well-informed decisions regarding where to invest your money.

Choosing Sides: Medical or Adult-Use?

The old adage that there are two sides to every story certainly applies to cannabis. In the case of cannabis, the two sides are medical and adult-use. *Medical cannabis* is prescribed by doctors to treat a long list of health conditions, including chronic pain, nausea, multiple sclerosis, cancer, epilepsy, arthritis, glaucoma, migraines, and more. Adult-use cannabis is for getting high, relaxing, enhancing certain sensory experiences or activities, and so on.

In some ways, the differences between medical and adult-use cannabis are barely distinguishable. Some growers and manufacturers supply both market sectors, and medical and adult-use consumers use many of the same products. In states where medical and adult-use cannabis are both legal, dispensaries serve both consumer groups.

However, as an investor, you're wise to consider some key differences between medical and adult-use marijuana and how these differences may influence your investment decisions.

REMEMBER

According to BDSA, consumers spent $10.9 billion on cannabis worldwide in 2018. BDSA projects that global consumer spending on cannabis will reach $40.6 billion by 2024 as it becomes legal in more areas. About two-thirds of this spending is expected to be for adult-use, and the remaining third for medical marijuana.

Investing in medical marijuana

Medical marijuana is an attractive option to some investors for numerous reasons, including the following:

>> Medical marijuana is legal in more states and more countries and is generally more widely accepted than adult-use cannabis, so businesses in this sector face less government and public resistance.

>> Medical marijuana provides relief to patients with a variety of health conditions, so demand for it is likely to be higher than for medications that treat specific conditions.

>> Medical marijuana may help governments address certain healthcare issues, such as the opioid epidemic and the high costs of Medicare.

>> Taxes are much lower on medical marijuana, so businesses that serve this market tend to have higher profit margins than businesses that cater to adult-use consumers.

Although cannabis-based medicines produced by pharmaceutical companies are technically medical marijuana, they're more a part of the pharmaceutical industry than the cannabis industry. As an investor, consider treating pharmaceutical cannabis as a third category — medical, adult-use, and pharmaceutical.

Investing in adult-use marijuana

Most of the excitement over investing in marijuana is focused on the adult-use market for a number of reasons, including the following:

>> Bigger market/more demand

>> Greater diversity of products

>> Increased public awareness

Unfortunately, investing in adult-use marijuana has an equally long list of potential drawbacks, including the following:

>> A change in legislation or enforcement can quickly turn the tide on adult-use consumption or drive more sales to the black market. (See Chapter 3 for more about the potential impact of changes in legislation and enforcement.)

>> High taxes not only reduce profit margins but also drive more sales to the black market, where dealers don't pay taxes and can afford to offer products for less.

>> Public awareness is a double-edged sword. A news story highlighting a potentially serious hazard of consuming cannabis can drive sales down quickly, as illustrated in the sidebar, "Vaping illness sinks sales."

>> Until the industry settles down, you're likely to see plenty of mergers and acquisitions. In addition, as legalization grows, big companies that are well established in other markets are likely to enter and drive the smaller companies out of business. Predicting winners and losers in such an environment is even more challenging than usual.

Recognizing Different Cannabis Business Types

Like many industries, the cannabis industry consists of diverse businesses ranging from those that grow cannabis to those that manufacture and sell products. The industry also supports a wide range of ancillary businesses that never come into contact with cannabis, including fertilizer manufacturers, delivery services, banks, law firms, real estate investors, and many more.

In this section, I introduce you to different business types that form the core of the cannabis industry — businesses that grow, produce, and sell cannabis products — so you have a better understanding of what these different companies do (and make) and you have some insight into their operations. In the section, "Considering Ancillary Businesses," I describe businesses that operate at the periphery of the core businesses while profiting from those core businesses.

TIP

As you evaluate cannabis companies, consider whether they're vertically integrated or at least have some degree of supply chain integration that ensures delivery of a final product to consumers (see the sidebar, "Vertically integrated or not"). If a company doesn't own the supply chain or have close relationships with other companies in the supply chain, it will be more susceptible to disruptions in operations.

VERTICALLY INTEGRATED OR NOT

A *vertically integrated* company is one in which the supply chain is owned by the company. In the cannabis industry, the term is used to describe companies that grow, manufacture, package, and sell cannabis products. Vertical integration is often referred to as the "seed-to-sale" experience. Some jurisdictions encourage or require cannabis companies to be vertically integrated, whereas others discourage or prohibit vertical integration.

Cultivation

Cultivation involves growing and harvesting the plants, which technically makes grow operations part of the agriculture industry. Cultivation involves the following activities:

>> Procuring and preparing space for growing plants indoors or outdoors.

>> Starting plants from seeds or cuttings.

>> Breeding plants to create new strains.

>> Growing and harvesting plants.

>> Separating the useable buds from the plants and disposing of *green waste* (parts of the plant not used to produce consumable products) in accordance with government regulations.

>> Drying, curing, and trimming the harvested bud.

>> Arranging for third-party lab testing for mold, contaminants, pests, and potency.

>> Packing and perhaps transporting products to manufacturers and retail locations.

>> Tracking and reporting all processes as required by law to government regulatory agencies.

If you're thinking of investing in a grow operation, consider the following factors that impact profitability:

>> Agricultural products are commodities, so grow operations comprise the lowest profit-margin segment of the industry. Companies can improve their profitability by increasing efficiency or by making up in volume what they lack in profit margin.

>> The cost of entry into this segment of the market is high due to expenses of procuring space to grow plants, setting up for the first crop, and complying with extensive government regulations.

Manufacturing

In the cannabis industry, a manufacturer is often referred to as a *manufacturer of infused products* (or MIP, for short). MIPs are in the middle of the supply chain, obtaining bud from growers and using it to make a variety of products (vape oils, tinctures, lotions, edibles, and so on) that they then sell to dispensaries and other retailers, which sell to consumers.

REMEMBER

From an investor's perspective, numerous factors can impact an MIP's value. Before investing in an MIP, consider the following:

>> Laws that prevent the transportation of cannabis products across borders create a significant barrier to a manufacturer's ability to expand distribution and increase revenue.

>> Vertically integrated cannabis companies are less susceptible to disruptions in the supply chain. For example, in Canada, some manufacturers struggled because cultivators couldn't keep pace with growing demand when cannabis was legalized. In some jurisdictions, delays in approving dispensaries can place pressure on manufacturers from the other direction of the supply chain.

>> In jurisdictions where cannabis has just been legalized, the launch of derivative products, such as edibles and vapes, could lag behind the availability of bud, negatively impacting manufacturers.

>> As legalization grows, large tobacco, alcohol, beverage, food, and pharmaceutical companies are likely to enter the market and either acquire competing MIPs or drive them out of business.

In addition to these concerns, every aspect of the manufacturing process has its own challenges and risks. MIPs typically have their own extraction, kitchen, and packaging operations. Before investing in a company, you should understand the basics of these operations, as described in the following sections.

Extraction

Extraction involves various processes that pull the active ingredients from the plant to create *concentrates* — products that contain higher potencies of desirable substances. Various extraction methods are used that involve subjecting the harvested and cured plant matter to temperature (heat or cold), pressure, solvents, or a combination of the three. The result is an oil or semi-solid product (such as resin), which is much more potent than the flower from which it was extracted. Concentrates may be sold or used as ingredients in other products, such as vape oils, edibles, and lotions.

Extraction operations can be complex, costly, and dangerous due to the following factors.

>> **Complexity:** A variety of extraction methods are available to produce different extracts for use as is or in different products. Knowledge and expertise with the different extraction methods and extracts requires a high degree of education and training. Recruiting and retaining someone with this expertise can be challenging and costly.

>> **Cost:** Extraction is a costly operation in terms of machines, materials (including solvents), safety equipment, and training. A single apparatus for performing CO_2 or H_2O extraction, for example, may cost hundreds of thousands of dollars.

>> **Danger:** Some extraction processes involve heat, compression, and volatile and potentially toxic chemicals. Safety is key, which means everyone involved must be well trained and deeply committed to complying with all government safety regulations.

REMEMBER

Many companies specialize in extraction, selling extracts to MIPs or directly to dispensaries and other retail outlets. They may cultivate their own plants or source bud from one or more cultivators. However, in some cases, the extraction process is part of a larger MIP.

Kitchen

Kitchen operations involve using the oil extracted from cannabis as an ingredient in consumer products, including vape oil, edibles, lotions, tinctures, and soaps. Although a kitchen can be a separate cannabis business, it's usually part of a larger MIP operation.

The main challenges that industrial cannabis kitchens must overcome are in the form of burdensome rules, regulations, and inspections. They must meet the high standards already in place for restaurant and industrial kitchens plus regulations that apply specifically to cannabis.

Kitchens must be kept impeccably clean, and inspections and detailed tracking and reporting can be costly and burdensome for companies.

Packaging

When you consider all the steps required to produce a consumer cannabis product, packaging may seem like an afterthought, but this stage of the process has its own challenges, such as the following:

>> Choosing the right packaging material for different products to preserve freshness and comply with safety regulations, such as child-proofing.

>> Complying with packaging and labeling regulations, which can be very detailed and subject to change.

>> Developing branding and designs that make products stand out against the competition.

>> Ensuring that the packaging is cost-effective (to preserve profit margins).

Processed product brand

A *processed product brand* is a company that develops and markets its own unique products and sells them to retail outlets. The company may be a vertically integrated MIP or contract with one or more cultivators and MIPs to grow, produce, package, and distribute its products to retailers. For example, a processed product brand may develop its own brand of vape devices and vape oils, market them to consumers, and sell them to medical and adult-use dispensaries in one or more states or countries.

As a brand owner, the company focuses primarily on coming up with new product ideas and establishing a strong brand presence. It can then outsource cultivation, manufacturing, distribution, and sales to other businesses or take on these operations itself.

REMEMBER

The big challenge comes when a processed product brand wants to expand distribution across borders, which often poses a legal problem. The brand can't simply expand distribution by shipping products outside its home state or province. It needs to either set up cultivation and manufacturing operations in the target jurisdiction or partner with other companies that are already established in that jurisdiction.

Retailers/dispensaries

Cannabis retailers run the dispensaries and other retail outlets that sell products directly to consumers. Depending on the rules and regulations in a given jurisdiction, dispensaries may be allowed to cater to medical marijuana consumers, adult-use consumers, or both.

Dispensaries and other cannabis retail outlets face a host of challenges, including the following:

» In the U.S., where cannabis is still federally illegal, dispensaries are an obvious target for federal law enforcement, so they can be a risky venture.

» Even in jurisdictions in which cannabis is legal, sale of cannabis may be restricted in certain areas, or residents may present strong resistance to having a cannabis retailer in their neighborhood.

» Retail locations must comply with set-back rules from schools, playgrounds, houses of worship, and other areas, which can make site selection difficult.

» Rules and regulations governing cannabis retail outlets are often complex, and penalties for non-compliance are stiff. If a business is selling both medical and adult-use cannabis, it's likely to face regulations similar to those that would apply to both a liquor store and a pharmacy.

Device makers

Device makers design and manufacture grinders, vaporizers (such as vape pens), and various smoking devices for consuming cannabis. The two big advantages to investing in device makers are that they're less closely regulated than companies that deal directly with the plant and extracts, and they can generally distribute their products across state lines without concern over breaking any federal laws.

Vaping is one of the most popular cannabis consumption methods. You can invest in this market segment by putting your money into either device makers or extraction operations, which supply the vape oils.

WARNING

Vaping technology is rarely proprietary, and when it is, the technology is often outdated before the patent is issued. Vape pens quickly go in and out of fashion in terms of style, shape, and delivery mechanisms. Think twice before investing in a vaping device startup, because the market is saturated and very difficult to penetrate with a new device. If you're dead set on investing in a vape company, look for one with strong management, revenues, and earnings.

Considering Ancillary Businesses

Businesses don't have to be in the cannabis industry to profit from it and to offer investors other avenues for getting into the market. Traditional businesses that have existed long before cannabis achieved legal status in any state or country also stand to profit. Often referred to as "ancillary" businesses, these traditional establishments provide products and services that support cannabis companies, such as fertilizers and pesticides, grow lights, banking and payroll services, marketing and advertising, and many more.

In this section, I introduce you to some of the ancillary business types that are likely to profit from the cannabis industry, and provide some guidance on what to look for before investing in these establishments.

TIP

If you have an aversion to financial risk, ancillary businesses offer a safer (though not totally safe) alternative to investing in cannabis. Even if the entire cannabis industry were to fold, your investment wouldn't be entirely obliterated. The ancillary business could continue to operate and profit by serving other customers. As you evaluate ancillary businesses to invest in, consider the portion of revenue coming in from cannabis business — some ancillary businesses depend more than others on the success of their cannabis customers.

Breweries

Breweries can be both primary and ancillary cannabis businesses. Many breweries are entering the core market with their own cannabis-infused beers and other beverages. Others serve the industry as CO_2 (carbon dioxide) suppliers.

The fermentation process that produces beer naturally creates CO_2, a greenhouse gas, which is normally vented out of the brewery and into the surrounding air. Cannabis cultivators feed CO_2 to their plants to fuel growth. Some extraction processes also require CO_2. To reduce their carbon footprint and create another source of revenue, breweries have begun to capture and store their excess carbon dioxide and sell it to cannabis cultivators and companies that produce extracts.

Banking, payroll, and other cash management services

In any countries where cannabis is legal, traditional banks and other financial institutions can serve cannabis businesses as they do other businesses. In the U.S., however, where cannabis is federally illegal, some banks and financial institutions may shy away from cannabis businesses. For example, as I was writing this, branded credit card companies prohibited cannabis transactions on their networks, forcing dispensaries to operate as cash-only businesses. (Many have ATMs on site to provide customers with convenient access to cash.)

Financial regulations and restrictions on cannabis businesses have opened opportunities for banks and other financial institutions geared specifically to cannabis businesses, including third-party electronic payment processors and specialized payroll services.

WARNING

Investing in banks and other financial service providers that focus on serving the cannabis industry can be risky for a couple reasons. First, they may attract more attention from regulators, increasing their risk of suffering costly penalties. Second, if laws change to allow federally insured banks to do business with legitimate cannabis businesses, competition from more established banks and financial institutions will put pressure on financial service providers whose clientele are mostly cannabis businesses.

THE SAFE BANKING ACT

The Secure and Fair Enforcement (SAFE) Banking Act of 2019 proposes that banks in the U.S. be permitted to offer loans and other banking services to Cannabis-Related Legitimate Businesses (CRLBs), including contractors and vendors that never touch the plant. It passed the House of Representatives on September 25, 2019 by a vote of 321 to 103 but has since been delayed in the Senate. It has strong support among state attorneys general and financial service organizations.

If the bill passes, it will prohibit federal regulators from taking any of the following actions against banks or financial service organizations that do business with CRLBs:

- Terminating or limiting deposit insurance.

- Prohibiting a depository institution from providing services to a CRLB or penalizing them for doing so.

- Encouraging or incentivizing a depository institution to refuse service to a CRLB.

- Taking any adverse action in respect to a loan made to a CRLB.

However, the bill doesn't give CRLBs and financial institutions carte blanche. If the bill passes, strict rules and regulations will remain in place to ensure that all transactions can be traced to legitimate activities. For example, a CRLB that has cash from sales prior to cannabis being legalized in the state in which it operates will not be free to deposit that cash in a federally insured bank, because the bank will not be able to prove that the money came from legitimate business transactions.

Blockchain and other technologies

Blockchain is best known as the technology behind the cryptocurrency bitcoin, but its uses extend far beyond those of enabling bitcoin transactions. Blockchain functions as a secure, shared, digital ledger that's being used more widely to track everything from vehicle service records to real estate transactions. It's very useful in the cannabis industry, because it can be used to track product from seed to sale, simplifying the task of managing and monitoring the supply chain, complying with complex regulations, facilitating tax collection, and much more.

Numerous tech companies, including IBM, are heavily invested in blockchain and are using it to develop solutions for a variety of industries and government organizations. Smaller tech companies are also getting involved, many of which are developing products and services specifically for the cannabis industry.

WARNING

Be careful about investing in blockchain in the hopes that it'll ride the coattails of cannabis growth. The marriage between cannabis and blockchain is unholy at best. Cannabis businesses are trying to shed the decades-old perception that revenues are laundered and not properly reported. Blockchain and the related cryptocurrency offerings give cannabis consumers and companies a way to discreetly transact, but do little for the overall value of a particular cannabis business. Plenty of money will be made coupling blockchain and cannabis, but this is a nascent and risky proposition at best.

Delivery services

Grocery stores and restaurants are increasingly offering delivery services to their customers, and cannabis businesses are beginning to follow this trend. One factor contributing to the popularity of delivery services in the cannabis industry is the fact that new customers are often reluctant to visit a cannabis dispensary to buy product.

Unfortunately, with cannabis, unlicensed delivery services are a target for state regulators in their attempts to clamp down on illicit cannabis businesses. This pressure on delivery services makes it difficult for small players to survive and compete. Industry experts believe that as regulations on delivery services become clearer, smaller delivery services will begin to consolidate and start looking for opportunities to go public to attract capital to fuel their growth.

WARNING

Before investing in a delivery service, be sure you understand the geographical limitations of the associated licenses and the market demand for delivery in your prospect's territory. Delivery is an overcrowded vertical as well. You need only look at the trouble Ease (a well-known delivery brand) has had to understand the risks associated with this service. You're going to want to know who's providing product for delivery services to gauge demand for delivery.

Another factor that may threaten the survival of dedicated cannabis delivery services is the fact that many dispensaries may simply hire their own delivery staff.

Grow equipment manufacturers and suppliers

Given the fact that the entire cannabis industry is based on the ability to grow the plants, it's no surprise that specialized equipment is needed, especially for growing cannabis indoors. Specialized equipment includes grow lights, air conditioning and ventilation systems (including fans and ducts), hydroponics systems (to grow in nutrient-rich solutions instead of soil), grow tents, and grow pots.

As an investor, you can look for companies that cater specifically to professional cultivators or home growers or consider larger, more established companies that produce lighting and ventilation equipment for homes, businesses, and industrial or agricultural applications.

TIP

Companies that specialize in equipment for growing cannabis may have a bigger potential upside as demand for cannabis grows. However, if you have a low appetite for risk, look for well-established companies that have a broader base of customers extending beyond the cannabis industry, such as companies that manufacture grow lights for large agricultural operations, or lighting or air conditioning equipment for industrial use.

Marketing, public relations, and advertising firms

Due to regulations that govern the marketing and advertising of cannabis to consumers and the challenges of overcoming negative attitudes toward cannabis, a number of marketing and advertising firms specialize in serving cannabis businesses. These firms typically create and manage marketing and advertising campaigns that include the following:

>> Social media and influencer marketing

>> Search engine optimization (SEO)

>> Pay-per-click (PPC) advertising

>> Email marketing

>> Event planning

>> Branding

>> Packaging design

TIP

Before investing in a cannabis-focused marketing and advertising firm, check its client list to be sure the firm serves a number of successful cannabis companies.

Professional employer organizations

Professional employer organizations (PEOs) provide staffing services for companies, handling recruitment, hiring, and in some cases even payroll. Because the cannabis industry is growing so quickly, finding skilled and unskilled employees is often a challenge for businesses. PEOs help cannabis businesses meet that challenge and scale their workforce during peak periods of production and sales.

When qualifying a PEO, examine the management team's track record and its experience in PEOs in other industries. PEOs are a new trend in cannabis, and they frequently serve larger, better-funded cannabis companies as well as publicly traded companies.

TIP

PEOs are a service business, so the health of the company depends on the number and size of service contracts that company holds. To identify the best prospects in this arena, compare client lists and related service contracts.

Pharmaceutical and biotech companies

Although adult-use and medical marijuana draw the majority of investors' attention, pharmaceutical and biotech companies seeking to profit from cannabis often go unnoticed. Small biotech and large pharmaceutical companies alike are researching the active ingredients in cannabis in the hopes of discovering new medical uses for them. As they succeed and as the Food and Drug Administration (FDA) and Drug Enforcement Agency (DEA) recognize these products as pharmaceuticals instead of as illicit drugs, these companies are well positioned to profit from cannabis.

REMEMBER

Pharmaceuticals have three big advantages over the medical marijuana available through dispensaries:

>> Pharmaceutical cannabis is legal across the nation, not just in states where medical marijuana is legal.

>> Insurance companies reimburse for pharmaceuticals but not for medical marijuana.

>> Pharmaceuticals are exempt from sales tax in nearly every state.

When evaluating biotech and pharmaceutical companies, use many of the same criteria that you would to evaluate established pharmaceutical companies. Consider how much a company has invested in medicinal cannabis research (in both time and money) and look at its portfolio of pharmaceuticals, with an emphasis on companies that have existing patents on cannabis-based medications.

Investments in private biotech and pharmaceutical companies are a long play. Don't expect swift returns.

Real estate

The cannabis industry needs land and buildings to grow, process, and sell cannabis products, and these real estate assets are often in short supply due to several factors:

>> Zoning laws that restrict where cannabis can be grown, processed, and sold

>> Inability or reluctance among banks to loan money to cannabis businesses

>> Inability or reluctance among insurance companies to insure cannabis operations

>> Strict security, fire, and safety regulations in place for cannabis businesses

If you're interested in investing in the cannabis real estate market, you have several options:

>> Sell or lease land or buildings to cannabis businesses. Be sure to lease the land/building at a premium that takes into account the limited real estate options for cannabis businesses.

If this is the approach you decide to take, team up with a real estate broker and an attorney who understand the local cannabis market and the rules and regulations that are in place where you plan to invest. Profiting from cannabis-focused real estate investments requires specialized knowledge and expertise.

>> Invest in a cannabis-focused real estate investment trust (REIT).

Because cannabis is federally illegal in the U.S., obtaining an accurate property appraisal when you decide to sell the property can be a challenge. The property should be valued at the market price of the land plus the value of a location that's permitted for a cannabis business. That makes the land/building more valuable, but you may have a hard time selling that notion to a buyer.

Security services and security equipment suppliers

Cannabis is primarily a cash business, and both cannabis and cash attract thieves, so safety and security are key issues across the supply chain — from growers to dispensaries. As a result, security companies stand to profit from the industry through the sale of equipment and services, including access control solutions, fences and gates, safes, security doors, video surveillance, armored vehicle transportation, armed guards, and cyber-security.

REMEMBER

Like PEOs, security providers are service businesses, so the health of the company depends on the number and size of service contracts that company holds. To identify the best prospects, compare client lists and related service contracts.

Software companies

Like any modern business, cannabis businesses benefit from the use of computers and software, and many software companies develop products specifically for the cannabis industry. Software includes specialized point-of-sale systems for dispensaries, seed-to-sale inventory tracking/supply chain management systems, B2B marketplace software, cannabis delivery software, and more.

WARNING

The biggest risk when entering the software space is that many technologies become dated within 18 to 36 months. Many cannabis companies using industry-specific software solutions won't engage in long-term contracts and often change providers every few quarters, depending on the scope of services.

Chapter **3**

Understanding the Political, Cultural, and Regulatory Landscape

A s a cannabis investor, you can expect to experience more uncertainty in the cannabis market than in other more stable markets, largely due to changes in the political, cultural, and regulatory landscape and to the high costs and complexities of doing business. These factors place additional pressures on the industry as a whole as well as on individual companies, which can often drive companies out of business or influence decisions regarding restructuring, acquisitions, and mergers. Cannabis investors should be prepared for a wild ride until acceptance and legalization of cannabis become more widespread and the industry becomes more established. This could take several years or even decades, and may possibly never happen.

Before investing in cannabis, you would be wise to familiarize yourself with the politics, culture, and regulations that may impact cannabis demand, availability, and costs. Information and insight into these factors enable you to make well-informed decisions about whether to invest in cannabis and where to put your money if you do invest.

In this chapter, I bring you up to speed on the political, cultural, and regulatory landscape in which cannabis businesses operate, and I encourage you to conduct your own research to access current information.

Recognizing the Impact of Laws on the Industry

When discussions arise about the legality of cannabis, they usually revolve around growing it, selling it, or possessing it. However, cannabis laws and the enforcement of those laws also impact the industry, influencing everything from where different cannabis businesses can operate and under what conditions, to the taxes and fees they pay and ultimately the cost and availability of the product.

Complications and confusion often arise over differences in laws and regulations at the federal, state, and local levels. For example, in the U.S., cannabis is illegal at the federal level, legal for medical use in many states, legal for both medical and adult use in several states, and prohibited for sale and possession in many municipalities within states where it's legal.

In 2013, Uruguay became the first country to officially legalize cannabis for both medical and adult use. In 2018, Canada became the second country and the first G7 member to legalize cannabis. In the provinces of Quebec and Alberta, the legal age is 18; in the remainder of the country, it's 19. In New Jersey, before voters even had a chance to vote on a proposition to legalize adult-use marijuana, more than 50 local governments had already passed laws banning its sale or possession.

In this section, I bring you up to speed on federal, state, local, and international marijuana laws in the hopes that by knowing the laws, you'll be better prepared to ride the waves that are sure to rock the cannabis industry as its future unfolds.

Getting up to speed on U.S. federal law and enforcement

In the U.S., in the 1800s, marijuana was used as an ingredient in many medicinal products sold in pharmacies across the country, but by 1931, 29 states had outlawed it, citing research at the time that linked the use of marijuana with violence, criminal activity, and other deviant social behaviors.

Federal regulation didn't occur until President Franklin D. Roosevelt signed the Marihuana Tax Act of 1937, which required every person who sold, acquired, dispensed, or possessed marijuana to register with the Internal Revenue Service

(IRS), pay taxes on their transactions, and complete an order form that required the name and address of both buyer and seller and the amount of marijuana being sold or bought. Although the act did not specifically criminalize marijuana, it came to be used in that way.

In 1970, the Supreme Court overturned the law, and Congress repealed it but simultaneously passed the Controlled Substances Act, designating marijuana a Schedule 1 controlled substance based on the belief that it had a high potential for abuse, no currently accepted medical use, and a lack of accepted safety regarding the use of the drug. Adding marijuana to the list of Schedule 1 controlled substances (along with heroin, LSD, ecstasy, and magic mushrooms) effectively made it illegal for anything other than very limited research.

WARNING

In particular, the following activities are federal crimes:

>> Transporting cannabis across any state line, even if it's transported from one state in which it's legal directly to another.

>> Flying with cannabis, because it enters into federal airspace.

>> Possessing or using marijuana on federal land, including national parks and forests.

THE COLE MEMORANDUM

During the Obama administration, on August 29, 2013, United States Deputy Attorney General James M. Cole issued a trio of memos including the Cole Memorandum to all United States attorneys general. The memo informed the state attorneys general that due to limited resources, the U.S. Department of Justice would not be enforcing federal marijuana prohibition in states that legalized and effectively regulated and enforced their own marijuana laws.

The memo directed the state attorneys general to "not focus federal resources in your states on individuals whose actions are in clear and unambiguous compliance with existing state laws providing for the medical use of marijuana." Instead, states were encouraged to address federal priorities, for example, "by implementing effective measures to prevent diversion of marijuana outside the regulated system and to other states, prohibiting access to marijuana by minors, and replacing an illicit marijuana trade that funds criminal enterprises with a tightly regulated market in which revenues are tracked and accounted for."

This memo was rescinded under the Trump administration in January 2018 by Attorney General Jeff Sessions. The impact of the rescission in individual states has yet to be determined, but it's a cause for concern because it indicates that the feds may be leaning toward greater enforcement of the federal prohibition of marijuana.

Federal laws and their enforcement impact cannabis businesses and investors in the following ways:

>> Because transporting cannabis across state lines is illegal, cannabis businesses that want to expand sales into other states must duplicate their operations in those states. They can't take advantage of economies of scale simply by shipping their products across state lines.

>> The Bank Secrecy Act (BSA) and federal money-laundering statutes discourage banks from offering services to cannabis businesses. (Passed in 1970, the BSA is a U.S. law that requires financial institutions in the U.S. to assist federal agencies in detecting and preventing money laundering.) Violations can result in steep fines and imprisonment of bank officials. Inaccessibility to basic banking services increases the costs and complexities of operating cannabis businesses.

REMEMBER

Some banks are starting to serve cannabis businesses, and the Financial Crimes Enforcement Network (FinCEN), the financial intelligence unit of the U.S. Department of Treasury, offers guidance to banks on how to comply with regulations when serving marijuana and ancillary businesses. However, compliance places an added burden on banks to police the marijuana businesses they serve. In addition, the Department of Justice reserves the right to prosecute banks for working with these businesses.

>> Without basic banking services, cannabis businesses have no access to the capital markets, which are useful for raising money for development and growth. They need to rely on private investors, which provides private investment opportunities but at a very high risk.

>> According to the principles of contract law, any contract in breach of public policy is void and unenforceable, which is a major concern for investors or funds regarding any investment contract's legitimacy. This concern serves as another obstacle to cannabis businesses seeking to raise investment capital for development or expansion.

>> Cannabis businesses are required to pay income taxes, but filing tax returns (federal and state) constitutes self-incrimination. In addition, without banking services, cannabis businesses must pay their taxes in cash, which is inconvenient, costly, and risky.

>> Due to the 280E provision in the IRS tax code, cannabis businesses are prohibited from deducting ordinary business expenses from their gross income, thereby significantly increasing their tax burden and negatively impacting their profitability.

>> Bankruptcy protections are unavailable for cannabis businesses in the U.S. Without the option to restructure, cannabis businesses are often forced to shut down when they encounter credit issues. As a result, creditors may have difficulty collecting their debts, which discourages them from loaning money to cannabis businesses in the first place.

>> Fear among potential customers of losing a federal job, student financial aid, the right to own a firearm, or eligibility for federally subsidized housing can put downward pressure on cannabis sales.

>> If marijuana is legalized at the federal level, the entire business environment will change, allowing large, well-established companies in other industries, such as alcohol, tobacco, and pharmaceuticals, to compete for market share.

So, what does this mean for investors? Regulations generally move in a direction that favors growth and investment opportunity. At this time, more than two-thirds of Americans live in a jurisdiction that has some form of legal cannabis. The country is trending toward a repeal of prohibition, but that will likely be a slow and clumsy process from a regulatory standpoint.

If you're looking to invest in licenses and permits, consider states with a more limited number of granted permits. States that limit the number of permits make those permits more valuable by doing so. You also want to consider states that have constitutions providing for voter referendums. As you do, you'll notice that most states that allow for referendums are west of the Mississippi and business friendly. There's a historical reason for that. Those states joined the union in the 19th century, and their state constitutions are based on the Spanish and French democratic models that allow voters to pass laws by referendum. As a result, and generally speaking, states with voter referendum and business-friendly regulatory environments tend to have legislation providing for some degree of legalized cannabis.

WARNING

Be careful when you're considering investing in any company whose licenses are based on narrow zoning laws. I've invested in real estate that was once coveted because it was zoned for cannabis only to have the city loosen its zoning restrictions six months later. I paid a premium for the property, only to see its value drop when zoning laws made more real estate available for cannabis businesses. I could have avoided that mistake by researching more thoroughly what was on the ballot or what was being discussed by the zoning committee.

TIP

Keep an eye on the Strengthening the Tenth Amendment Through Entrusting States (STATES) Act, which would amend the Controlled Substances Act (CSA) so that any state-legal cannabis activity would no longer be considered illegal under federal law. The STATES Act would also solve the cannabis banking problem, because the federal money-laundering statute is triggered only for illegal activities. Likewise, because the 280E provision applies only to revenue generated by illegal means, cannabis businesses would be able to deduct their business expenses just like any legal business. Although the STATES Act has bipartisan support and was passed by a large margin in the House of Representatives, as of this writing, the bill was hung up in the Senate.

Brushing up on state cannabis laws

Although cannabis is federally illegal, each state has the right to legalize it within its borders and set the rules and regulations for personal and commercial growth, production, transportation, sale, possession, and use. States fall into one of the following five categories.

>> **Fully legal:** Both medicinal and adult use are allowed.

>> **Fully illegal:** No medicinal or adult use is allowed or decriminalized (see the final item in this list for more about decriminalization).

>> **Medical and decriminalized:** Medical use is legal, and possession and use is decriminalized.

>> **Medical only:** Marijuana is legalized only for medical use, which in some states allows only cannabidiol (CBD) oil use (CBD doesn't contain the psychoactive ingredient THC).

>> **Decriminalized:** Possessing or using small amounts of marijuana will not lead to arrest, prosecution, prison time, or a criminal record (decriminalization details vary by state).

TIP

The easiest way to find out where each state in the U.S. stands on legalization is to search the web for "marijuana legal states." You'll see a color-coded map like the one shown in Figure 3-1. State marijuana laws change frequently, so access a map from a reliable source that has current information, such as weedmaps. com/learn/laws-and-regulations.

State laws and enforcement of those laws can negatively impact cannabis businesses and investors in several ways, including the following:

>> Every state in which marijuana is legal has numerous rules and regulations that apply to marijuana growers, producers, sellers, and distributors. These rules and regulations govern everything from verifying the identities of buyers to packing, labeling, and tracking products, and all of them add to the cost and complexity of doing business.

>> Marijuana taxes vary by state, with adult-use marijuana typically taxed at a much higher rate than medical marijuana. Higher taxes add to the product cost and can drive sales to illegal sellers, negatively impacting sales for legal businesses.

>> States vary in the number of legal cannabis businesses they allow, how much they charge for licenses, and how quickly they implement legalization, which can all impact how successful cannabis businesses are in each state.

» Some states require marijuana businesses to reserve large amounts of cash before applying for a license. This practice encourages *rolling up* marijuana businesses — a method that involves acquiring and merging small businesses to increase their collective value. In these states, large marijuana businesses have a distinct advantage over smaller operations.

» State laws may stipulate residency requirements for investors in cannabis businesses.

» Some states in which marijuana is legal are less stringent in enforcing laws against illegal sales, which can negatively impact sales for legal businesses.

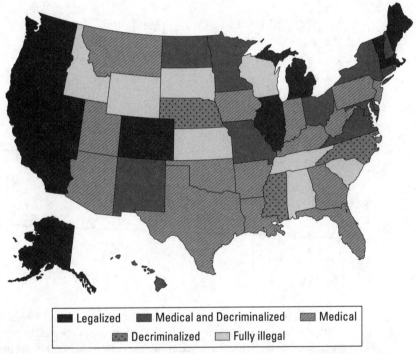

FIGURE 3-1:
Check out an online map to determine overall legal status.

Legend: Legalized | Medical and Decriminalized | Medical | Decriminalized | Fully illegal

©John Wiley & Sons, Inc.

Considering local laws, too

In states where cannabis is legal, local municipalities can separately regulate its growth, production, and sale within their borders. They are also allowed to add taxes and fees to commercial efforts above and beyond those of the state. In some cases, municipalities can completely ban commercial endeavors. For example, Colorado Springs permits medical sales but has continued to ban adult-use dispensaries. Penalties can vary significantly from one municipality to another.

These variations and costs can negatively impact the sales and profits of cannabis businesses, even in states in which cannabis is legal.

Examining cannabis laws in other countries

As an investor, you want to know about a cannabis company's range of operations — specifically, the countries it serves around the world. A company that operates in several countries may be less susceptible to changes in laws and regulations than a company operating in only one country. In addition, a company's global reach reflects its ambitions for growth. Here's a list of countries in which cannabis is legal or decriminalized to some degree:

>> Australia

>> Canada

>> Germany

>> Italy

>> Mexico

>> The Netherlands

>> New Zealand

>> South Korea

>> Spain

>> Switzerland

>> Uruguay

>> U.S. Virgin Islands

REMEMBER

Carefully research each market before investing in companies that operate in it. Examine the laws and enforcement of those laws, cannabis demand, the costs of doing business, competition from illegal sellers, and other factors to gain a better understanding of the potential for sales, profits, and growth, as well as the risks involved.

Riding the Waves of Politics and Culture

Cannabis has a long history of use in many areas, including medicine, textiles, religion, and even magic (in the ancient world). Perspectives about the plant, its uses, and its users have changed frequently around the world, especially over the last 100 years. In the U.S., cannabis has been a lightning rod for debate among politicians, scientists, and citizens over whether it has medicinal benefits and whether those potential benefits outweigh the potential risks, especially with respect to adult use.

As an investor, you want to stay tuned to the news and the opinions of the day, because attitudes toward cannabis can change overnight and significantly impact the value of any investments you have in the industry, especially in the short term. A single study concluding that marijuana poses a significant danger to a user's health or to society overall could derail any positive momentum in the industry.

In this section, I highlight the areas of focus, so you know what to look for, and I bring you up to speed on the political and cultural climate surrounding cannabis as of the writing of this book.

Checking the nation's pulse

Legalization of cannabis for both medical and adult use in the U.S. began as a movement with early activists coming from the more traditionally recognized user demographics of artists, musicians, and the so-called stoner culture. However, growing acceptance, along with expanding numbers of states legalizing use, has begun to show that cannabis acceptance is a very big tent, encompassing people from every demographic of age, race, income, gender, location, and political party.

This section explores the factors that are driving people to change their attitudes about cannabis, examines the prevailing attitudes and perspectives, and encourages you to stay abreast of the ever-evolving social and political climate.

Acknowledging the drivers of change

Acceptance and use among the middle-American, middle-income, middle-aged white constituency has come mostly from three drivers.

>> **Monetary impact to the community:** With Amendment 64 in Colorado, voters approved adult-use cannabis with an extremely high tax burden (on consumers and the industry) that directs funds to the state's rural education efforts through a grant program for school construction projects. Colorado was the first state to implement voter-approved adult-use cannabis sales, and the resulting state income from sales tax, excise tax, and fees has provoked revenue-envy among other states across the country, forcing both politicians and voters to sit up and take notice. In any state where adult-use (recreational) cannabis use is legal, the taxes and fees are fairly steep and show some promise of easing state budgetary constraints.

>> **Reduction in stigma due to medical marijuana:** After a few states legalized medicinal marijuana, more people started to accept its value as a health management tool. Increasingly, people are hearing from friends, relatives, and acquaintances who have had success using marijuana in many forms to help mitigate symptoms related to severe and chronic illness, as well as more mundane aches and pains. Specifically, the use of marijuana to alleviate nausea and stimulate appetite in cancer patients, along with the support of physicians, has helped drive the narrative that marijuana can be used as medicine.

REMEMBER

In addition, statistics showing the drop in fatal opioid overdoses in states where marijuana is legal have helped drive the awareness of its benefits to society. One study estimated that "legalization and access to adult-use marijuana reduced annual opioid mortality in the range of 20 to 35 percent, with particularly pronounced effects for synthetic opioids."

>> **The rising tide of positive media coverage:** Traditional media outlets have begun to join bloggers in their efforts to expose more people to the well-researched and substantiated facts about marijuana. As marijuana messaging becomes more positive in the press, it's beginning to alleviate fears and break down resistance to legalization.

Recognizing differences in attitudes about medical and adult-use cannabis

The difference in public perception regarding medical versus adult marijuana use is reflected in how it's taxed — medical marijuana is taxed at a significantly lower rate. Medical use is gaining acceptance quickly, as witnessed by the growing number of states legalizing it. Adult use is still mired in stigma but working to break through.

Growing numbers of scientific research studies demonstrating the value of cannabis for treating symptoms associated with many diseases, illnesses, and ailments are helping people recognize marijuana's medicinal value. Add to this the thousands of media articles, publications, blog posts, and positive word of mouth about medical usage, and the world is beginning to turn toward a positive perspective on at least one segment of the industry.

Keeping pace with evolving attitudes

As perspectives related to medical cannabis change, sometimes at lightning speed, limited numbers of early adopters are turning into an avalanche of support. This has been translating to additional support for adult use as people share their success stories through the press, social media, and word of mouth.

The dire warnings of societal destruction have failed to materialize, and even some ardent opponents have acknowledged the value of the industry and the benefits to individuals. Some dramatic pivots have occurred, even with constituencies that had virulently opposed cannabis, as they've hopped on the bandwagon. For example, former Speaker of the House, John Boehner went from staunch opposition to joining the board of directors of a cannabis company!

As attitudes evolve, turn to social media and the Internet to follow the discussion. With half the customer base under 35 years old, online and mobile interactions are leading the charge, and bloggers, along with cannabis websites, are a primary source of information.

Debunking misconceptions of cannabis and users

Many of the anti-cannabis voices have harped on the myths of unintended consequences and unfounded allegations to drive fear of legalization. The largest misconception is rooted in the negative stereotype of the "stoner" culture. The reality is a much broader and more inclusive demographic.

Many of today's cannabis dispensaries break with the stereotypical image of the old "head shop." The background music isn't exclusively reggae or heavy metal, and you're now much less likely to see the walls adorned with Jamaican flags and pictures of Bob Marley. The only black lights you're likely to see are those used by receptionists along with sophisticated ID scanners as they check for ID authenticity, age, or medical card compliance before allowing customers to enter secured "budrooms" for purchase. (A *budroom* is an area inside a dispensary where products are displayed and sold; it's often set up like a jewelry store, with products stored under glass.) Online sales also have high hurdles to protect against underage use.

Cannabis is becoming big business, and companies are building sophisticated marketing and branding designed to be welcoming and to appeal to all legal-aged demographics. Market share based on price and exclusivity is creating brands that cater to upscale clientele with store space that can look like a high-end jewelry store or a tasteful, yet hip, hangout.

Clientele are breaking old molds, too. In 2017, BDSA's profiles of cannabis dispensary shoppers showed that about half of them were aged 21 to 35, and the other half were older. Six in ten had college degrees or higher education. Nearly half lived in the suburbs. About half were married with children. Sixty-two percent were employed with an average annual income of $74.9K.

Many misconceptions about cannabis and its users fall into the category of myths of "unintended consequences" — the idea that legalization will result in vast increases in homelessness, crime, black market activity, overdose, impaired driving, addiction, and teen use. Science and research have debunked these myths:

>> Homelessness and crime have not increased due specifically to legalization of cannabis. After controlling for increased populations and traditional movement of people, the increases in homelessness are in line with those locations that have not legalized, and the levels are what are expected in those locations, regardless of cannabis use.

>> Statistics show that black market activity has actually decreased in areas with legal adult use.

>> Due to a lack of receptors in specific areas of the brain, people have no biological means to overdose on THC alone or to become biologically addicted (though emotional addiction or habitual use is as likely as with other substances and habits such as chocolate or exercise). No reported and confirmed deaths have been linked specifically to cannabis overconsumption.

>> Teen use has not increased in states with legalization. U.S. numbers show that teen marijuana use is currently holding at its lowest level in 20 years.

>> Impaired driving from marijuana alone is a small fraction of the rate of impaired driving reported by law enforcement. In Colorado, statistics show that number to be close to six percent of all reports.

Examining activism

The original effort to legalize marijuana was started at the grassroots level by individuals with a great deal of passion and an understanding of the long odds necessary to overcome years of fear and prejudice against cannabis. The focus was on marijuana as medicine and its value in alleviating symptoms, such as seizures and nausea, associated with certain illnesses, such as epilepsy and cancer.

Generations of Americans growing up since the Nixon era's War on Drugs and the "Just Say No" campaign of First Lady Nancy Reagan in the 1980s had developed the perspective that equated marijuana with other Schedule 1 substances.

Yet these early activists were able to overcome steep hurdles, going directly to state constituencies with amendments on statewide ballots that succeeded in demonstrating the will of the people and the power of well-researched facts. As early-adopter states demonstrated success with regulation, state revenue generation, economic drivers, and resident acceptance, more formalized groups began to organize.

WHAT'S A SCHEDULE 1 SUBSTANCE?

The legal foundation of the U.S. government's war against drug abuse is The Controlled Substances Act, which is part of the Comprehensive Drug Abuse and Control Act of 1970. As a result of these acts, the U.S. Drug Enforcement Agency (DEA) divides controlled substances into five categories called "schedules," based on each drug's safety, potential for addiction and abuse, and whether it has any legitimate medical use:

- Schedule 1 substances are deemed to have no accepted medical use and a high potential for abuse. They include heroin, LSD, marijuana (cannabis), ecstasy, methaqualone (commonly referred to by the brand name Quaalude), and peyote ("magic mushrooms").

- Schedule 2 substances are also considered dangerous and are deemed to have a high potential for psychological or physical dependence. They include cocaine, methamphetamine, methadone, hydromorphone, meperidine, oxycodone, fentanyl, Dexedrine, Adderall, and Ritalin.

- Schedule 3 substances carry a low to moderate potential for physical or psychological dependence. They include ketamine, anabolic steroids, testosterone, and products containing less than 15 milligrams of hydrocodone per dose or less than 90 milligrams of codeine per dose.

- Schedule 4 substances are deemed to have a low potential for abuse and a low risk of dependence. They include Xanax, Soma, Darvon, Darvocet, Valium, Ativan, Talwin, and Ambien.

- Schedule 5 substances consist of products that contain limited concentrations of narcotics — typically cough suppressants, antidiarrheal medications, and analgesics.

In response, groups opposing the legalization of marijuana became more active, as well. They were often heavily funded by industries that have seen marijuana as a threat to market share for their own products (such as pharmaceutical medications), and bolstered by equally passionate individuals who believe that marijuana is a dangerous drug.

However, as the tide has turned, the grassroots constituencies promoting cannabis have successfully recruited professional trade organizations to join their cause, such as Colorado Leads and the Cannabis Trade Federation. These organizations are working to secure the industry as a whole and to further the march toward legitimacy through professionalism and promotion of industry-standard practices as seen in many other established industries.

Tuning into cannabis culture

Until recently, the perception of the cannabis culture has been aligned closely with the stoner culture as portrayed in popular movies such as Cheech and Chong's *Up in Smoke* and *Fast Times At Ridgemont High*, in which Sean Penn plays Jeff Spicoli, a failing high school student who routinely gets high before class, emerging from a VW van surrounded by clouds of smoke.

While these and other Hollywood comedies always portray a stereotype of the cannabis culture, the parody is mixed with the realities of Jamaican reggae culture and generations of real users consuming the illegal substance. An era of tacit acceptance began when military personnel used cannabis during deployment in Vietnam and returned to the U.S. with a newfound appreciation of its calming effects and, in some cases, the counterculture that had formed around it.

Cannabis has been grown, sold, transported, and consumed around the world, developing its own subcultures along the way and helping to shape the identity and perceptions of those locations. Amsterdam is a prime example. As the character Vincent, played by John Travolta in the cult classic *Pulp Fiction*, puts it:

> It breaks down like this: it's legal to buy it, it's legal to own it, and if you're the proprietor of a hash bar, it's legal to sell it. It's legal to carry it, but that doesn't really matter 'cause get a load of this, all right? If you get stopped by the cops in Amsterdam, it's illegal for them to search you. I mean, that's a right the cops in Amsterdam don't have.

Along the way to legalization, many high-profile cultural icons, including Willie Nelson, Bill Maher, and Snoop Dogg, began to acknowledge their own consumption publicly, making it more acceptable to talk about. The consumption question was even raised during the 1996 U.S. presidential race, when then-candidate Bill Clinton remarked that while a student in England in the 1960s, he had experimented with marijuana but had "not inhaled."

Today's cannabis culture is as individualized as the people who consume it in one way or another for their own personal reasons, whether as medicine for symptom relief, enhancement of athletic performance, adult use for social activities, exploration of artistic appreciation, or relaxation. The culture is no longer defined by the Tetrahydrocannabinol (THC) for the "high," but includes other cannabinoids, such as CBD, and other benefits from the plant.

The culture has evolved to unapologetic and unabashed use by soccer moms and a growing number of professional athletes. Recent news stories showcase the increasing acceptance of cannabis use among high-profile athletes, with articles following NFL player Josh Gordon and his conflicts over consumption with the Cleveland Browns; New England Patriots coach Bill Belichick's perspectives on consumption by his players; ultrarunner Jenn Shelton, who was featured in *The New York Times* bestseller *Born to Run*; and ultrarunners Avery Collins and Jeff Sperber, who have sung the praises of adding cannabis to their workouts or recovery regimen; as well as admissions from multiple retired athletes, including NBA player Matt Barnes, who has remarked that he consumed prior to each game.

But not everyone in the traditional cannabis culture is happy about the transition to mainstream that has come with legalization and the professionalization of the industry. A segment of the consumer population continues to lament the decline of the counterculture. However, even as cannabis becomes more mainstream, the industry is likely to continue to cater to the counterculture as well, as evidenced by the industry's support of massive events such as the unofficial cannabis celebration holiday 4/20 on April 20th of each year, which is focused on the mass civil disobedience of public consumption.

Regardless, one thing is clear: the cannabis industry, use, and culture are growing around the world with no signs of stopping, and this growth is driving a huge shift in cultural diversity among cannabis users.

Accounting for the High Costs of Doing Business

The cannabis industry is brutal. Businesses are pressured from all directions. They can't get loans from federally insured banks or accept credit or debit card payments; they're not allowed to claim standard business deductions; they can't conduct business across state lines; and they struggle daily to comply with a long, growing, and ever-changing list of rules and requirements. You really have to wonder how any cannabis businesses survive — most don't. The profit margins are slim, and the room for error even slimmer.

In this section, I open your eyes to the high costs of doing business in the cannabis industry, so you're well aware of what any cannabis business you're thinking of investing in is up against.

Regulatory and compliance costs

When people read about the amount of money cannabis generates for governments, they generally think that's tax revenue collected from retail sales, but that's just a portion of their proceeds. Governments also claim revenue in the form of licensing fees and compliance fees and penalties. These fees, costs, and penalties vary considerably based on the type of business (for example, cultivation, manufacturing, or dispensary), and the state and location within the state.

License application fees and related costs alone can cost tens or even hundreds of thousands of dollars. Most groups and individuals who purchase licenses are very well funded. You generally need a lobbyist, an application consultant, and a lawyer who specializes in cannabis license applications to guide you through the process, which is highly political and frequently subjective. Lay people generally don't score licenses.

In addition to the cost and hassle of getting licensed, there are compliance costs, including the cost of training personnel, buying or leasing software to help with compliance, and the costs of generating and submitting regular reports. To add to the costs and complexities of doing business in the cannabis industry, any compliance violations can result in hefty fines and the possibility of the business losing its license.

Federal, state, and local taxes

Even though the U.S. has declared marijuana federally illegal, it still demands its share of any revenue a cannabis business generates. So, too, do state and local governments. Here's a list of taxes that most legal cannabis businesses are required to pay:

>> Federal income tax, which is calculated on total revenue instead of net profit, because cannabis businesses are prohibited from deducting business expenses. Also, cannabis businesses that don't use banks have to pay their taxes in cash and pay an extra 10 percent for the privilege.

>> Federal Insurance Contributions Act (FICA) taxes on wages paid to employees. FICA taxes cover Social Security retirement and disability, along with Medicaid costs.

>> **State taxes.** All states where marijuana is legal charge sales tax, which customers end up paying, but some states also include an excise tax that can be charged to customers or to businesses. For example, Alaska charges an excise tax on the transfer or sale of marijuana from a grow operation to a retail store or manufacturing facility.

>> **Business and occupation taxes.** In some states, such as Washington, anyone who holds a producer, processor, or retailer marijuana business license is required to pay a business and occupation tax.

>> **Cultivation tax.** California charges a cultivation tax on harvested cannabis that enters the commercial market.

>> **Municipal sales tax.** Some municipalities also charge a sales tax, although this is paid by the customer, not by the cannabis business.

Security costs

Cannabis businesses have two things that attract thieves: money and drugs. You've probably heard plenty of stories in the news about thieves driving cars or trucks through doors or walls in attempts to steal cash and product from retail locations and grow operations. Some locations have even been robbed during operating hours.

To remain viable, cannabis businesses must protect themselves, their staff, and their customers, and that protection comes at a price. Security costs typically cover the following:

>> Security expertise to evaluate the business location, install equipment, and train the staff on security protocols and all security requirements for the cannabis industry

>> Cameras coupled with enough secure storage for retaining video for the required number of days or weeks

>> External lights on motion sensors or timers

>> Locks, safes, secured cabinets, and lockable refrigerators (for items that must be kept cold)

>> Security staff (in some situations)

» Internal and external door-locking mechanisms with badged or passcode access

» Barriers, such as opaque exterior windows, to obscure the view of products in retail locations

» Security alarms

» Separate and secured storage areas

» Controlled delivery areas

Businesses also need to account for a higher cost of business insurance and the costs associated with failed or successful break-ins and thefts. For example, even if a plan to rob a business is foiled, one or more employees may be harmed or the building may be damaged.

Chapter 4

Sizing Up the Risks and Rewards of Cannabis Investing

Every investment has a risk/reward profile, and cannabis investments are no exception. Generally, the greater the risk, the greater the potential reward. Some investors choose to go all-in on cannabis, seduced by the opportunity to buy into an industry in its infancy, in the hopes that it becomes the next big thing. On the opposite end of the spectrum are wary investors who won't touch a cannabis stock with a ten-foot pole, afraid that the entire industry will crumble if the feds decide to crack down on cannabis or negative news about it hits the headlines.

Chances are good that because you're reading this book, you're closer to the middle of that spectrum — cautiously optimistic. You don't want to miss out on a potentially lucrative opportunity, but you don't want to lose your shirt, either. That's actually a pretty good place to start.

This chapter highlights the risks and potential rewards of investing in cannabis. My hope is that it will nudge you to a position on the investment spectrum where you're more confident in your cannabis investment decisions, while calling your attention to risks and rewards you may currently be unaware of.

Weighing the Risks

Imagine what would happen to cannabis stocks if the U.S. federal government decided to enforce federal laws against it. What would happen to the price of cultivation stocks if growers engaged in a price war or grew quantities of marijuana that greatly exceeded demand (as oil-producing countries frequently do)? What would happen to your investment portfolio if a company you heavily invested in turned out to be a total scam — and never even existed?

These are only a few of the risks inherent in cannabis investing. This section describes these and other risks that can quickly turn hope to despair. Knowing about these risks can help you steer clear of bad investments, more accurately identify good investment opportunities, and reduce your exposure to risk if you ultimately decide to invest in cannabis.

TIP

See Chapter 15 for advice on how to minimize risks while maximizing gains. You can also minimize risks when buying shares in a company by using stop and limit orders to your advantage, as explained in Chapter 11.

Falling victim to con artists

One of the most potentially devastating mistakes you can make as a cannabis investor is to fall victim to someone who's intentionally trying to cheat you out of your money. This occurs more often than most people realize. Con artists frequently target cannabis investors specifically, for several reasons:

>> Cannabis is a hot industry, in which investors are often looking to score big, so they're more susceptible to being seduced by promises of big returns and low risks.

>> Plenty of news stories and articles have been published to lead people to believe that making lots of money in cannabis is relatively easy. As a result, con artists don't have to work very hard pumping up opportunities for investors.

>> Novice investors, who don't know how to investigate and evaluate a business and its management team, or someone selling securities, are easy prey. In addition, if an investor lacks knowledge of the industry, he might not even recognize warning signs, such as someone posing as a CEO who knows nothing about cannabis.

>> Victims are less reluctant to report being fleeced because 1) they feel stupid, and 2) cannabis is federally illegal, so they might be afraid of the legal repercussions of reporting their attempt to invest in a federally illegal drug.

Con artists typically engage in investment schemes that can be broken down into two categories: investment fraud and market manipulation.

Investment fraud

WARNING

Investment fraud involves selling counterfeit securities or securities in a business that doesn't exist. To avoid falling victim to investment fraud, watch for the following warning signs:

>> Guarantees of high returns, typically accompanied by promises of no to low risk.

>> Unsolicited offers; for example, someone contacts you via email, text, social media, or a phone call to present you with an attractive investment opportunity.

WARNING

Don't click any links, respond to any messages, or talk to anyone about an investment opportunity who contacts you "out of the blue." You should be the person initiating contact with an individual or company you already screened, as explained in Chapter 7.

>> The person selling the securities is unlicensed and unregistered. Use the search tool at www.investor.gov to find out if the person selling the securities is licensed and registered. Every stockbroker in the U.S. is required to have a Central Registration Depository number. Also be sure that the person is who she claims to be and isn't posing as a licensed stockbroker.

Market manipulation

Con artists often engage in pump-and-dump schemes to manipulate stock prices, so that they can buy low and sell high. They'll use email, texts, and social media to encourage people to invest in a supposedly hot stock. If enough people buy into the fake news, the share price spikes, and the con artist dumps his shares.

WARNING

To avoid becoming a victim of pump-and-dump schemes, beware of the following red flags:

>> The U.S. Securities and Exchange Commission (SEC) recently suspended trading of the company's stock. To check this, visit www.sec.gov/litigation/suspensions.shtml.

>> The company recently changed its name, industry, or business plan multiple times. To find out, research the business as explained in Chapter 7.

>> The company's press releases present information that seems too good to be true.

WARNING

If an investment opportunity sounds too good to be true, it probably is.

Investing in an overvalued company

Probably the greatest risk with buying legitimate marijuana stocks is that valuations of these stocks have increased so rapidly that share prices greatly surpass the companies' growth prospects. Many marijuana companies aren't yet profitable, making the challenge of determining a reasonable price to pay for shares even more difficult. In more established industries, you can use ratios such as price-to-earnings (P/E), price-to-sales (P/S), and price-to-cash flow (P/CF) to evaluate share price and compare it to that of other competing companies, but these ratios are less reliable indicators when companies haven't yet turned a profit.

Using historical sales is also problematic. Prior to October 17, 2018, when adult-use marijuana became legal in Canada, marijuana companies such as Canopy Growth generated revenue only from the country's medical marijuana market. As a result, any valuation metrics based on trailing sales — for example, price-to-trailing 12-month sales or enterprise-value-to-trailing 12-month sales — make the stocks appear to be priced ridiculously high. The same is true of GW Pharmaceuticals; the biotech's historical revenue doesn't include any sales for Epidiolex, the first FDA-approved prescription cannabidiol (CBD) oil for seizures.

Because using historical data is so unwieldy, investors must rely on forward-looking growth projections such as the price/earnings-to-growth ratio (PEG) to determine whether stocks are valued reasonably. And that opens up another can of worms.

CEOs of marijuana-cultivation companies sometimes estimate the size of the global marijuana market at $150 billion or higher. With a potential market that large, a stock with a *market cap* (the total market value of a company's outstanding shares of stock) of around $10 billion doesn't seem too expensive because a $150 billion market leaves substantial room for the company to grow. However, that $150 billion figure is inflated. It's based on a United Nations estimate of the global marijuana market *including sales of illegal marijuana*. If you subtract illegal sales from that $150 billion figure, you get a legal market size that's more like $30 billion. Using that figure, a stock with a market cap of $10 billion is expensive because it has little room to grow.

REMEMBER

Most illegal use is for recreational purposes, which remain illegal at the national level in all but two countries, Uruguay and Canada.

Someday, recreational marijuana may be legalized throughout much of the world. In the meantime, be careful about projections, valuations, and estimates of how large the marijuana market is likely to be. Always question whether the estimates and projections you're looking at are realistic.

REMEMBER

Arcview Market Research and BDSA conducted an extensive analysis, and they estimate that the global marijuana market will increase from $9.7 billion in 2017 to $32 billion by 2022.

So will all marijuana stocks compete for a share of that $32 billion market within a couple of years? No. The U.S. accounts for $23.4 billion of the total. Canadian marijuana stocks listed on the Toronto Stock Exchange (TSX) can't maintain their listing and conduct significant operations in any area where marijuana is illegal at the federal level, which, for now, includes the U.S. That means determining valuations of Canadian marijuana stocks based on growth projections should focus only on the Canadian market and markets outside the U.S.

Also consider the potential impact of future supply-demand imbalances. A supply *glut* (a situation in which supply far exceeds demand) is predicted for the Canadian marijuana market by 2021, perhaps earlier, based on the rapid expansion of production capacity that many Canadian marijuana growers are undertaking. A supply glut would drive down prices for cultivators, thereby driving down profits and placing downward pressure on their share prices.

Valuation risks also apply to cannabinoid-focused biotech stocks. For example, estimates of peak annual sales for Epidiolex vary widely. While highly optimistic analysts project peak annual sales of more than $2 billion, some of the more pessimistic analysts think that the CBD drug could account for sales of less than $300 million per year. Which estimate you use makes a huge difference in determining how attractively priced GW Pharmaceuticals stock is to you right now.

Accounting for dilution risks

Dilution occurs when a company issues new shares to generate additional capital for funding operations or expanding the business. The value of existing shares decreases as a result of the higher number of *outstanding shares* — the total number of shares investors own, including those held by company insiders.

Why is dilution often bad for current shareholders? Suppose a company has 10 million outstanding shares trading at $10 per share, giving the company a market cap of $100 million. If you own 1 million shares, your investment is worth $10 million. Now suppose the company issues 10 million new shares. Assuming the market cap remains constant, each share (old and new) is now worth $5 rather than $10 due to dilution. Your investment that was worth $10 million would now be worth only $5 million.

While dilution is a risk for many kinds of stocks, it's especially problematic for a lot of marijuana stocks. Because of legal barriers that have prevented access to borrowing from banks, Canadian marijuana businesses have had limited choices available for generating capital to fund operations and growth. Many of these companies use an approach referred to as *bought deal financing*, whereby an investment bank or syndicate agrees to buy all of the securities a company issues at a predetermined price. While this approach allowed marijuana companies to raise much-needed cash, it also dramatically increased their numbers of outstanding shares and diluted the value of existing shares.

WARNING

Dilution risks for at least some marijuana businesses could diminish as they become consistently profitable. Until that happens, though, dilution remains a serious threat for investors to consider.

Weighing the risks of potential commoditization

One risk that applies especially to marijuana growers and to royalty and streaming companies is the potential for *commoditization* — the process by which a product becomes indistinguishable from other similar products, at which point the only factor distinguishing one product from another in the same market is price. All agricultural crops are commodities, and marijuana is an agricultural crop that may eventually be commoditized.

The idea behind a *cannabis streaming company* is relatively simple. Cannabis companies looking to expand their growing capacity or some other aspect of their operations, but without the adequate financing to do so, go to a third party, such as a better-funded company (or in Canada, an institution), and raise capital. In exchange for funding, the financier receives a royalty percentage of that business. Generally speaking, a streaming company has no recurring costs and no daily maintenance expenditures to worry about. It's merely about making deals and reaping high-margin returns by selling what you receive from the stream at current market prices.

Agricultural crops aren't the only commodities. Precious metals, such as gold and silver, are commodities, too. So are resources including crude oil and natural gas. Other types of products can be commoditized as well, such as memory chips, storage devices, and other components of personal computers. Any product for which price is the only or dominant differentiating factor among multiple vendors is a commodity.

Commoditization weakens the pricing power for producers. Companies can't raise prices for their products without causing demand to fall. For example, if one gas station raises the price of fuel significantly higher than its competitors, it will lose business as customers choose to fill up at other gas stations offering lower prices. After all, gas is gas.

When demand is greater than supply, commoditization isn't a big problem. But when supply exceeds demand, as will eventually happen in Canada, commoditization could hurt marijuana growers, particularly smaller ones. This is because they don't have the same *economies of scale* — cost savings that result from increased size and scope of operations — that larger producers have.

Recognizing the possibility of changes in how federal marijuana laws are enforced

Although many states in the U.S. have legalized medical marijuana, adult-use marijuana, or both, their laws are in direct violation of federal marijuana laws. During the Obama administration, the official federal policy was to avoid interfering in states that had legalized marijuana. In other words, the Obama administration told federal law enforcement to back off and let state and local law enforcement handle the issue in legal states.

However, in January 2018, U.S. Attorney General Jeff Sessions rolled back the Obama-era policies. His move cleared the way for U.S. federal attorneys to prosecute anyone who possesses or sells marijuana, including medical marijuana. Sessions had a long history of opposition to legalizing marijuana before becoming attorney general. His opposition continued after taking the top spot in the U.S. Department of Justice.

When Jeff Sessions was essentially fired by Donald Trump, Attorney General William Barr was appointed, and the U.S. cannabis industry breathed a collective sigh of relief. Barr claims he still opposes federal legalization. However, his approach to the issue is a direct contradiction to that of Sessions, who once quipped that "good people don't smoke marijuana."

Barr is on record saying, "I am accepting the Cole Memorandum for now, but I have generally left it up to the U.S. attorneys in each state to determine what the best approach is in that state." Barr further testified during the hearing: "I haven't heard any complaints from the states that have legalized marijuana."

President Trump has expressed support for medical marijuana and a willingness to leave laws pertaining to recreational marijuana to the states. In April, Senator Cory Gardner (a Republican representing Colorado) announced that the president pledged to support "a federalism-based legislative solution to fix this states' rights issue once and for all."

REMEMBER

Keep in mind that federal legalization is by no means guaranteed, and that, in the meantime, companies face highly disparate regulations and enforcement depending on where in the country they operate.

RAIDED IN LOS ANGELES

A possibility always exists that the federal government will come in and shut down a business that's operating lawfully in a state that has legalized cannabis. In advance of a March 2016 voter referendum that made marijuana laws more business friendly, the feds conducted a spate of raids on marijuana businesses operating legally (according to California law) in Los Angeles.

I was an owner in a dispensary in Los Angeles that was raided in January 2016. The business was shut down despite operating lawfully in California, and the case took three months to resolve in court. It was ultimately dropped, but it was costly and derailed our plans to raise capital and to sell the business.

Considering the impact of state and local regulation and enforcement

Whether state and local governing bodies are too restrictive or not restrictive enough in regulating marijuana and enforcing state marijuana laws, either approach can negatively impact legal sales and profitability of marijuana in that state. For example, if a state legalizes marijuana but doesn't crack down on illegal marijuana operations at the same time, consumers are likely to continue to buy their marijuana on the black market, where it's cheaper because it's not being taxed and where they don't have to present identification to make a purchase.

In addition, as long as most states still outlaw recreational marijuana, a black market based on cross-state exports will flourish. States can chip away at illicit intrastate operations by easing regulations and limiting local control, but they need to be careful not to embark on a frenzy of deregulation. Lower prices and more legal cannabis businesses are the goals. For example, Oregon may have gone too far in lowering the barrier to entering the legal market. Its glutted market has added more fuel to the interstate black market because cultivators export their product across state lines due to small profit margins in the legal market. This suggests that there are Goldilocks conditions for marijuana legalization: regulate too much, and not enough legal dispensaries will enter the market; regulate too little, and prices will plummet, negatively impacting the profits of legal operations and fueling the cross-state black market.

REMEMBER

As an investor, you're wise to keep your finger on the pulse of state and local regulations and law enforcement affecting any legal cannabis businesses you've invested in or are considering investing in. Any change in rules or regulations or how they're enforced can negatively or positively impact sales, revenue, and earnings, and therefore the company's value.

Evaluating risks associated with obtaining banking and financial services

Even if businesses operating in the U.S. cannabis industry aren't prosecuted, they face another risk on an ongoing basis — obtaining banking and financial services. Because selling marijuana is illegal at the federal level, banks or other financial institutions that handle money made from marijuana-related businesses could be accused of *money laundering* (that is, concealing the origin of money earned illegally).

Many banks have opted to steer clear of dealing with marijuana businesses because of the risks of running afoul of federal laws. Their reluctance has resulted in marijuana businesses being forced to operate on a cash-only basis. One downside is that it makes companies more susceptible to robbery. An even greater problem, though, is that it limits their ability to obtain capital needed for expansion.

Fortunately, some banks and credit unions have started doing business with U.S. cannabis companies. As a result, the risks for marijuana-related businesses in regard to obtaining banking and financial services have lessened in recent years.

In addition, some U.S. companies are working to sidestep the issue of raising capital by listing on Canadian stock exchanges (such as the Canadian Securities Exchange, or CSE). MedMen, for example, is based in California, but its stock is listed on the CSE. Unlike the TSX, the CSE doesn't prohibit marijuana businesses with U.S. operations from listing.

Anticipating the impact of possible supply and demand imbalances

At first glance, the cannabis supply chain is straightforward (see Figure 4-1). Cultivators grow the plants and provide harvested plants directly to distributors and/or to manufactures (who create various products from the plant, then provide those products to distributors). Distributors then ship the plants and products to retail locations, including dispensaries, and to delivery services, which deliver the products directly to consumers.

However, the cannabis supply chain is susceptible to potential supply and demand imbalances along with other challenges, such as the following:

>> If states fail to cap production (cultivation) licenses, supply quickly exceeds demand and available shelf space. Wholesale prices drop, and cultivators struggle and perhaps go out of business, creating the opposite problem — insufficient supply to meet the demand, in which case retailers and delivery services suffer.

>> The same problem occurs if too many local jurisdictions prohibit retail locations. Cultivators and manufacturers create products but have limited outlets to sell to.

>> If jurisdictions issue too few licenses for growing or manufacturing cannabis relative to the number of retail licenses, prices rise and retailers can't obtain enough product to meet demand.

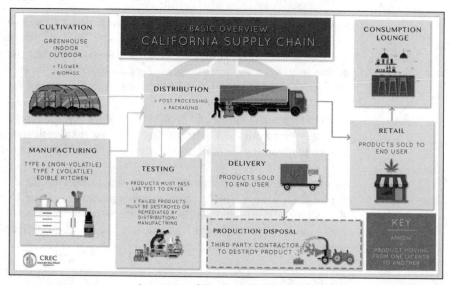

FIGURE 4-1:
The cannabis supply chain.

Image courtesy of Cannabis Real Estate Consultants – cannabisrealestateconsultants.com

Vertically integrated companies avoid these supply chain imbalances by controlling the entire supply chain. A vertically integrated cannabis company grows, manufactures, distributes, and sells product to consumers, so it can deal with any supply-demand imbalances internally as they arise.

Another, less obvious supply and demand imbalance that can impact a company's profitability is the labor market. Having the expertise not only to grow, manufacture, and sell cannabis but also to manage the business and build and manage a supply chain is essential for a company to profit and grow. As the industry grows, people who understand the rapidly changing regulatory environment and can help set up complicated distribution networks — not to mention rapidly scaling production — will be in extremely high demand.

In many cannabis companies, purchasing and inventory are still done on an ad-hoc basis, which opens opportunities for cost savings and operational efficiencies. It also exposes companies to risks if they grow too fast without solid supply chain processes and people in place. The blank-slate state of these supply chains also opens up exciting possibilities for true professionals who won't have to disrupt any existing ways of doing things.

If the labor market can't supply people with the requisite expertise, cannabis companies will struggle to grow.

Considering the possibility of business failure

The cannabis industry is highly competitive, and companies struggle to turn a profit. At the same time, the industry attracts speculators — people who trade stocks as though they're spinning the roulette wheel in Las Vegas. They ignore the value of the company and its profit potential, focusing instead on media hype and the irrational exuberance of other investors to drive up share prices in cannabis companies.

I strongly encourage you to be an investor and not a speculator. Carefully vet cannabis companies before investing in them. The industry has a high rate of business failures, and U.S. companies have virtually no federal bankruptcy protection, so if a company becomes insolvent, investors are likely to walk away with nothing. Meet the CEOs and senior managers in person and vet their backgrounds. Run a criminal background check on any and all managers and board members before investing. Look for any criminal histories, bankruptcies, securities violations and secure references where you're able. There are fortunes to be made as there were when alcohol prohibition was repealed. However, there are also huge risks in markets that are not yet fully regulated.

Assessing the Potential Rewards

Obviously, people who invest in cannabis want to profit financially, and they can certainly do so. People who know what they're doing and have fortune on their side are already reaping the financial rewards of investing in cannabis. However, you may also want to consider some of the personal rewards of investing in the industry, such as the following:

>> Getting in at or near the bottom of a new and growing industry (or company) is always exciting. By investing in cannabis, you're not only motivated to follow the story of the company's and industry's growth, but you also play a small role in those stories. Over time, as you gain more knowledge and experience, you may choose to play an even bigger role.

>> As an investor, you have the opportunity to take part in the marijuana culture, even if you choose to experience it only vicariously. You're contributing in a small way to making marijuana more readily available to more consumers, both for medicinal and adult recreational purposes.

>> If you benefit from medicinal marijuana or enjoy consuming it recreationally, investing in it is a way to help introduce those benefits to others while profiting from your investment. You're investing in a product you believe in.

>> By investing in medical marijuana, you're helping to increase research into new medications and bring them to market, potentially helping to alleviate some physical suffering in the world.

Deciding Whether Investing in Cannabis Is Right for You

Only you can decide whether investing in cannabis is right for you. In the following sections, I present some factors to consider when making your decision. You would be wise to consult your financial advisor and perhaps your life partner, as well.

Considering your investment goals

Before investing in any company, exchange traded fund, mutual fund, or other investment vehicle, be sure the investment fits with your investment goals. What do you want or need money for, how much do you need, and when do you need it? These are questions you need to answer when setting your investment goals. Maybe you decide you need a million dollars by the age of 65 to retire comfortably or you need $250,000 by the time your children graduate high school to be able to pay for their college (or at least a certain portion of it). Maybe you're investing to build a nest egg for a down payment on a house.

Investing in cannabis may or may not be a good fit for your investment goals. For example, if you're relatively young and have considerable time to ride out the ups and downs of the industry, cannabis may be the right fit. In contrast, if you're older or you need investments that are safer or more liquid, cannabis may be a poor choice. If you have a lot of money to play with (money you can afford to lose), investing in a private company may provide you with the best opportunity to realize significant gains. On the other hand, if a loss would subject you to considerable financial strain, you should probably steer clear of private investments at least until the industry becomes more established.

TIP

Regardless of your investment goals, diversification is always a good idea. Don't put all your nest eggs in one basket. Spread your investment dollars across different industries, companies, and securities (stocks, bonds, and cash).

Assessing your own risk tolerance

Risk tolerance is the amount of risk you're willing to take on to realize potentially bigger returns. Several factors contribute to influencing a person's risk tolerance, including the following:

>> Investment goals

>> Timeframe (the amount of time you have before you need to cash in your chips)

>> Other financial assets and resources

>> The amount of money you could reasonably afford to lose

>> Your own personal tolerance for risk taking

REMEMBER

On the spectrum of low to high risk, cannabis investing falls solidly at the high-risk end. It is speculative. However, doing your homework and investing in solid, well-managed companies can significantly reduce your exposure to risk while increasing the possibility of earning handsome returns.

2
Doing Your Homework

IN THIS PART . . .

Recognizing the different ways to invest in cannabis, including public versus private investments, investing in exchange traded funds (ETFs), and joining a venture capitalist group.

Finding leads on cannabis investment opportunities by using online tools and apps, industry news publications, connections to private equity and venture capital funds, and consulting with qualified brokers.

Analyzing a cannabis business's fundamentals to ensure that you're investing in a profitable company or a company that demonstrates the potential to become profitable.

Conducting technical analysis to track market trends in an attempt to buy low and sell high.

» **Deciding whether to invest in foreign companies**

» **Choosing between businesses that touch the plant and those that don't**

» **Investing in stocks, exchange traded funds, or mutual funds**

» **Financing startups as a venture capitalist**

Chapter 5

Exploring Your Investment Options

A s with other industries, cannabis offers a variety of ways to invest. You can put up money to finance a privately held company in exchange for a share of that company, buy stock in a publicly traded company that is or isn't listed on one or more of the major stock exchanges, or buy shares of cannabis-focused exchange traded funds (ETFs). You can invest domestically or abroad. You can buy and sell (or lease) real estate to cannabis companies. You can even invest in cannabis by starting your own cannabis business (but that's outside the scope of this book).

This chapter introduces you to your cannabis investment options, so you can make well-informed decisions of how to invest your money. In the process, I steer you clear of some of the riskier investment options.

Comparing Public versus Private Investment Options

In terms of ownership, all companies can be divided into two groups.

>> **Private companies:** A private company is owned by its founders, managers, or a group of private investors. Shares of a private company aren't bought and sold in the stock markets.

>> **Public companies:** A public company is owned by its shareholders, who purchased shares of the company via an initial public offering (IPO) or secondary offerings, which involve private investors selling their shares (a *non-dilutive offering*) or the company creating and selling additional shares, which *dilutes* (reduces) the value of existing shares.

A key difference between privately owned and publicly owned companies is the degree of transparency. Publicly owned companies are required by law to publish certain financial reports regularly, and they're likely to attract more attention from analysts, who can provide insight into the company's financial health and potential for profitability and growth. As a result, you have more information about private companies on which to base your investment decisions.

Another difference between private and public equity investments (shares in a company) is how investors are compensated. Private equity investors generally receive regular distributions, whereas public investors reap their benefits in the form of rising stock prices, and cash out only when they sell shares.

REMEMBER

If you buy a stock and sell it for a profit, that profit is a taxable capital gain. Also, if you're investing in the hope of generating income, keep in mind that publicly traded cannabis companies rarely pay dividends to their investors. They usually roll any profits they earn into running the business or expanding.

As an investor, you have the option to invest in private or public companies. In the following sections, I explain the basics of investing in both private and public companies, the pros and cons of each option, and some of the requirements you need to meet to be able to invest in certain privately owned companies.

Understanding how companies raise capital

Obviously, new companies need money (capital) to get started, and existing companies often need capital for expansion. To raise capital, they generally have two options.

>> **Equity financing:** With equity financing, the company sells a stake in the business to shareholders, essentially making them partial owners of the company and giving them a claim to a portion of the company's earnings.

>> **Debt financing:** With debt financing, the company borrows money with the intention of repaying the loan at some point. A company can borrow money from a bank or sell bonds to investors.

REMEMBER

Bonds generally carry less risk than stocks, because in the event that a company is forced to liquidate, bondholders have a higher priority in being repaid. Shareholders have the last claim on any cash remaining after the company sells off its assets. On the other hand, shareholders have the potential to reap bigger returns by selling their shares for a higher price if the company succeeds. Shareholder also generally have more input in how the company is run.

On a small level, you can think of your investment options in terms of financing a friend's or relative's business startup. You can loan the person a certain amount of money and draw up a loan agreement that stipulates the following:

>> The amount of the loan

>> When the loan will be repaid

>> The interest rate

>> The payment frequency (for example, monthly payments)

>> Any collateral you can take ownership of if the loan isn't repaid

>> Other conditions of the loan

Your other option is to buy shares in the company. For example, you can choose to invest $75,000 to own half the company, in which case you're entitled to a certain percentage of the profits (whatever the two of you agree to). Instead of a loan agreement, you draw up a shareholder agreement with certain stipulations, such as the following:

>> Which decisions require shareholder input and agreement

>> When financial statements will be provided

>> How any profits from the venture (or sale of the business) will be shared

WARNING

Before investing in any business, even if it's being started by a close friend or family member, I strongly encourage you to consult with a qualified business lawyer to draw up a binding agreement and have all parties sign off on it. Also, before investing in a company you're unfamiliar with, when you don't personally know the owner and management team, carefully research the company, as explained in

Chapter 7. Con artists are constantly on the lookout for eager investors to fleece, especially would-be cannabis investors.

Investing in private companies

Investing in a private company offers two key benefits: you share more directly in the company's profits (assuming the company is profitable) and, possibly, in its decision-making. Three potential drawbacks are increased risk, less access to information about the company, and lack of *liquidity*; that is, your money is tied up in the company until it goes public or is sold, or someone buys you out. Due to the nature of these drawbacks, private investment is generally reserved for more sophisticated investors with deep pockets, and institutional investors, such as pension funds, mutual funds, and endowments, which can pool money from many individuals.

WARNING

Because private companies are subject to less oversight from government agencies and from analysts, before investing in a private company, you should carefully vet the management team, including ordering background checks on team members. See Chapter 7 for details.

How you invest in a private company generally corresponds to the stage of the company's development:

>> When a business is just getting started, you can get in at the bottom as an angel investor. *Angel investors* are usually friends or family members who provide startup capital in exchange for ownership equity or convertible debt (a loan that can later be converted to shares in the company). You can also find angel investor groups or networks online or by asking a reputable financial advisor.

>> When a cannabis business has gotten off the ground and demonstrates some long-term potential, you may be able to invest in it as a venture capitalist. As a *venture capitalist*, you become a member of a group of investors that provide capital, managerial expertise, and other assistance to help the business grow and become more profitable. See the section, "Investing as a Venture Capitalist," for details.

>> After the venture capitalist stage, you may be able to engage in *mezzanine investing*, which generally involves providing financing in the form of convertible debt. If the company defaults on the loan, your investment is converted into shares in the company.

>> In later stages of a private company's development, you may be able to enter the realm of *institutional investors* — individuals or groups that trade securities in large quantities, such as banks, credit unions, insurance companies, pension funds, hedge funds, endowments, and mutual funds.

THE IMPORTANCE OF DUE DILIGENCE

I had a good friend who invested in what he thought was a private cultivation facility in the desert in California back in 2017. He met the mayor of the town (so he could make sure the licenses were real), visited the property and building, and met the cultivator. Unfortunately, the "plant visit" was a carefully orchestrated scam. The mayor and all the other people my friend met were actors, and they took him to the cleaners.

Before you invest in any business venture, perform your due diligence. Hire an independent private investigator, as I recommend in Chapter 7, to perform background checks on all the people involved. Costly? Yes, but even more costly is investing tens of thousands of dollars (or more) in a business that doesn't and will never exist.

Remember, money attracts thieves, and this is especially true in the cannabis industry, where people eager to score huge returns on their investment become easy prey.

If you decide to invest in privately held companies, consider joining a reputable investment group with experience investing in cannabis companies. The collective knowledge and experience of an investment group combined with the fact that risk is distributed among group members, helps to reduce your exposure to risk.

WARNING

Before joining any investment group, carefully research the group and its members. Independently verify all the information the group provides.

Many private investment opportunities are generated by word of mouth, and transactions are relatively informal. Larger and more sophisticated businesses work with investment bankers to make shares in the company available to private investors. Investment bankers help with structuring the value of private shares or *paid-in capital* (payments received from investors in exchange for shares). Investment bankers can also help companies test the investment demand and set an investment date.

The company and bank work together to publish a *private placement memorandum (PPM)*, which is similar to a prospectus for public companies. The PPM explains how the investment is structured and what investors can expect in terms of distributions (their share of the company's profits). The offering of a private placement is generally very similar to an IPO.

The PPM also establishes the requirements for investors. Because private placements are less regulated than public investments, they usually come with higher risks and therefore are generally geared toward more sophisticated investors. Also, unlike public investments, private companies may solicit commitments over time from investors, in which case these companies want investors with deep pockets. Usually, private investors must be accredited, meaning their net worth must meet a specified minimum. Accredited investors can be individuals, as well as institutions such as banks, mutual funds, or investment funds.

WARNING

Be very careful when pursuing private investment opportunities, especially informal, word-of-mouth opportunities. If it looks and feels like a gold rush, it's probably a scam.

Investing in public companies

Investing in public companies has two big benefits: you have more information on which to base your investment decisions, and your investments are more *liquid* — you can quickly and easily buy and sell stocks and bonds through a brokerage. As a result, investing in public companies generally carries less risk, but at the cost of generally lower returns.

Average investors predominantly invest in public companies, typically by buying and selling shares on one of the major stock exchanges, such as NASDAQ, NYSE, TSX, or AMEX. This approach is less risky than private investment because the Securities and Exchange Commission (SEC) in the U.S. and the Canadian Securities Administrators (CSA) oversee publicly traded companies, in their respective countries, to a certain degree before allowing them to be listed on the major stock exchanges.

REMEMBER

Less risk doesn't mean no risk. Stock prices can rise and fall significantly for however long you hold a stock, and businesses can fold, which could result in you losing your entire investment.

To invest in public companies that aren't traded on the formal stock exchanges, you can purchase shares over the counter (OTC). Shares traded OTC generally don't meet the stringent financial reporting and listing requirements of the major stock exchanges. Shares in a company may also be relegated to OTC status if their price falls below a certain dollar amount, such as $1.00, which is why these shares are commonly referred to as *penny stocks*.

You can buy and sell unlisted stocks OTC through certain brokerages (see Chapter 9 for details). If you're looking to buy and sell OTC shares online, make sure the online discount broker allows OTC trades — some do, some don't. Also, carefully research companies before investing in them, regardless of whether they're OTC or listed on one of the major exchanges (see Chapter 7 for details).

REMEMBER

In the U.S., cannabis is still federally prohibited, which creates another layer of risk for investing in U.S. cannabis stocks, most of which are traded OTC. The SEC can delist a publicly traded cannabis stock at any time, leaving the company with little legal recourse because of the federal prohibition. Delisting of cannabis stocks has become less frequent over the years, but it still occurs.

Investing Domestically or Abroad?

Many countries have legalized cannabis for medical or adult recreational use, as listed in Table 5-1, but this doesn't mean these countries offer great investment opportunities.

The markets outside the U.S. and Canada are generally not mature consumer markets, which means these markets carry additional risks for investors. First, you have to take into account local regulations, differences in business culture, and the complexities and delays in getting deals done. Second, when investing in markets outside the U.S. or Canada, you're subject to tax codes that are often in flux or aren't as clear as those at home. Finally, the U.S. prohibits cannabis imports even to states that have legal cannabis, so foreign companies can't expand into those markets.

TABLE 5-1   **Countries Where Cannabis Is Legal**

Country	Medical Use	Adult Recreational Use
Argentina	CBD legal, partially medically legal	Decriminalized
Australia	Legal	Partially decriminalized
Canada	Legal	Legal
Chile	Legal	
Columbia	Legal	Decriminalized
Croatia	Legal	
Czech Republic	Legal	
Cyprus	Legal	
Germany	Legal	Decriminalized
Greece	Legal	
Ireland	Legal	
Israel	Legal	
Italy	Legal	
Jamaica	Partially legal	Decriminalized
Lithuania	Legal	
Luxembourg	Legal	
Macedonia	Legal	
Mexico	Legal	Decriminalized
Norway	Legal	
The Netherlands	Legal	
New Zealand	Legal	
Peru	Legal	
Philippines	In progress	
Portugal	Legal	
Poland	Partially legal	
Puerto Rico	Legal	
South Africa	Decriminalized	Decriminalized
Switzerland	Legal	
Thailand	Legal	

Country	Medical Use	Adult Recreational Use
Turkey	Legal	
United Kingdom	Legal	
Uruguay	Legal	Legal
United States	Varies by state	Varies by state
Zambia	Legal	

Uruguay is an allegory for what can happen in markets outside the U.S. It was the first country to legalize marijuana at the federal level in December 2013, but due to a series of political delays, the new law wasn't implemented until late 2017, and pharmacies didn't start getting licenses to sell THC products until 2018.

Before investing in a foreign cannabis market, familiarize yourself with the laws, cultural sensitivities, and available legal remedies in the event you need to go to court. See Chapter 14 for details.

Investing in Cannabis or Ancillary Businesses?

Businesses that profit from cannabis can be divided into two groups — those that touch the plant, and those that don't (commonly described as "ancillary" or "no-touch" businesses).

Plant-touching businesses do just as the name suggests: they handle the cannabis plant in some form, cultivating, distributing, processing, or selling it. These tend to be the businesses most people think of when they imagine the cannabis industry:

>> Cultivators (growers)

>> Manufacturers, which create products such as vape oils and edibles

>> Dispensaries (cannabis retailers)

>> Laboratories involved in product testing

>> Cannabis delivery services

Businesses that come into contact with the plant are generally subject to the strictest regulations facing the industry, and many must navigate complicated licensing processes before they can get started. They're also at the greatest risk of getting shut down if the feds decide at some point to enforce federal laws against cannabis. As a result, these "touch" businesses are where the money's at, supporting the age-old adage, "No risk, no glory."

Ancillary businesses support the cultivation, processing, and sale of cannabis products without coming into contact with the plant. These businesses include the following:

>> Manufacturers and sellers of equipment and supplies, such as grow lights and fertilizers

>> Agriculture technology (ag-tech) companies

>> Industry-specific supply-chain-management platform developers

>> Point-of-sale (POS) payment processors

>> Construction firms that specialize in cannabis buildouts

>> Various professionals or firms that specialize in serving cannabis businesses, including law firms, marketing and public relation (PR) firms, professional employer organizations (PEOs), cash or payroll management firms, security and armored car services, and delivery services

These ancillary businesses are the same as those needed to support business processes in other industries. While they're also subject to strict regulations, as the entire industry is under the careful watch of the states, they tend to avoid the most stringent rules, such as licensing application processes. Investments in these businesses carry less risk (at least in the U.S.), but generally lead to lower returns.

REMEMBER

Investing in touch versus no-touch cannabis businesses depends on the specific business, your risk tolerance, the return on investment you're looking for, and your ability to evaluate a business's potential.

STARTING A CANNABIS BUSINESS?

One way to invest in cannabis is to start your own business, a topic that's beyond the scope of this book. If you're considering starting your own cannabis business, the first question you should ask yourself is whether you want to operate a touch or no-touch business, which is no small consideration. Running your own dispensary, for example, may sound like a fun way to make lots of money, but understanding the rules, capital requirements, and licensure process are critical, and getting started is a huge challenge. If you're serious about running a plant-touching business, be realistic about all that it entails.

Buying and Selling Cannabis Stocks

The large majority of people who choose to invest in cannabis do so by buying and selling shares of public cannabis companies on the big stock exchanges or OTC. Buying and selling shares of public companies is quick, easy, and inexpensive. In a matter of minutes, you can set up an account with an online broker, such as E*TRADE or Fidelity, transfer some money from a bank account to your online broker account, and start buying and selling shares.

In this section, I describe various ways you can choose to buy, own, and sell stock in public companies. See Chapter 9 for more details about choosing a broker or buying shares directly from a company. Chapter 11 explains how to place buy and sell orders.

Going mainstream with listed stocks

Listed securities (stocks or bonds) are those that investors can buy and sell on the major exchanges, such as the New York Stock Exchange (NYSE) and NASDAQ in the U.S. and the Toronto Stock Exchange (TSX) in Canada. Securities must meet a number of requirements to be listed on a major stock exchange. Although each exchange has its own standards for listing or delisting securities, the standards typically cover total market value, stock price, the number of publicly traded shares, and the number of shareholders the company has. Exchanges also require that companies adhere to certain rules regarding corporate governance to address the interests of all stakeholders, including shareholders, company executives, customers, suppliers, financiers, and so on. To be listed, a company is also required to pay a substantial listing fee, which generally indicates that the company is profitable or at least well financed.

Here are a few cannabis companies listed on major stock exchanges in the U.S.:

>> Aurora Cannabis Inc. (NYSE: ACB)

>> Canopy Growth Corporation (NYSE: CGC)

>> Cronos Group Inc. (NASDAQ: CRON)

>> GW Pharmaceuticals PLC ADR (NASDAQ: GWPH)

REMEMBER

Due to the stringent requirements for being listed on a major exchange, listed companies are generally considered to be of higher quality than those that aren't listed. If you're a casual investor or just getting started in cannabis investing, strongly consider trading in listed securities exclusively.

Bargain hunting with unlisted, over-the-counter stocks

Over-the-counter (OTC) stocks aren't traded on a regulated exchange such as the NYSE or NASDAQ. In most cases, they're trading OTC because they don't meet the stringent listing requirements of the major stock exchanges. In addition, most unlisted companies have a market capitalization of $50 million or less, indicating that they're relatively small, unproven players.

WARNING

Be aware that unlisted companies aren't required to provide much information about their finances, their business operations, or their products, as is required for companies listed on the regulated stock exchanges. Take their statements with a grain of salt and do your own research (see Chapter 7 for details), especially in cannabis where little market data is available for vetting companies and making well-informed investment decisions.

Often referred to as "penny stocks," because they generally trade for less than a dollar, unlisted stocks are popular with some investors. For a relatively small investment, you can purchase a substantial number of shares. If the share price doubles or triples (or jumps even more than that), you can sell for a handsome return, and if it drops, you hopefully haven't lost much, or so goes the reasoning behind this investment strategy.

Personally, I don't subscribe to that line of reasoning. Consistently successful investors put their money into well-managed companies with good ideas. Regardless of whether you buy listed or unlisted stocks, look to invest in quality companies. Before investing in any company, do your research, as explained in Chapter 7.

WARNING

OTC securities are frequently instrumental in pump-and-dump schemes. Con artists buy a large block of shares and then use social media and email to heavily promote the company. If the hot stock tip goes viral, it can create a quick spike in the price of the stock, at which point the perpetrator sells all his shares. When the price drops, all the other greedy (I mean eager) investors lose their money (or most of it). OTC stocks are perfect for these schemes because they're relatively unknown and unmonitored compared to exchange traded stocks.

Diversifying with exchange traded funds

Marijuana stocks have been increasingly popular among investors, but they're also highly volatile, as evidenced in 2019. Stock prices soared for many cannabis companies at the opening of the Canadian adult-use (recreational) market in late 2018 only to give up their gains and then some in the months that followed. Many of the big players, including Aurora Cannabis Inc., Tilray, and Canopy Growth Corporation, took a beating in 2019 and haven't really recovered (as of mid-2020). The experience taught many investors that diversification may be the best strategy when investing in speculative areas, such as the marijuana sector.

One way to quickly and easily diversify while focusing your investments in the cannabis industry is to buy cannabis exchange traded funds (ETFs). An ETF is like a mutual fund in that it contains a mix of investments in different companies, but it trades over the course of the day like a stock. Mutual funds, on the other hand, can be bought only at the end of the day with the share price based on a calculation of the average value of the securities held by the fund. (See the section, "What about mutual funds?" for details.)

Marijuana ETFs invest in companies that

>> Grow, distribute or sell marijuana.

>> Research the medical uses of marijuana, such as those in the pharmaceutical and biotech industries.

>> Have significant interest in cannabis, such as companies in the alcohol and tobacco industries.

Although only a limited number of cannabis ETFs are available, those ETFs offer wide exposure to many of the biggest players in this budding industry.

REMEMBER

Although ETFs aren't actively managed to any great extent, they do have fund managers that choose cannabis companies to invest in. Before buying shares of any ETF, vet the fund manager with the same scrutiny you would vet any ETF or mutual fund manager in non-cannabis industries.

TIP

A great resource for researching and analyzing cannabis ETFs is ETFdb.com. During the writing of this book, ETFdb.com listed the nine strongest ETFs in the cannabis space as follows (note that a couple of items in this list are exchange traded notes [ETNs]; see the next section for details):

MJ	ETFMG Alternative Harvest ETF
YOLO	AdvisorShares Pure Cannabis ETF
MJJ	Indxx MicroSectors Cannabis ETN
THCS	Cannabis ETF
POTX	Global X Cannabis ETF
TOKE	Cambria Cannabis ETF

ACT	AdvisorShares Vice ETF
MJO	Indxx MicroSectors Cannabis 2X Leveraged ETN
CNBS	Amplify Seymour Cannabis ETF

Betting on an index with exchange traded notes

Like ETFs, exchange traded notes (ETNs) trade on a stock exchange and track a benchmark index. However, ETNs differ from ETFs in the following ways:

>> An ETN is sort of like a bond, in that it's a corporate debt security issued by a bank. However, unlike a corporate bond that has a stated rate of interest, an ETN's value is based on the performance of the index it tracks.

>> While an ETF holds assets, such as stocks, commodities, or currencies, which form the basis for the ETF's price, an ETN holds no assets.

>> ETFs distribute taxable dividends, whereas ETNs don't, so ETNs have certain tax advantages for long-term investors.

>> ETNs aren't susceptible to tracking errors, as ETFs are. A *tracking error* is the difference between the performance of the ETF and the index it tracks. With an ETN, you own a note with a rate of return promised by the issuing bank.

ETNs are commonly used to invest in areas that are difficult to invest in, such as commodities and securities, which makes them suitable for investing in the cannabis industry as a whole.

WARNING

The two drawbacks of ETNs are that they're not as liquid as ETFs and that they carry some degree of credit risk based on the issuing bank. If the bank that issued the ETN goes belly up, you can lose your investment.

What about mutual funds?

Mutual funds have been a staple for investors looking to diversify since the early to mid-1900s, and they remain popular to this day. However, you won't find many cannabis-focused mutual funds. The exception, in the U.S., is American Growth Fund Series II E (MUTF: AMREX). This fund was organized and incorporated in Maryland in 1958 but reorganized in July 2016 to focus on the cannabis industry. It's the first and, as far as I know, only marijuana mutual fund available in the U.S.

Mutual funds and ETFs have much in common. Both fund types consist of a mix of many different assets and represent a common way for investors to diversify. However, be aware of key differences in how they're traded and managed. You can trade ETFs the same way you trade stocks, throughout the day, whereas you can purchase mutual funds only at the end of each trading day based on a calculated price. Also, in general, mutual funds (except for index funds) are more actively managed, meaning a fund manager makes conscious decisions regarding which assets to include in the fund's portfolio. ETFs, on the other hand, usually are passively managed and based more simply on a particular market index. Mutual funds tend to have higher fees and higher expense ratios than ETFs, reflecting, in part, the higher costs of being actively managed.

Buying and selling shares of Canadian cannabis companies

Because cannabis is federally legal in Canada, many of the bigger and better-covered cannabis stocks are traded on various Canadian exchanges. If you're wondering whether you can buy shares of Canadian companies when you're not a Canadian citizen, the answer is yes. You have two options:

» Buy stock in Canadian cannabis companies that are listed on one of the U.S. stock exchanges, such as the NYSE or NASDAQ. Several hundred Canadian firms have listed their stocks on U.S. exchanges. The NYSE alone hosts 120 listings from Canada with a combined market value of $1.3 trillion.

» Buy stock in Canadian cannabis companies that aren't listed on one of the U.S. stock exchanges. You just need to find a broker or online broker that enables you to buy and sell stocks on one of the Canadian stock exchanges. Several online discount brokers, such as E*TRADE, facilitate the process of buying shares in Canadian companies. (See Chapter 9 for more details.)

Here are your Canadian stock exchange options:

» The Toronto Stock Exchange (TSX), which has subsets such as the TSX Venture Exchange. TSX is Canada's leading stock market, so if you're looking to purchase equities on a Canadian exchange, TSX is the place to go.

» The Canadian Securities Exchange (CSE)

» The Montreal Exchange

» NASDAQ Canada

» The NEO Exchange (formerly called CNQ)

Investing as a Venture Capitalist

If you have deep pockets (and preferably extensive knowledge of the cannabis industry or some part of it), you may want to invest in cannabis as a venture capitalist. As a venture capitalist, you provide financing in exchange for an equity stake in the company. As such, you increase your exposure to risk but also have the opportunity to earn a massive return on your investment. Assuming the company is successful, you can eventually sell your shares at a profit. Or, if the company is bought out, you receive a portion of the proceeds.

Venture capitalists are common in certain industries, such as technology and pharmaceuticals. They're less common in the cannabis industry because of the difficulties in evaluating the assets and value of cannabis startups.

WARNING

Don't go it alone. To mitigate the risk, join a venture capitalist group that has members with extensive knowledge of the cannabis industry. If you choose not to belong to such a group, create your own investment team by hiring people with the knowledge and expertise to properly vet a cannabis business, including the business's management team. As a venture capitalist, you're going to be expected to invest a significant amount of money in the operation, so be sure to allocate some of that money toward making sure the investment opportunity is legitimate. Recognize how risky that proposition is in a market with federal prohibition and ever-changing regulatory environments.

» **Keeping your finger on the pulse of the cannabis industry**

» **Getting leads on cannabis exchange traded funds**

» **Investing privately as part of an investment group**

» **Finding a broker who knows the industry**

Chapter **6**

Digging Up Cannabis Investment Opportunities

I f you Google "how to find cannabis investment opportunities," the search results are likely to include more links to resources for helping cannabis businesses find investors than for investors to find cannabis businesses to invest in. In other words, many cannabis businesses and people wanting to start cannabis businesses are looking for investors to finance their startups or grow their existing businesses. Finding these companies may not be a huge challenge because *they* are looking for *you.*

WARNING

The problem is that you should generally steer clear of anyone who's actively trying to get you to hand over your money because so many cannabis investment opportunities are scams. You want to track down legitimate cannabis businesses that have a good chance of earning a profit. Obviously, a general web search isn't going to present you with such a list, so the question becomes, *How do I find legitimate and promising cannabis investment opportunities?*

In this chapter, I answer that question by highlighting the most reliable and reputable resources and methods for tracking down leads on cannabis investments.

Using Online Investment Tools and Apps

Just because you can't Google your way to a definitive list of the top 100 cannabis investment opportunities in the world, that doesn't mean you have to unplug and use old-fashioned methods to find investment opportunities in this industry. Plenty of online investment research tools are at your disposal to aid in your search, including websites, apps, online newsletters, reports, and stock screeners. The Internet has made it cheaper and easier than ever to get information about businesses to invest in.

Finding decent investment tools and resources online these days is also relatively easy. In this section, I present some free online investment tools you can use to track down cannabis investment opportunities. Some are more general resources, whereas others focus specifically on businesses in the cannabis industry.

TIP

Sample these tools, choose a few you like, and then spend some time learning how to use them. Don't try to master all of them. Going deeper with a few tools is likely to deliver better results than having a broad understanding of a wide range of tools.

TIMES ARE CHANGING

Before the dawn of the Internet, investors had to subscribe to one or more of the major financial news services such as the *Wall Street Journal* or *Standard & Poor's (S&P)* to obtain reputable information and insight into businesses (or hope that the local library subscribed to these publications). Subscriptions were expensive (and still are). Other investors would spend hours or days pouring through the *S&P* annual volumes.

Now, you're a mouse click away from powerful online tools and resources, many of which are free or very inexpensive to use and provide more information, to boot. Another advantage is that many of these tools provide screeners that enable you to filter your search and focus on businesses that meet your criteria.

Cannabis Stock Trades

Cannabis Stock Trades (www.cannabisstocktrades.com) is an investor news and information site that features several online tools and resources you're likely to find very useful in finding and choosing cannabis investment opportunities. These tools include the following.

>> **Model Portfolio:** This is a cannabis stock buy list of the most promising cannabis stocks from around the world. The portfolio includes a mix of longer-term investments based on fundamentals, and shorter-term trades based on technical chart formations and momentum.

>> **Trade Alerts:** These are email alerts for changes in the Model Portfolio, along with notifications of cannabis stocks you may want to add to your watchlist.

>> **Stock Analysis:** This offers daily stock analysis and discussion, providing insight into cannabis stock investment opportunities. Experts do the research for you and provide detailed reports to help guide your investment decisions.

>> **Member-Only Newsletter:** This newsletter keeps you posted on initial public offerings (IPOs), earnings reports, new product releases, regulatory updates, and more.

>> **Access to an Expert:** As a member, you can contact the editor of Cannabis Stock Trades to ask questions, make requests, and chat via email and the comments section.

You'll need to subscribe for the good stuff, but as I was writing this, Cannabis Stock Trades was offering a free two-week trial.

Yahoo! Finance

Yahoo! Finance (finance.yahoo.com or ca.finance.yahoo.com) is an old-school favorite for obtaining quotes, charts, information, and news related to a broad range of investment securities. On top of that, it offers watch lists, screeners, and calculators, and has built a stable of original video programs that cover the gamut of financial topics. Most of the newer online investment resources are unlikely to unseat Yahoo! Finance in its lead position because Yahoo! has always been a great news aggregator, which is exactly what you need to thoroughly research businesses and trends.

Click Watchlists (in the toolbar near the top of the home page) and then scroll down the page and click the link for Cannabis Stocks to access a list curated by Yahoo! If you can't track down the Cannabis Watchlist on the Watchlist page, click in the search bar at the top of the page, type "cannabis list," and click Cannabis Stocks Watchlist in the drop-down menu that appears. This list covers companies in horticulture, pharmaceutical research, and ancillary businesses.

Morningstar

Morningstar (www.morningstar.com) has developed into one of the best investment resources available. It's especially known for its mutual fund analyses and the easiest place to find any mutual fund's prospectus (that goes for exchange traded funds [ETFs], as well). I tend to focus more on the articles, which provide great insights into specific industries and companies. Morningstar, like Yahoo! Finance, also offers watch lists, screeners, fund comparisons, and a portfolio analyzer.

REMEMBER

Morningstar is best for researching specific stocks, mutual funds, ETFs, and other investment vehicles you already know about. It's less helpful for discovering investment opportunities you're unaware of. However, if you're looking for leads on cannabis investment opportunities, you can head to Morningstar's website and use the search bar near the top of the page to search for "cannabis" or "marijuana." The search results will probably include links to companies you haven't heard of. They'll also include links to articles and videos that may contain additional leads and insights.

FINVIZ

There are many great stock online screeners, but FINVIZ (finviz.com) is one of the best free versions around. A *stock screener* filters through thousands of stocks based on the criteria you specify and spits out the results in under a second.

To dig up leads on cannabis stocks, click in the search box near the top of the home page, type "cannabis," and you'll get a list of companies with "cannabis" in their names.

REMEMBER

FINVIZ is better for researching cannabis companies *after* you find a company you're thinking of investing in. It's not the greatest tool for tracking down leads on cannabis companies you don't already know about.

ETFdb.com

ETFdb.com is my favorite site for researching and comparing similar ETFs. It has several free investment tools, including the following:

>> **ETF Screener** for filtering and screening ETFs based on your specified criteria

>> **ETF Country Exposure Tool** to identify ETFs that offer exposure to securities in specific countries

>> **Head-to-Head ETF Comparison Tool** for comparing the performance of similar ETFs

>> **ETF Stock Exposure Tool** to find ETFs that offer significant exposure to a specific stock

>> **ETF Performance Visualizer** to view the annual performance of every existing ETF, making it easy to track annual trends and identify hot and cold spots in the market

TIP

Although ETFdb.com is a great site for evaluating and comparing ETFs, it's also very useful for finding cannabis/marijuana ETFs. Use the search tool near the top of the page to search for "cannabis." The search results will contain links to several articles about cannabis ETFs, along with a link to ETFdb.com's Marijuana ETF List (ETFdb.com/themes/marijuana-etfs).

FeeX

FeeX (www.feex.com) is one of my favorite free tools for examining ETF and mutual fund fees. Fees are one of the biggest drags on investment performance. Paying too much in fees can cause you to lose out on a great deal of money over time.

FeeX analyzes your portfolio and calculates your costs. If a similar fund is available with lower management fees, FeeX will suggest it for you and show you how similar it is. It will also show you how much more you could potentially earn over time by switching to the recommended fund.

TIP

Use FeeX after you make a preliminary selection of a cannabis ETF or mutual fund to see similar funds with lower fees and possibly a superior performance profile.

FRED

Federal Reserve Economic Data, or FRED, is the economic database hosted by the Federal Reserve Bank in St. Louis. If you're into financial and economic data, this is the only place to go. You can compare current and historical data or build your own graphs and charts. I use it for research.

The Marijuana Index

The Marijuana Index (`marijuanaindex.com`), or North American Marijuana Index, tracks the leading cannabis stocks in Canada and the U.S. It's broken down into a sub-index for each country based on where the company's business operations are primarily focused.

One of the best features of The Marijuana Index is that it weeds out (funny, huh?) companies that lack a business strategy focused on the legal marijuana industry, and it requires that constituents of the index have more than 50 percent of their operations focused on the marijuana industry. By choosing to invest in companies listed on the index, you can be certain that they're legitimate cannabis companies. For additional coverage of The Marijuana Index, turn to Chapter 10.

WARNING

Investing in legitimate companies, whether they're focused on cannabis or something else, still carries risk.

Marijuana Stocks

Marijuana Stocks (`marijuanastocks.com`) features a full list of marijuana stocks along with cannabis industry news and articles. Open the List of Marijuana Stocks menu, near the top of the home page, and choose Focus List or Marijuana Stocks to Watch to view some of the leading companies in the industry. To the right of the resulting list of leading companies is a more comprehensive list of marijuana stocks, including a number of penny stocks, which I generally discourage investors from speculating on (see Chapters 5 and 9 for more about penny stocks).

Barchart

Barchart contains a good list of publicly traded cannabis companies, which you can access by visiting `www.barchart.com/stocks/sectors/cannabis-stocks`. After pulling up the list, click the plus sign next to a company's ticker symbol to view additional details about the company and the performance of its stock, including a daily chart reflecting the stock's performance over the past 30 days and links to news articles about the company.

Apps

If you're more into apps than websites, here are some of the best apps for tracking down leads on cannabis stocks and keeping up on cannabis industry news.

Yahoo! Finance

Yahoo! Finance is great for any stock news, so it makes a great app for tracking marijuana stock news. It enables you to track the performance of your portfolio, obtain real-time stock quotes, and compare stocks. The basic version is free, but the premium version starts at $34.99 per month and comes with exclusive tools.

Get the app at `apps.apple.com/us/app/yahoo-finance/id328412701`

Marijuana Handbook

This is the ultimate guide to understanding marijuana. It has a gigantic database of facts, cookbooks, dispensary maps, and information on over 175 different strains. While this app isn't directly related to marijuana stock news, it's a great starting point for investors new to the cannabis industry. No free version is available, but the full version is only $2.99 — a worthwhile investment to become a marijuana expert.

Get the app at `apps.apple.com/us/app/marijuana-handbook-lite/id477750914`

Scutify

Scutify is a completely free app that contains learning tools for beginner investors, along with interactive discussions. Both traders and investors can post articles to share with the community. Think of this as a social network and educational resource for stocks. You can even set it up to send you news updates about any stocks you want to follow.

Get the app at `www.scutify.com/apps.html`

Market Watch

Market Watch is another free app that's useful across the entire stock market. One of its best features is its ability to get real-time updates on topics that matter to you. These include business news and analysis, market data, a watch list, and article sharing.

TIP

This app seems to work better on a full-featured computer than on a smartphone, but the app is great for when you're on the go.

Because marijuana stocks are still relatively new, marijuana app development is still in its infancy. Keep on the lookout as more app developers realize the potential for this market and create new apps to help investors track stock news. You might even decide to take your earnings from your own marijuana stock portfolio and invest in creating the next amazing app!

Get the app at apps.apple.com/us/app/marketwatch-news-data/id336693422

Staying Abreast of Cannabis Industry News

The past eight years have experienced an explosion of cannabis industry newsletters. One of the oldest and most respected is Marijuana Business Daily (mjbizdaily.com). Bookmark this site and use it to get up to speed on marijuana business news and to keep pace with industry trends. Check out the menu near the top of the home page to familiarize yourself with the site's offerings, including the following.

>> **News by Topic:** Instead of just lumping together all the news as many marijuana business news sites do, Marijuana Business Daily breaks it down into relevant categories, including Recreational Marijuana, Legal and Regulatory, Marijuana Cultivation News, International News, and News by State.

>> **Investing:** Investor resources are broken down into two sections:

- **Investor Intelligence Virtual Briefings**, which (according to the website) keep you "apprised of the current state of affairs related to cannabis investing, helping you understand where the opportunities and pitfalls can be found during these uncertain times."

- **Investor Intelligence Business Resources**, which are in-depth reports; two examples are an investment assessment of the North American Vape Market and the Annual Marijuana Business Factbook, the latter of which I strongly encourage you to read from cover to cover.

>> **Data Charts:** This page features industry statistics, data, and charts that provide valuable insight into the state of the industry as a whole.

>> **Business Resources:** These resources are mostly for cannabis business owners and management, but if you're looking for a deep dive on a topic that might influence an investment decision, they can be helpful.

>> **Company News Releases:** When cannabis companies issue press releases, they're sent to Marijuana Business Daily, and you can access them on the Company News Releases page. This is a great way to stay current with industry happenings.

I encourage you to subscribe to Marijuana Business Daily to receive a daily email message with news and information about the industry.

TIP

In 2020, Marijuana Business Daily produced the biggest industry event of the year, MJBizCon (mjbizconference.com/vegas). As a marijuana investor, you'll find that this event is a great opportunity to network and learn the business end of marijuana directly from industry experts.

Although Marijuana Business Daily is my top source for cannabis news and information, here's my complete list of favorites, including newsletters, blogs, and industry magazines:

>> **Baker blog** (www.trybaker.com/blog) This blog is mostly of interest to cannabis business owners and management, but occasionally contains posts that may be of interest to investors.

>> **BDSA** (bdsa.com) To access cannabis industry and business analytics, check out the items on the Resources menu, especially the blog.

>> **Canna Newswire** (cannanewswire.co) This website gives you access to a broad range of cannabis industry news and insights.

>> **Cannabis Business Executive newsletters** (www.cannabisbusiness executive.com/newsletters) Register to receive weekly newsletters delivered to your inbox about breaking industry news and information.

>> **Cannabis Industry Journal** (cannabisindustryjournal.com) This website offers frequent articles that highlight cannabis businesses making the headlines.

>> **Cannabis Product News** (cannaproductnews.media) Use this website to access news about the latest solutions in cultivation supplies and equipment, software, packaging, shipping and distribution, and more, which can be helpful in digging up leads on cannabis businesses that serve growers and processors.

>> **Cannabis Weekly** (cannabisweekly.co) Register here for cannabis industry articles delivered to your inbox weekly.

>> **Dentons US Cannabis Newsletter** (`www.dentons.com/en/insights/newsletters/us-cannabis-newsletter`) This website offers mostly articles about what's happening in politics regarding cannabis legislation.

>> **Ganjapreneur newsletter** (`www.ganjapreneur.com/subscribe`) Register to receive news about issues that matter to cannabis activists, business owners, and career seekers that may also contain some insight into cannabis companies in the news.

>> **GreenScreens blog** (`greenscreens.tv/about-us/blog`) This website mostly contains posts of interest to dispensary owners and managers, but also occasional posts that may help investors identify potential investment opportunities and find out more about the industry.

>> **Hemp Industry Daily** (`hempindustrydaily.com`) Open the News by Topic menu and choose Hemp Finance, Investing and Banking News to access news more relevant to investors.

Hemp Industry Daily focuses on news related to companies more active in hemp and CBD products than THC products.

>> *High Times* **magazine** (`hightimesinvestor.com`) Open the News menu and select the category that interests you: Business, Environment, Laws, Legalization, Politics, or World.

>> **Leafly's cannabis news** (`www.leafly.com/news`) You can access a broad range of cannabis news and information for investors, business owners and managers, and consumers. Use the menu on the left to view articles specific to certain categories, such as Politics, Industry, and Canada.

>> **Marijuana Moment** (`www.marijuanamoment.net`) Visit this website to stay current on news related to the politics, business, and culture of cannabis, which is useful for tracking and maybe even forecasting industry trends.

>> **Marijuana Retail Report** (`marijuanaretailreport.com`) This website lets you access news and information geared to recreational retailers, accessories retailers, and wholesalers.

>> **New Cannabis Ventures** (`www.newcannabisventures.com`) Visit this website for quality news on the most promising cannabis companies.

Be sure to explore the New Cannabis Ventures website menu to access areas specifically for investors, including cannabis investor news (under News), resources (under Resources), and the Global Cannabis Stock Index (under Indices).

>> **New Frontier Data analyst reports** (newfrontierdata.com/analyst-reports) This is a great resource for gaining insight into key developments, trends, risks, and opportunities in the cannabis industry.

An old adage among seasoned investors is that as soon as an investment opportunity appears in the news or trade publications, it's already too late to invest. That rule of thumb contains some truth, but you can find tremendous insight in cannabis investment and trade publications that can steer you in the direction of where the industry is heading and perhaps find good prospects that haven't been in the news yet.

Conduct your own thorough due diligence on any company in which you are thinking about investing. Don't rely solely on the work of a reporter, blogger, or analyst.

Many corporate profiles in cannabis industry rags are pay-for-play and glorified puff pieces for companies. You want a balanced view of your investment prospect. I have listed nearly 20 different cannabis investment and trade publications, blogs, and newsletters that cover many of the more conspicuous, well-marketed investment opportunities. I suggest you check out all the resources I listed and subscribe to those that speak to you and make you feel informed.

Some of the most promising young companies aren't covered in the investment and financial publications. Use these publications to get to know the business, and then network your way to the better opportunities that haven't been publicized yet.

Cannabis investment and trade publications benefit you, as an investor, in several ways, including the following:

>> They assist you in identifying trends in the industry, as you continue to read about the industry over time.

>> They keep you informed of any changes in legislation that could negatively impact your investments or open new opportunities.

>> They increase your knowledge and understanding of the cannabis industry, so you can make well-informed investment decisions and engage in more fruitful discussions with management teams and brokers. When you know more of what you're talking about, you're better equipped to ask tough questions.

Scoping Out Opportunities in Exchange Traded Funds

In Chapter 5, I cover cannabis ETFs extensively and provide a list of some of the leading ETFs in this sector. Here are a couple of resources for tracking down cannabis ETFs specifically:

>> ETFdb.com's Marijuana ETF List (ETFdb.com/themes/marijuana-etfs)

>> Daily Marijuana Observer's Cannabis ETFs databases (mjobserver.com/databases/cannabis-funds/marijuana-etfs-list)

If you use an online discount broker, such as E*TRADE or Fidelity, you can use the site's ETF selector or simply search the site for "cannabis etf" to find a list of cannabis ETFs to invest in.

WARNING

The quality of an ETF is directly proportional to the knowledge and experience of the fund manager, who decides which companies to include in the fund's portfolio. (This is true of mutual funds, too.) I think many of the cannabis ETFs are immature, and the fund managers generally don't have direct cannabis industry experience. These fund managers often rely on third-party information to evaluate prospects, which provides them with limited investment options.

Before buying shares of any ETF, vet the fund manager with the same scrutiny you would vet any ETF or mutual fund manager in non-cannabis industries. Here are a few criteria for vetting a cannabis ETF or mutual fund manager.

>> **Experience in the cannabis industry:** Check out the manager biography in the prospectus to find out what sort of experience he has. Chances are, you'll find few, if any, fund managers who have experience in the cannabis industry, which is one of the drawbacks of cannabis ETFs.

>> **Focus on the fund:** The prospectus should show the total number of funds the fund manager oversees. Any more than three, and the fund manager may be spread too thin.

>> **Skin in the game:** Read the fund's prospectus to find out how the fund manager is compensated to ensure that compensation is tied in some way to the fund's performance. Also check to see how vested the manager is in the fund — how many shares does she own?

>> **Good risk/performance track record:** As you compare funds in terms of performance, also compare their standard deviation or degree of volatility to see how much risk the manager has taken to achieve that corresponding

performance. A good indicator to look at is the *information ratio* — the measure of a fund's returns beyond the returns of a benchmark, usually an index, compared to the volatility of those returns. A high information ratio indicates that the fund manager is able to achieve higher returns for the fund without exposing investors to heightened risk.

TIP

You may be better off creating your own diversified portfolio based on your own research and due diligence. (For more details about researching cannabis investment opportunities, turn to Chapter 7.)

Finding Private Equity and Venture Capital Funds and Firms

Private equity funds buy and invest in private companies with the hopes of either adding significant value or restructuring the company to then re-sell or hold long term. Like any high-growth industry, the cannabis industry has attracted a long list of private equity funds, ranging from marijuana-focused funds to general health and consumer-focused funds that invest in companies doing business in the cannabis space.

Following is a list of private equity firms that invest in cannabis. You can check out each firm's website to find out more about their performance-specific investment criteria, such as minimum investment to become a member.

REMEMBER

Research the management teams of each firm to be sure the principals have cannabis industry experience.

>> Ancient Strains (https://www.ancientstrains.ca)

>> Cannabis Capital Inc. (http://www.cannabiscapitalinc.com)

>> Casa Verde Capital (https://www.casaverdecapital.com)

>> DCM (https://www.dcm.com)

>> Doventi (http://www.doventi.com)

>> Entourage Effect Capital (https://entourageeffectcapital.com)

>> Grays Peak Capital (https://grayspeakcapital.com)

>> Green Growth Investments (http://www.greengrowthinvestments.com)

>> Hypur Ventures (https://hypurventures.com)

- » LaMarch Capital, LLC (http://lamarchcapital.com)

- » Lerer Hippeau (https://www.lererhippeau.com)

- » Lizada Capital, LLC (http://www.lizadacapital.com)

- » McGovern Capital, LLC (https://www.mcgoverncapital.com)

- » Merida Capital Partners (https://www.meridacap.com)

- » Panther Consulting, LLC (https://www.pantherconsultingllc.com)

- » Privateer (https://privateer.co)

- » Skytree Capital Partners (https://www.skytreepartners.com)

- » Tress Capital, LLC (https://www.tresscapital.com)

- » Tuatara Capital, L.P. (https://tuataracapital.com)

- » Tusk Ventures (https://tusk.vc)

- » Winklevoss Capital Management, LLC (https://winklevosscapital.com)

Getting Investment Leads from a Broker

Some stockbrokers are more savvy than others when it comes to investing in cannabis. They may stay abreast of industry news and may have gleaned insight from working with other clients who invest in the industry. If you trade through a broker, consider picking her brain to see whether she has any good cannabis investment leads. If you have a financial advisor, I encourage you to consult and work closely with her to choose cannabis investments that support your overall investment goals.

REMEMBER

Even if you use a savvy broker, I encourage you to perform your own due diligence to carefully vet any leads (see Chapter 7 for details). Your broker may be able to bring your attention to companies you haven't discovered yet and possibly provide a second opinion on any companies you're considering. (See Chapter 9 for more about finding and working with a broker.) In addition, brokers and financial advisors typically have access to more powerful tools and resources for analyzing investment opportunities than those made available online for free.

Chapter **7**

Researching Cannabis Businesses and Stocks: Fundamental Analysis

nvesting in cannabis is like crossing a hostile frontier in search of gold; charlatans and snake oil salesmen lurk at every turn, the terrain is uncharted, and you have no guarantee of survival. If you strike gold, or in this case, green, you just might land an opportunity to build generational wealth. But boom can turn to bust in the blink of an eye if you choose the wrong investment.

Imagine what life must have been like for people such as Joe Kennedy, investing in alcohol businesses a few years before prohibition was repealed. The regulatory environment was uncertain and risky, support for alcohol was growing among the electorate, and the opportunity was ripe for building financial empires. That's the landscape in cannabis today.

Cannabis is as big as the coffee market and is both a legal and black-market business. More than 40 states in the U.S. have legalized or at least decriminalized marijuana to some degree, yet the plant is still prohibited by the federal government and has been deemed a Schedule 1 narcotic. Fortunes can be made, but the risks are tremendous.

Eliminating risk is impossible, but you can significantly reduce it by performing your due diligence. In this chapter, I explain how.

Grasping Fundamental Analysis Basics

Fundamental analysis is an approach to evaluating a security's intrinsic value based on a number of factors, such as the business's assets, liabilities, earnings, and management team; market conditions; the competitive environment; the overall state of the economy; legislation that is likely to impact the industry; analyst opinions, and so on. This method of stock analysis is commonly presented in contrast to *technical analysis* — an approach to predicting the future value of a security by analyzing trends in trading activity such as price movement and trading volume. (See Chapter 8 for more about technical analysis.)

In this chapter, I explain how to perform fundamental analysis on any security or business you're thinking of investing in, and I offer additional guidance for researching cultivation businesses (which grow the plant) — see the section "Evaluating Cannabis Cultivation Businesses."

WARNING

Thorough due diligence and careful analysis have no substitutes; before investing in any cannabis business, do your homework. As the Cold War was nearing its end, on several occasions, then President Ronald Reagan repeated the Russian proverb "Trust but verify" in the context of nuclear disarmament discussions with the Soviet Union. In the context of investing in cannabis, I suggest you trust nothing and verify everything. Here are a few general guidelines to follow (I provide more detailed guidance throughout this chapter):

>> Don't invest in any business you can't fully vet.

>> Don't invest in any cultivation business you haven't seen, any technology you haven't tested, or any license you haven't vetted with a credible attorney who specializes in such matters.

>> Background check all business owners, managers, and operators. Employing the services of a private investigator before investing in a management team is well worth the cost. (See the section, "Assessing the management team," for details.)

>> Add a few reputable cannabis investment newsletters and online portals to your reading list before investing in the sector. I highly recommend Arcview's annual *The State of Legal Cannabis Markets* report, which is replete with state-by-state and sector-by-sector marketing and business analysis. (Visit arcviewgroup.com/research/reports to order the report.) Arcview also

holds conferences, and its website provides a great deal of market information for novice cannabis investors. I also recommend the following websites:

- `mjbizdaily.com`
- `www.fool.com`
- `www.cannabisbusinesstimes.com`
- `www.cannabisbusinessexecutive.com/newsletters/`
- `www.ganjapreneur.com/subscribe/`
- `www.leafly.com/news`
- `420intel.com`
- `www.mpp.org`

» Check investor blogs, chatrooms, and message boards before investing in any cannabis stock, and identify and talk to seasoned cannabis investors. I have gained some great insights from visiting certain websites, and reading posts on message boards and conversations in chatrooms, including the following:

- InvestorsHub (`investorshub.advfn.com`)
- Next Green Wave (`www.nextgreenwave.com`), a cannabis company that shares some good information
- 420 Investor (`marketfy.com/item/420investor`)
- Cannabis Stock Trades (`www.cannabisstocktrades.com`)
- Yahoo! Finance (`Finance.Yahoo.com`) for information on specific stocks and ETFs

WARNING

Not everyone who acts like a cannabis investment expert is a financial wizard or even remotely qualified to weigh in on the health of cannabis companies. Short sellers (who bet against stocks) also participate in discussions for the purpose of creating downward pressure on stocks, so they don't have to *cover* (buy back stocks they borrowed to close out an open short position; see Chapter 12 for more about shorting stocks). Chat rooms and discussion forums are full of hot air, so take a lot of what you read with a grain of salt. However, some people who engage in these discussions closely follow cannabis stocks and really do know what they're talking about.

» Talk to brokers in Canada and the U.S. to verify that your prospect is real, compliant, and listed on a credible exchange. (See Chapter 9 for guidance on working with investment brokers.)

>> Before investing in a publicly listed cannabis operation, read all its public filings and ask questions. See the section, "Evaluating the company's financial health," for details.

>> Whenever necessary, employ the services of qualified lawyers and accountants who specialize in cannabis businesses. A growing number of attorneys and CPAs serve the cannabis market.

Researching Any Company You're Thinking of Investing in

Investors who consistently make money know the value of what they buy before they pay for it. The less you know about the value of a security or a business, the more speculative the investment. When investing in cannabis, which is already a risky venture, you need to know even more about what you're planning to buy. In this section, I explain how to find out everything you need to know.

Assessing the management team

If you're investing in a dispensary or cultivation operation, or even a distribution company, you likely want to invest with someone who has been in the business since before the dawn of legalization — a team with a proven track record and a reputation for operating honorably. To properly vet a cannabis management team in cultivation, manufacturing, dispensary operations, or distribution, take the following actions:

>> Hire a private investigator to run background checks on the managers and operators of the business. The investigation should focus on any felony records, bankruptcies, and securities fraud. Make sure the managers, particularly on the operational side, don't have criminal histories that could complicate the process of raising capital or selling the company. Most credible operators in the cannabis business got their start in the black market, and many of them have criminal records for growing, trafficking, and selling marijuana. Arrests and convictions for these crimes generally don't prevent an operator from securing licenses or raising capital. Violent crimes and securities fraud, however, do pose a problem.

TIP

I use private detectives. I highly recommend James E. Canner from Parkside Investigations in New York. He is a decorated, 25-year law enforcement veteran with the New York City and Long Beach Police Departments. You can also find licensed private investigators in most major cities by doing a basic Google search. Check with the Better Business Bureau before choosing a private investigator.

» Hire a lawyer who specializes in cannabis transactions and understands the regulatory environment to look into the management team you're prospecting. An increasing number of lawyers are specializing in cannabis business. Most of the lawyers who understand the regulatory environment have a background in criminal defense.

REMEMBER

Choose a lawyer specific to the state in which the business you're thinking of investing in operates. You can find many of these attorneys through a basic Google search. I recommend a Los Angeles-based attorney named Eric Shevin (www.shevinlaw.com) for any general information you're seeking. Shevin is, in my estimation, one of the most respected regulatory experts in U.S. cannabis law.

» Make sure the operator/manager has the title and assignment rights to the business you're prospecting. Check the licensing board in the state or municipality of the business. You can also have your lawyer or private investigator check it out. Also, have your lawyer examine the license and ascertain the most current review of the license with the state and local government.

» Check management's credentials. Is the management team qualified and competent?

» Check the company's mission statement. Is the management team executing against the company's stated mission? If not, why not? Properly managed companies are aligned from the top down with the company's mission. Misalignment ultimately negatively impacts a company's profitability.

» If you're thinking of investing in a dispensary, have friends stop by unannounced to make sure the operation is worthy of your investment. Find out who the manager is and run a background check on them. Make sure the operator isn't the target of any legal action in the state or city where the dispensary is located and that the operator is on the license that allows the dispensary to conduct business. If the operators check out, and they have reasonably clean backgrounds and are able to operate the dispensary lawfully, then you're ready to proceed to financial due diligence.

» If you're investing in a cultivation business, tour the facility with someone who has cultivation experience. Find out where the cultivator's products are sold and distributed and check for product reviews on sites like WeedMaps (weedmaps.com) and Leafly (leafly.com).

UNDERSTANDING THE CANNABIS CULTURE

Most successful and credible cannabis industry operators got their start in the black market. They represent a very particular personality type who is comfortable operating outside the limits of the law. They have a high-risk tolerance and are used to working off a handshake. I know many industry pioneers who have bought homes and cars with cash — I'm talking duffle bags stuffed with hundreds.

When I ran my hydroponics retail gardening enterprise, a sort of Home Depot for marijuana cultivators, many of my customers, all of whom were commercial marijuana cultivators, refused to share their last names, let alone Social Security numbers and tax IDs. The overwhelming majority paid on time and honored their word, but they all retained a certain degree of paranoia and suspicion when it came to paperwork. That's changing but the black-market legacy is intrinsic to cannabis business culture.

As cannabis becomes more mainstream and financial, health care, and consumer-products professionals look to crowbar their way into this hot new sector, you have to be just as diligent screening a management team from Wall Street and Main Street as you would a team that got its start in the black market. I've seen many arrogant Wall Street titans enter the cannabis industry thinking they knew it all and could simply take over and run a business in which they had no prior experience. I've watched these white-collar professionals think they could change the culture of cannabis to suit their needs and practices. They tend to underestimate the cannabis industry pioneers and get fleeced in the process.

To size up a cannabis management team at a publicly traded company, here's what you do:

>> Check to see if the C-level executives have prior cannabis industry experience. The best public company management teams are those with both cannabis and financial industry experience. Make sure the CEO has some past experience in the cannabis industry. Professionals who understand, respect, and learn from the cannabis culture tend to excel in the space.

>> Make sure any sales, marketing, and business development executives have prior cannabis industry experience. Of course, if you're investing in technology or another ancillary business, consider other, more relevant factors.

>> Run background checks on the chief executive officers (CEOs) and chief financial officers (CFOs); make sure they don't have any Security and Exchange Commission (SEC) or Canadian Securities Exchange (CSE) violations. You can search the SEC database at www.sec.gov/litigations/sec-action-look-up for specific names to find out if an individual has a record of SEC violations. In

Canada you can conduct your search at www.securities-administrators. ca/disciplinedpersons.aspx.

>> Read any and all press releases about and interviews involving the company's C-level executives. Chances are good that all or some of them have been active on the cannabis conference circuit. To find press releases and interviews, search for the person by name and title on Google or Google News. You may also find relevant information about the C-level executives on LinkedIn or on the company's website.

TIP

Start with the company's website and with corporate press releases, so you can put your Google search in context. For example, if a CEO is quoted in a press release regarding the acquisition of a new asset, put the CEO's name and the name of the asset in your search bar and see what comes up.

>> Reference check the management team's prior work experience as though you're interviewing them for a job. Start by asking for management team bios and resumes, and then check their LinkedIn profiles, as well as their profiles on Facebook, Twitter, Instagram, YouTube, and so on. You can find out a lot about a person by looking at their social media profiles and what they post. Call former employers and make sure the managers you're vetting left on good terms.

Evaluating the company's financial health

Most people talk about investing in cannabis, which places the emphasis on *cannabis*, when the emphasis should be placed on *business*. As an investor, you want to know whether the company is financially healthy, and you do that by examining fundamentals, such as revenue history, debt ratios, profit margins, and growth.

REMEMBER

Many cannabis businesses are all-cash operations and are therefore difficult to audit and ultimately value. Regulations change all the time in cannabis, generally for the better, but any cannabis investment in the U.S. still carries substantial regulatory risk. Start by examining the company's legal position, and then work toward developing a clear insight into its financial health. Here's how:

>> Make sure the business is licensed and operating lawfully. To do so, check the state and municipality in which the business is operating to ensure it's licensed. You can also search Dun & Bradstreet's business directory at www. dnb.com. Have your lawyer review the license and validate it against state and local government records.

>> Check for pending lawsuits or criminal actions against the business or its operators. Hire a private investigator to ensure a thorough vetting of any cannabis operation you're thinking of investing in.

>> Obtain the company's most current financial statements, business plan, and *pro forma* projections. (The term *pro forma* is used to describe information provided as a courtesy or to satisfy minimum requirements.) For publicly traded companies, you can obtain this information by searching the company's ticker symbol on the exchange where the company is traded or via the company's website. Any and all *pro forma* projections should be included in the financial statements.

TIP

For a public company, check out its 10K. A *10K* is a comprehensive report about a publicly traded company's financial performance, which the SEC requires the company to file annually. To access all reports a company has filed with the SEC, including its 10Ks, search for the company in the SEC's Electronic Data Gathering, Analysis, and Retrieval (EDGAR) database at www.sec.gov/edgar/searchedgar/companysearch.html.

REMEMBER

With private companies, ask the CEO or CFO for all financial information about the company to date, including any and all annual income tax filings. If the CEO or CFO has a problem sharing this information, run, don't walk, away from the investment.

>> Examine the company's financial statements closely, paying special attention to the following details.

- **Revenue:** Check the income statements over the history of the business, especially over the last few quarters, to ensure increasing revenue growth. A business with declining growth is a big red flag.

- **Expenses:** Check the profit and loss (P&L) statements to see whether expenses are staying flat, decreasing, or increasing. If expenses are increasing, be sure they correspond to increases in revenue. Ideally, you want to see increasing revenue with flat or decreasing expenses. Increasing expenses without a corresponding increase in revenue growth may be a sign of poor management.

- **Debt ratios:** Check the P&L statements for debt ratio (total debt divided by total assets), debt-to-equity ratio (total debt divided by total equity), and debt service coverage ratio (total net annual operating income divided by total annual loan payments). Generally, a ratio below 0.4 (40 percent) is considered healthy. Anything above 0.6 (60 percent) makes borrowing money difficult. However, an extremely low ratio (near zero) may be a sign that the firm doesn't leverage debt sufficiently to finance growth.

- **Cash balance:** Check the balance sheets for the cash balance over the past several quarters. Ideally, you want to see a positive cash balance, but a cash balance that's too high and growing may be an indication that the company should be paying dividends or reinvesting the cash to fuel growth. Another concern is if the company's cash balance suddenly drops, which is common among fledgling companies in a new industry when management spends too much too quickly. The rate at which a company spends money is commonly referred to as its *burn rate*.

- **Profit margin:** Calculate the company's profit margins over the last several quarters or years to determine whether the business is profitable. Use the following formula to calculate profit margin: Net Profit divided by Net Sales or Revenues equals Net Profit Margin. You can find the company's net profit and net sales or revenue numbers on its income statement.

- **Price-to-earnings (P/E) ratio:** This ratio helps to gauge the a company's share price relative to its earnings per share. P/E ratios vary by industry. For a mature cannabis industry, an average P/E ratio will likely be around 20, so anything below that is reasonable.

- **The company's return on investment (ROI):** A company's ROI indicates whether a company is using its capital efficiently to fuel growth. Various methods are used to calculate ROI; one easy method is to divide the company's net profit by its total assets.

- **Customer acquisition and retention:** Examine customer acquisition and retention numbers. (You can obtain these numbers from the CEO or chief revenue officer.) A healthy company retains existing customers while regularly adding new customers. If a company is having trouble acquiring or retaining customers, this could be a reason not to invest in it.

» Examine the company's long-term strategy. (See the section, "Looking at the company's business strategy," for more details.)

TIP

Before investing in a private company, consider hiring an accredited accountant who has a background in the cannabis industry to audit the business and verify all financial statements.

Evaluating startups and investments in licenses

TIP

The criteria listed in the previous section may not apply to investments in a startup, such as a new cultivation buildout or a license to operate in a newly deregulated market. (See Chapter 5 for more about investing in startups or licenses.) Investment opportunities like those are much harder to value and vet, especially licenses. License values vary greatly from market to market and can change on a dime, depending on the regulatory and business landscape in a given market. The best approach in these scenarios is to consult with an attorney who has done a number of these transactions to get a sense of what the market will bear.

In most startup scenarios, you're investing in the viability of the business plan, the underlying assets and licenses that allow that business to operate lawfully, and the strength of the management team. Investing in a cannabis startup is not for the faint of heart. If you're going to make the leap, don't invest money you can't afford to lose. Cannabis startups are among the riskiest in the realm of all startups. They are notoriously hard to vet.

TIP

Hire a good private investigator, lawyer, and accountant to analyze the business alongside you and do some real, on-the-ground due diligence; for example, before investing in a cultivation buildout, do the following:

>> Check to be sure the cultivator/gardeners have signed off on the buildout plan. Cultivators are like artists; they're very fussy about how their facilities are built.

>> Talk with the cultivator and contractor to be sure both have prior cannabis industry experience and are working in concert.

>> Check with the state and municipal regulators to ensure that the real estate assets are compliant, zoned, and financially sustainable. (This is a good job for your lawyer or accountant.)

>> See and touch all assets before making your investment to ensure that the business is a real thing.

The same is true if you're thinking about opening a new dispensary or investing in one. Have your lawyer check all the licenses and make sure the retail location is zoned for a dispensary and is compliant with all state and local regulations. Review the business plan, management team, and financials, as explained in the previous sections.

WARNING

Take your time investigating your investment prospect. If the principals in the deal try to rush you or tell you someone else wants the deal if you don't move right away, then tell them to close that other deal. Don't be hustled into investing before you've performed your due diligence.

Looking at the company's business strategy

A *business strategy* is a long-term plan to start and grow a successful business. Four broad business strategies are diversification, product development, market penetration, and market development. Business strategies are important because you want to make sure any investment prospect is responding to the market's needs and trends.

Most publicly traded companies have a corporate website where you can find a presentation deck for investors, which typically includes the company's business (or growth) strategy. Private companies are less likely to publish that kind of information. Regardless of whether you can access this information online, the best way to be sure you have the current growth strategy and business goals is to arrange for the management team to walk you through the corporate overview and then to ask specifically about the growth strategy. The company may ask you to sign a non-disclosure agreement; many companies consider their growth strategies to be proprietary.

When evaluating a company's growth strategy, be sure that it tracks to revenue and earnings. Owners and managers can have great visions for the future of the company, but if the company doesn't have a plan for becoming profitable, it's not a good investment. Also, if the company has an exit strategy, meaning a strategy to eventually sell the company or take it public, ask the management team to explain how the growth strategy and corporate goals track to that mission.

Evaluating the internal consistency of the company's business strategy, goals, objectives, tactics, and policies is also important:

>> *Business strategy* is the company's long-term plan to start and grow the business. For example, a company's overall strategy could be to offer the highest-quality cannabis on the market. A competitor's strategy might be to offer the most affordable cannabis on the market.

>> *Goals* are general statements of desired achievement, such as a 20 percent increase in efficiency, 10 percent annual revenue growth, and 5 percent improvement in customer satisfaction.

>> *Objectives* are measurable targets the organization must hit to achieve its goals. For example, if the goal is 10 percent annual revenue growth, objectives may be 2.5 percent quarterly revenue growth.

>> *Tactics* are specific steps or actions taken to achieve objectives. For example, if the objective is 2.5 percent quarterly revenue growth, one tactic could be to grow the sales force, whereas another tactic could involve building more dispensaries.

>> *Policies* are principles and guidelines that direct and limit the scope of the company's (and its employees) actions.

For a company to achieve success, its goals, strategy, objectives, and policies must all align to form an integrated whole. Any conflicts among these factors inhibit the company's ability to achieve its goals. For example, if a family-owned business wants to grow rapidly while maintaining family control and ownership, the goal (rapid growth) is in direct conflict with the objective (family control and ownership). In business, you can't have it both ways.

WARNING

Proceed cautiously when you encounter a business in which management doesn't know the difference between goals, strategy, objectives, tactics, and policies. A lack of clarity on the differences among these factors increases the risk that a company will fail. For example, if management confuses policies with goals, goals can become platitudes (meaningless statements) that fall short of getting everyone in the company moving in the same direction, executing the company's strategy, and meeting its goals. Another example is management that thinks becoming bigger is a strategy without considering how management will handle the operation, or even if bigger makes financial sense for the company.

A company may find some degree of success without having a strategy in place, but that usually happens only in the absence of any real competition, when the company has a lot of room to make mistakes. For a company to efficiently and effectively execute a strategy, it must be clearly documented and communicated to everyone in the organization. Documenting and communicating strategy keeps all managers and employees on the same page, literally and figuratively.

Management must also understand the strategy well enough to effectively coordinate and delegate tasks and measure performance. Many companies use objectives and key results (OKRs) to quantify objectives and results as a way of measuring and documenting success (or lack thereof). Without a system in place for quantifying and measuring outcomes, a company has no basis on which to evaluate whether its strategy is working. Additionally, if a company fails to clearly document its business strategy, regardless of whether it's successful, it won't be able to easily replicate the strategy in any new ventures or acquired businesses.

REMEMBER

Cannabis is a rapidly changing business in a complex and varied universe of regulations, trends, culture, and business models. Investigating and evaluating a company's business strategy is a challenging process based on capricious trends and elusive data. For example, in 2018, vape pens and all the related products were all the rage. Then, sadly, in 2019 a number of users died, mostly young people, turning the tide against vaping, nicotine, and THC and CBD consumption, even though the cause of deaths was ultimately traced to an additive (vitamin E acetate). Suddenly legislators, educators, physicians, and parents were calling for an end to vaping. That one setback had a seismic negative impact on the vape industry, requiring vape companies to reinvent themselves and change course to survive.

Checking out the company's competitive position

When evaluating any investment, examine the company's competitive position within its market. The analysis and vetting process varies depending on the investment category, for example, whether you're investing in a cultivation operation or dispensary. If you're thinking of investing in a cultivation operation, do the following to evaluate the operation's competitive position:

>> Obtain a copy of the prospect's license to cultivate in the jurisdiction where it will operate, and authenticate the license with the licensing authority that issued it.

>> Check with the licensing authority in the same jurisdiction to find out the number of cultivation licenses available, the number that have been or are being issued, and the number that have been granted.

>> Find out where the cultivator's product can be sold and whether the sale (retail or wholesale) requires any additional license, and, if it does, whether your investment prospect has or will have such a license.

>> Determine whether the cultivator has brands, strains, and products on the shelves of the top-selling dispensaries in the market where it can sell or distribute products.

>> Consult with a local cannabis attorney who specializes in mergers and acquisitions (M&As) and regulatory issues for additional input and insight on the cultivator's potential for success.

If you're considering investing in a dispensary, do the following to evaluate its competitive position in the market:

>> Obtain a copy of the prospect's license to operate and authenticate the license with the licensing authority that issued it.

>> Check with the licensing authority to verify that the license is valid.

>> Ask the licensing authority how many dispensaries are licensed to operate in the same market.

>> Visit competing dispensaries to see how they're performing. Ask the budtenders what their top-selling brands are and how much product they're selling on a daily basis.

>> If your prospect is already operating, check out reviews of the dispensary and its competitors on weedmaps.com and leafly.com. You can also do a general web search and check customer reviews on other sites such as Yelp.

If you are investing in a publicly traded company, all the same fundamentals apply when evaluating the competition. Pot stocks, as they have been called for years now, are notoriously volatile and don't often track to the *intrinsic value* of the company (the measure of what the asset is actually worth, which varies according to the financial model used to determine it). You want to review earnings reports, any and all press releases, and quarterly and annual filings. You can easily do this by looking up the ticker symbol on the website for the exchange where your prospect is being traded. For example, if your prospect is a Canadian stock traded on the CSE, go to `thecse.com` and enter the ticker symbol to get the latest trading information, press releases, and filings. You will find everything you need there to determine whether your prospect is a healthy company, and whether it's undervalued or overpriced.

There is no substitute for good management, a solid strategy, and basic fundamentals. Take your time with your competitive analysis. Track down the CEOs of these various companies and email them the questions you have. The better CEOs will respond or at least forward your query to an investor relations professional.

TIP

Don't be shy about reaching out to management. As a CEO of a publicly traded Canadian marijuana company, I really appreciate hearing from prospective investors. I am eager to talk about my company and wish more prospective investors reached out when contemplating an investment.

Checking any insider buying or selling

For public companies, investigate whether anyone working inside the company is buying or selling shares in the company. For example, if a company looks like a great investment opportunity but everyone in the C-suite (CEO, COO, CFO, and so on) is sell their shares, that's a huge red flag. In contrast, if key personnel are buying more shares, that could be a positive sign.

Insiders who buy or sell stock must file reports that document their trading activity with the Securities and Exchange Commission (SEC), which makes the documents available to the public. You can view these documents on the SEC's website, which maintains the EDGAR database. Just click "Search for Company Filings." Some of the most useful documents you can view there include the following:

>> **Form 3** is the initial statement that insiders provide. They must file Form 3 within ten days of obtaining insider status. An insider files this report even if he hasn't made a purchase yet; the report establishes the insider's status.

>> **Form 4** shows the insider's activity, such as a change in the insider's position as a stockholder, how many shares the person bought and sold, or other relevant changes. Any activity in a particular month must be reported on Form 4 by the 10th of the following month.

>> **Form 5** is an annual report covering transactions that are small and not required on Form 4, such as minor, internal transfers of stock.

>> **Form 144** serves as the public declaration by an insider of the intention to sell *restricted stock* — stock that the insider was awarded, received from the company as compensation, or bought as a term of employment. Insiders must hold restricted stock for at least one year before they can sell it. After an insider decides to sell, she files Form 144 and then must sell within 90 days or submit a new Form 144. The insider must file the form on or before the stock's sale date. When the sale is finalized, the insider is then required to file Form 4.

REMEMBER

Companies are required to make public the documents that track their trading activity. The SEC's website offers limited access to these documents, but for greater access, check out one of the many websites that report insider trading data, such as MarketWatch.com and Bloomberg.com.

Looking into warrants and convertible securities

Cannabis stocks provide the same variety of security structures you would find in any stock, including stock warrants and convertible securities.

REMEMBER

Businesses can structure warrants and convertibles creatively and design them to suit their needs and the needs of prospective investors. Before investing in stock warrants or convertible securities, be sure you understand how they differ in structure, risk, and potential upside, as explained in the following sections.

Stock warrants

A *stock warrant* is a contract that secures an investor's right to purchase the underlying stock or bond at a predetermined price in the future. They're usually used to sweeten a deal for prospective investors; for example, in exchange for $20,000 cash from an investor, a company may offer a $20,000 bond plus the option to buy 1,000 shares of the company at $1 per share (the *exercise price* or *strike price*) by some future date (the *expiry date*). If the share price is $7 by the expiry date, the investor still has the right (but no obligation) to buy up to 1,000 shares for $1 per share, essentially earning an additional $6,000 on the contract.

The value of a warrant is made up of two components — the time remaining before the expiry date and warrant's intrinsic value. The more time left until expiration, the greater the value of the warrant, because the share price has more time to rise in value. *Intrinsic value* is based on the current share price and the strike price; for example, $7 per share minus $1 per share equals $6 per share (the warrant's intrinsic value per share).

Stock warrants offer the following advantages:

>> Warrants provide two ways for you to profit: you can exercise the warrant if the price exceeds the strike price or sell the warrant to another investor.

>> A warrant offers the potential to earn a large return on a relatively small investment.

>> You can receive a warrant contract in addition to a bond or preferred stock in exchange for your investment in a company, so you can earn money from your investment in two ways.

Stock warrants carry two potential disadvantages:

>> You don't enjoy the benefits of stock ownership until you purchase the underlying asset.

>> A warrant becomes worthless if the market value of the asset drops below the strike price.

TIP

Approach warrants as a perk for making a direct investment in a company and to diversify your risk, not as the sole factor in deciding whether to invest in a company. You should be comfortable with the company's growth strategy and revenue horizon, so you have a reasonable chance of profiting from the stock warrant. As CEO of a cannabis company, I've used warrants to attract strategic high-net-worth and angel investors who were sitting on the fence.

Convertible securities

Convertible securities became a popular option for cannabis companies in 2019, when the industry experienced a historic downturn. Struggling to secure financing through traditional channels and high-net-worth individuals, these companies started to issue convertible securities to raise capital quickly. A *convertible security* is an investment that can be converted from one security type (typically a bond or preferred stock) into another (such as common stock). The number of shares is determined by the *conversion ratio*; for example, a conversion of 50 to 1 means that investors can convert one bond with a $1,000 face value to 50 shares of common stock.

The key advantage of investing in convertible securities is that you can earn a significant rate of return if the company's stock price is undervalued, especially if the company doesn't pay a dividend.

The main risk is centered on the likelihood that the company defaults on your investment, in which case you stand to lose it entirely. Perform your due diligence as explained earlier in this section, looking closely at the management team and all financial statements, especially the P&L statement. Also be aware of the constantly fluctuating regulatory and consumer demands inherent in a vertically integrated company and how they impact the company's ability to secure financing.

My mention of *fluctuating regulatory and consumer demands inherent in a vertically integrated company* refers to two factors:

>> The regulatory environment in cannabis is always changing. Every year more and more states loosen their restrictions on cannabis businesses. Also, local and state laws governing and taxing marijuana businesses change all the time. Those changes often relate to the politicians and legislators responsible for setting policy in a jurisdiction.

>> Consumer demand changes, based on new technologies and genetics that become available. For example, vaping became a strong trend and then contracted when reports of vaping-related deaths hit the media. Likewise, some strains, like Purple Haze, are popular among flower consumers and then shift when strains like Gelato come to the market.

Following analyst coverage and conference calls

Analyst coverage and earnings calls are a good way to research publicly traded cannabis companies. *Analysts* are financial professionals who generally specialize in an industry or a small collection of industries. They deliver research and valuation reports and make buy, sell, and hold recommendations. One of the leading analysts in the cannabis space is Viven Azer at Cowen. She's widely considered the first true cannabis industry analyst, and her work is the benchmark for all other analysts in the sector. Other reputable analysts in this space are Piper Jaffray, Michael Lavery, and Christopher Carey.

WARNING

Beware of analysts who provide positive coverage for companies that pay them to spread only good news. Many so-called experts traffic in rumors and feel-good stories to pump up the industry and specific companies. Stick with analysts who have a traditional financial industry background.

Conference calls, or earnings calls, provide another means to evaluate the relative health of cannabis companies. Unfortunately, most cannabis companies are still in their infancy, and few conduct regular earnings calls, but for those that do, listen for information, financial and otherwise, that goes beyond what's available in press releases. These calls, which are usually run by CEOs and CFOs, generally conclude with a question-and-answer period. This is an opportunity to ask direct questions about earnings, management, strategy, and growth. Participate in these calls, whenever they're available, as part of performing your due diligence.

REMEMBER

Private companies rarely offer the same degree of transparency through analyst reports and conference calls.

Digging up dirt

Whenever you're researching a potential investment opportunity, dedicate a portion of your due diligence to digging up dirt on the company. Hopefully, you won't come up with any dirt on a prospect, but you should make a serious effort to turn up anything that might challenge your eagerness to invest in that prospect. In the following sections, I point you in the general direction of what to look for.

Checking for lawsuits

The existence of any lawsuits filed against a company raises red flags about how the company is managed and whether any litigation could jeopardize the company's finances. Start by asking management to disclose any litigation against the company. Ask about any liens against the company's assets, as well as any judgments against the company. Starting with management may provide you with leads to investigate. In addition, what management tells you may raise red flags as you conduct your own investigation.

The following resources may come in handy when you perform your own independent investigation into whether the company has any lawsuits filed against it (all of these are fee-based for premium content):

>> **Dun & Bradstreet** (www.dnb.com) enables you to run a comprehensive report on a company to identify any lawsuits, liens, or judgments.

>> **LexisNexis** (www.lexisnexis.com) provides authoritative legal, news, public records, and business information with legal, tax, and regulatory publications.

Looking for any SEC suspensions or halts

The best way to see if a company has any security violations is by checking the SEC and CSA websites:

>> www.sec.gov/litigations/sec-action-look-up

>> www.securities-administrators.ca/disciplinedpersons.aspx

Evaluating Cannabis Cultivation Businesses

If the cannabis industry were a food chain, cultivation would be at the very bottom. Cultivators grow the cannabis on which the entire industry "feeds" — from manufacturer to dispensary to consumer, and everyone along that chain.

Before investing in a cannabis cultivation business, carefully consider several criteria, especially the background and credentials of the *grow master* (or *master grower*) — the person in charge of setting up and managing the cultivation operations. Other key criteria are the cost per gram of product and the cultivator's clientele. In the following sections, I provide guidance on how to evaluate these criteria.

Sizing up the grow master

The success of any cannabis cultivation business hinges on the expertise of its grow master. The grow master must have a thorough understanding of the entire life cycle of the cannabis plant as well as the light, water, and nutrients required for optimal growth of each strain. She needs to know how to grow indoors and outdoors, in soil or hydroponically, and on a commercial scale. Growing hundreds or thousands of plants commercially requires considerably more experience than growing a few plants as a hobby. Before investing in a cultivation business, thoroughly vet the grow master by checking the following.

>> **Experienced:** Make sure the grow master has several years' experience growing cannabis commercially. Great grow masters are a combination of botanist, chemist, and artist. Years of experience and education are required to grow safe, high-quality product.

>> **Licensed:** Grow masters must be licensed to operate lawfully. Consult your attorney to make sure the grow master is licensed in the jurisdiction where the business is or will be operating.

>> **Reputable:** Run a criminal and personal background check on the grow master to ensure that he hasn't been found guilty of any crimes that could negatively impact the business, such as theft or fraud. Also check references with past employers and with dispensaries, wholesalers, and distributors who've sold products made from cannabis grown by this grow master.

>> **Systematic/organized:** The top grow masters have standard operating procedures (SOPs) and protocols for lighting, nutrients, plant selection (genetics), and harvesting. You don't necessarily need to understand a grow master's methods; what's important is that he has effective methods in place to build and maintain a clean and efficient cultivation of the plant. Review all SOPs and any available test results from the grow master's previous crops.

Checking a grower's cost per gram

To evaluate a grow business's efficiency, look at its cost per gram of product. To calculate cost per gram, divide the total weight of the cannabis harvested over a given time period (in grams) by the total dollar amount spent to grow that harvest.

Costs include the following:

>> Rent (or mortgage interest)

>> Power and water costs

>> Cost of fertilizer

>> Amortized buildout costs

>> Security costs

>> Equipment costs — lighting, irrigation, climate control, and drying (curing) costs

>> Labor costs (for example, junior gardeners and trimmers)

>> Cost of genetics

You may not need to crunch the numbers yourself, because cultivators should be able to tell you their cost per gram, but double-check the numbers and the math. Every cultivator should be using cost per gram to track the cultivation operation's efficiency.

REMEMBER

The cultivator should be able to share a financial model that breaks down all the costs that go into calculating the cost per gram and provide you with a spreadsheet clearly detailing all the costs that go into growing a gram of marijuana, replete with amortization tables (which spread certain costs over several years). If a company doesn't have a financial model, run for the hills.

Comparing cost per gram

Cost per gram may vary considerably based on location and whether the business is growing premium, mid-market, or mass-market cannabis. Generally, higher-quality cannabis is more expensive to grow. All three product tiers can be profitable, but when investing in cultivation businesses, you need to know which market the business is targeting, so you don't end up comparing apples to oranges.

REMEMBER

What's important is that the cost per gram is competitive with that of other cultivation businesses serving the same or similar markets.

Considering the cultivator's clientele

You can tell a lot about a cannabis cultivation business by checking out its customers. If successful (and legally operating) manufacturers, brands, and dispensaries are buying their cannabis from the cultivator, you can rest assured that the cultivator is reputable and reliable. You still want to be sure that the cultivator's financials are healthy (that the business is profitable or on its way to becoming profitable), but knowing that it has satisfied customers gives you the peace of mind that it's growing and selling quality cannabis.

Ask the company's management for a list of its customers and obtain copies of the contracts the cultivator has with these customers. Then, check to see whether these customers are leaders in the marketplace. Are they mentioned in cannabis news or business publications? Are they competing against more successful businesses in the same class?

REMEMBER

Also be sure the clientele are operating lawfully. You want to make sure any dispensary to which a cultivator sells is licensed to sell. For example, before you invest in a grower, be sure the dispensaries it supplies are operating legally. Otherwise, a dispensary's legal problems can become the cultivator's legal problems.

Chapter **8**

Analyzing Market Trends: Technical Analysis

nvestors like to pretend that a stock's price reflects the value and profitability of the underlying company, but that's not always the case. Stock price is often based on an investor's opinion or the opinion of one or more analysts. Sometimes, the stock market is more like an auction and other times more like a popularity contest in which the most publicized company draws the highest bids. Often, emotion is the force that drives the stock market, not reasoned judgment.

Based on the belief that opinion and emotion play a role in driving the price of stocks and that the fundamentals are reflected in the stock price, many investors chart the movements of the market and the price of specific investment securities in an attempt to predict where they're heading and capitalize on those predictions. This is the realm of technical analysis and the topic of this chapter.

Prices of cannabis stocks are influenced just as much by emotion as the prices of stocks in other industries, sometimes even more so due to the popularity of cannabis. Technical analysis may be a useful tool in choosing which stocks to buy and sell, and perhaps even more importantly, when to buy and sell them.

Comparing Technical and Fundamental Analysis

When figuring out what to invest in, most professionals use one of two basic approaches: fundamental analysis or technical analysis (many use some combination of the two). The difference between the two approaches comes down to what determines a stock's value and price:

>> **Fundamental analysis** considers the value of the company, which ultimately depends on the value of its assets and the profits it can generate. Fundamental analysts are concerned with the difference between a stock's value, and the price at which it's trading. (See Chapter 7 for a detailed explanation of fundamental analysis and how to use it to size up cannabis businesses.)

>> **Technical analysis** tries to understand where a stock's price is going based on trading patterns, supply-and-demand dynamics (in terms of the supply and demand of shares), and investor behavioral patterns. Patterns in stock prices often repeat themselves because investors tend to behave in the same way in the same situations. Technical analysis doesn't try to figure out a fair price for a stock based on the company's value; it's used to predict where the price of that stock or investment is heading based on momentum.

In the following sections, I explain the main principles of technical analysis and highlight its pros and cons as compared to fundamental analysis. I also explain how to combine technical analysis with fundamental analysis, and I list some tools that'll come in handy if you choose this approach.

Grasping the principles of technical analysis

Technical analysis is sort of like forecasting the weather or predicting the future based on where events seem to be leading. It's not just guesswork; it's based on a few fundamental principles that I present in the following sections.

Price is all that matters

To a technical analyst, all that matters is the stock's price. They argue that all those fundamentals, such as the company's management team, the state of the economy, the state of the industry, consumer demand, and so on are reflected in the stock's price, so all you need to do is study the stock's price and where it's trending to make wise investment decisions.

Supply and demand set the price

Unlike fundamental analysis, which seeks to determine a fair price for a security based on the underlying value of the asset it represents (the company), technical analysis is based on the premise that supply and demand of shares determine the price, just as in other markets. When investor demand for shares exceeds supply, prices rise, and when supply exceeds demand, prices drop. This principle is as obvious as it is simple, but it's true to some degree — theoretically, if nobody is interested in buying stock in a company, the stock is worthless, even if the company is highly profitable.

REMEMBER

To a technical analyst, stocks are sort of like homes in that they're worth whatever someone is willing to pay for them.

The trend is your friend

The motto of the technical analyst is "the trend is your friend," meaning stock prices move in patterns that provide insight into what to buy and sell, and when. Following the trend is a bedrock principle in technical analysis. When a trend in the stock's price is established, its tendency is to continue.

REMEMBER

The three trend types are up, down, and sideways (but you knew that). (See the section, "Spotting and Monitoring Trends," for more information.)

Patterns repeat themselves

Another foundational idea in technical analysis is that history repeats itself in terms of trends in prices. The repetitive nature of price movements is attributed to market psychology; in other words, investors follow the same patterns over and over, reacting the same way to the same or similar events.

Technical analysts use chart patterns to analyze market movements and understand investor sentiments and behaviors. Although many of these charts have been used for more than 100 years, they're still believed to be relevant because people haven't changed that much.

Weighing the pros and cons of technical analysis

Like any investment strategy, technical analysis has advantages and disadvantages, pros and cons. In this section, I present a balanced view by highlighting each one.

The pros of technical analysis

Technical analysis has several advantages over fundamental analysis. Here's a list of some of the key advantages.

>> **Eliminates the need for detailed research:** No company research, background checks, reading financial reports, and so on are needed. All you need to do is focus on the price of the stock and where it's headed, and all that requires is examining a chart.

>> **Identifies entry and exit points:** Timing the market is always a risky approach, because world events and people are difficult to predict, but technical analysis can help you more accurately identify good entry and exit points, so you have a better idea of when to get in and when to get out. Chart patterns, candlesticks, moving averages, Elliot wave analysis, and other indicators are very useful for traders to make better-informed decisions regarding the timing of their trades.

>> **Keeps you a step ahead of other investors:** If you're doing technical analysis properly, you know what other investors are going to do before they do it, so you can act first. Fundamental analysis can't help you when it comes to identifying trend reversals before they happen.

>> **Delivers quick insight:** You can slice and dice charts to look at trends over whatever time period you desire. Technical analysis provides 1-minute, 5-minute, 30-minute, and 1-hour charts that can help you make quick decisions.

>> **Is flexible:** Technical analysis is helpful for short-term or long-term trading or swing trading (trying to profit from swings in price over a short period of time). Technical charts provide substantial data and insight on which to base buy and sell decisions. Support, resistance, chart pattern, market momentum, volatility, and trader psychology are just some examples of information provided by technical analysis and used by traders.

The cons of technical analysis

Technical analysis has some drawbacks. If it didn't, every investor in the world would use technical analysis to inform their buy and sell decisions. The fact that many do not is testament to some of its shortcomings, which include the following.

>> **Delivers mixed signals:** One technical indicator may send a buy signal, while another sends a sell signal, which can leave you clueless as to what to do. To overcome this limitation, many technical analysts look at a combination of technical indicators, patterns, trading volume, and moving averages.

>> **Lacks precision:** Trends may indicate a probable reversal in the near future, but that's only a probability, and you can never tell exactly when that trend reversal will occur. In the meantime, you could be losing money as you wait for the right point to buy or sell or after you actually buy or sell the security.

>> **Isn't exactly technical:** Technical analysis is a human approach that tracks human behavior in a particular market. In other words, just because it's called *technical* analysis doesn't mean that it's technical like the laws of physics. It's called technical analysis because the data you look at is technical. But the movement of the price of the underlying stock or investment is due to the cumulative decisions of many buyers and sellers who are human — and therefore, fallible.

>> **Requires interpretation:** Two analysts can look at the same charts and indicators and come up with conflicting opinions about buying, selling, or holding. The charts and indicators don't give you the answers; they only provide information and insight to inform your opinion. Getting good at interpreting the data requires practice.

REMEMBER

If you're a long-term, buy-and-hold investor, fundamental analysis is probably the better choice, because it helps you choose fundamentally sound businesses to invest in. Technical analysis is generally better for short-term investors, but keep in mind that short-term investing can be more costly in terms of taxes and fees.

Combining the best of both worlds

Fundamental and technical analysis aren't necessarily mutually exclusive. You can use them together to your advantage; for example, you can use fundamental analysis to find solid cannabis companies to invest in and then use technical analysis to identify buy and sell opportunities, so you're getting the best prices. Here are a few other ways you can use fundamental and technical analysis in tandem:

>> Conduct a search for cannabis stocks or ETFs, screen them using technical analysis to find which ones are trending up or down, and then perform fundamental analysis on the companies that interest you to determine whether their fundamentals are strong.

- » Use fundamental analysis to build a watchlist of stocks you are prepared to own based on fundamentals, such as the management team and the company's potential for growth; then use technical analysis to decide if and when to buy shares.

- » Use fundamental analysis to identify undervalued cannabis stocks, and technical analysis to highlight the members of that group that have strong positive momentum.

REMEMBER

Quantitative studies have found that a combination of value and momentum can be an effective stock-picking method. In essence, stocks trading on low valuations but with strong momentum tend to outperform.

- » Use fundamental analysis to identify cannabis growth stocks with high valuations and then technical analysis to identify good buying and selling opportunities. (Here, "growth" doesn't refer to cultivation but to stocks in companies whose revenues and earnings are expected to increase faster than the average company in the same industry.) Companies that have high growth rates and trade on high valuations often experience large corrections. In such cases, technical analysis can be used to identify points at which corrections are likely to occur and identify oversold levels that indicate a possibly good time to buy.

- » Use fundamental analysis to identify the fair value of a stock, and then technical analysis to trade within a specific range of prices based on that fair value. Here, you're engaging in swing trading — buying and selling shares as their prices rise and fall over a relatively short period of time.

- » Use fundamental research to determine which parts of a business cycle are most profitable for a company (expansion, peak, contraction, or trough), and use technical analysis to confirm anticipated trends and inform your buy and sell decisions.

TIP

Stocks can continue trading higher long after they become overvalued. Selling a stock just because it is expensive often means missing out on a large percentage of a rally. By following price and volume trends, you can more confidently hold the stock until the momentum is exhausted.

Gathering your tools

Technical analysts rely on two tools for identifying trends:

- » **Charts** (graphs) are the neat pictures that illustrate price movements (chart patterns).

- » **Data** includes price and volume information (along with technical and behavioral indicators derived from it).

Some technical analysts rely exclusively on charts, others exclusively on data, but most use both. However, whether they rely mostly on charts or raw data is of little consequence, because they're generally examining the same things:

>> **Prices** reflect the attitude of investors and the supply-and-demand of securities.

>> **Time** defines the period over which any given trend in price is defined. By examining a share's price over time, technical analysts identify trends that can help them predict future prices.

>> **Volume** is a measure of the number of shares exchanged, and when looked at in the context of price, can indicate the relative strength of a stock. For example, if volume suddenly increases while prices dramatically drop, you know that more people are selling than buying, perhaps due to some bad news about the company or industry.

>> **Width** provides insight into whether a change in price or volume is narrow (specific to a company or sector) or wide (evident across a sector or sectors).

Spotting and Monitoring Trends

Spotting trends in cannabis is challenging to say the least, and a great many trends have come and gone. For example, just a couple of years ago, vape pens were all the rage. Vape pen companies started popping up everywhere and raising a great deal of capital. Then came the bad news — a number of deaths and hospitalizations were linked to vaping. As a result, the vape market contracted, and investors in vape companies pulled back.

You can find trends in cultivation, processing, brands, technology, equipment, distribution, delivery services, and all other businesses that comprise and service the cannabis industry. Frequently, these trends emerge as the regulatory landscape shifts and as new markets, new processes, and new product categories emerge.

Examining different trends

Technical analysis focuses on three basic trends:

>> **An uptrend or bullish trend** exists when each successive high is higher than the previous high and each successive low is higher than the previous low.

>> **A downtrend or bearish trend** exists when each successive high is lower than the previous high and each successive low is lower than the previous low.

>> **A sideways trend or horizontal trend** shows that the highs and the lows are both in a generally sideways pattern with no clear indication of trending up or down (at least not yet).

It's easy to see which way the stock is headed in Figure 8-1. For a couple of months in 2017, Aurora Cannabis was a hot stock, rising in price from around $30 to nearly $140. (Note the dotted straight line in Figure 8-1. This is a *trendline*, which reflects the general direction in which the price of the stock is headed. See the section, "Following trendlines," for details.)

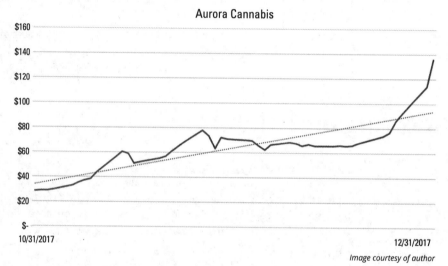

Aurora Cannabis

FIGURE 8-1:
Investors were bullish on Aurora Cannabis in late 2017.

In contrast, from March of 2019 to the same month in 2020, you can see an extreme downward trend in the price as it dropped from about $120 to less than $10 per share (see Figure 8-2).

In 2020, from March to May, you can see a horizontal trend as the price fluctuated in a small range between $8 and $10 per share (see Figure 8-3).

TIP

A sideways or horizontal trend shows a consolidation pattern, which may indicate that the stock will break out into an uptrend or downtrend.

FIGURE 8-2:
Investors were
bearish on
Aurora Cannabis
for an entire year.

Image courtesy of author

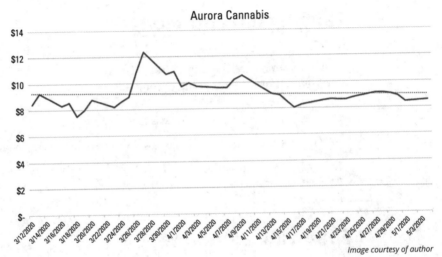

FIGURE 8-3:
The price of
Aurora Cannabis
stock showing a
sideways trend.

Image courtesy of author

Regardless of whether a trend is up, down, or sideways, you'll notice that it's rarely (closer to never) in a straight line. The line is usually jagged and bumpy because it's really a summary of all the buyers and sellers making their trades (see Figure 8-4). Some days the buyers have more impact, and some days it's the sellers' turn.

Technical analysts call the highs *peaks* and the lows *troughs.* In other words, if the peaks and troughs keep going up, that's bullish. If the peaks and troughs keep going down, it's bearish. And if the peaks and troughs are horizontal, you can expect an upturn or downturn.

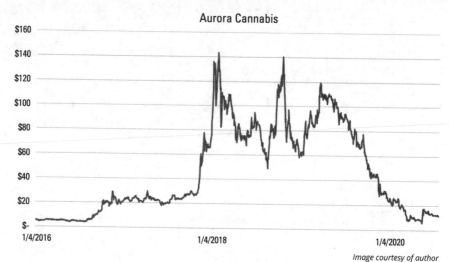

Aurora Cannabis

FIGURE 8-4:
Tracking the price of a stock is usually a bumpy ride.

Gauging a trend's length

With trends, you're not just looking at the direction; you're also looking at the trend's duration — how long it lasts. Trend durations can be (you guessed it) short-term, intermediate-term, or long-term:

» A *short-term* (or near-term) trend is generally less than a month.

» An *intermediate-term* trend is up to a quarter (three months) long.

» A *long-term* trend can last up to a year. And to muddy the water a bit, the long-term trend may have several trends inside it.

Following trendlines

A *trendline* is a simple feature added to a chart — a straight line indicating the general direction in which the price of a security is traveling. It's sort of like a piece of string stretched between point A and point B. Figures 8-1 through 8-3 each include a trendline (the straight, dotted line).

Trendlines indicate momentum in a certain direction and help to predict the future price of a stock. Theoretically, you can extend the trendline to see what the price is likely to be in the next hour, day, week, month, or year. However, trends also reverse based on rumors, news, and investor sentiment. As noted earlier, for example, a sideways trend often signals that a stock's price is about to increase or decrease.

WARNING

Don't rely solely on trendlines to make investment decisions. If you were to draw a trendline on Figure 8-4, it would show a steady increase in stock price over time, but given the large swings in the stock price over that time period, the stock price could soar or continue to drop.

Looking for resistance and support

The concepts of resistance and support are critical to technical analysis the way tires are to cars. When the rubber meets the road, you want to know where the price is going:

>> *Resistance* is like the proverbial glass ceiling in the market's world of price movement. As a price keeps moving up, how high can or will it go? That's the $64,000 question, and technical analysts watch this closely. Breaking through resistance is considered a positive sign for the price, and the expectation is definitely bullish.

>> *Support* is the lowest point or level that a price is trading at. When the price goes down and hits this level, it's expected to bounce back, but what happens when it goes below the support level? It's then considered a bearish sign, and technical analysts watch closely for a potential reversal even though they expect the price to continue to drop.

Check out the channel in Figure 8-5; it shows you how the price is range-bound between a trendline at the top that traces the highs and a channel line at the bottom that traces the lows. (A *channel* occurs when an asset is trading between two parallel trendlines.)

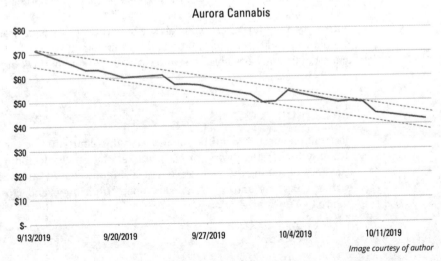

FIGURE 8-5:
Chart showing a channel.

Image courtesy of author

In Figure 8-5, the stock is zigzagging downward. Toward the end of the channel, the stock is getting more volatile as its price moves outside the original channel lines. This tells the trader/investor to be cautious and on the lookout for opportunities or pitfalls (depending on your outlook for the stock).

Referencing Technical Charts

Charts are to technical analysis what pictures are to photography. You can't avoid them because you're not supposed to. If you're serious about trading stocks (or ETFs, commodities, or whatever), charts and the related technical data come in handy. In the following sections, I describe different types of charts and chart patterns.

Getting to know the different chart types

Technical analysts use charts to "diagnose" an investment's situation the same way any analyst uses different tools and approaches. Different charts provide fresh angles for viewing the data. In terms of visualization and utility, the following are the four most common charts used in technical analysis.

Line charts

A *line chart* shows a series of prices plotted in a graph that displays how the price has moved over a period of time. The period of time can be a day, week, month, year, or longer. The prices usually chosen for a line chart are the closing prices for those market days. Figures 8-1 through 8-5 are all line charts.

With a yearlong line chart, you can see how the stock has progressed during the 12-month period, and you can do some simple analysis by identifying the peaks and troughs and possibly the strongest and weakest periods of the year for the stock's price.

Bar/column charts

Bar/column charts are a little fancier than line charts. While the line chart gives you only the closing prices for each market day, the bar/column chart gives you the range of trading prices for each day during the chosen time period. The bar for each trading day shows the stock's open, high, low, and closing prices (see Figure 8-6).

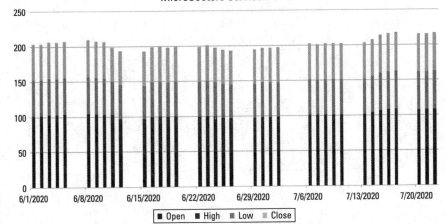

Image courtesy of author

FIGURE 8-6:
A sample column
chart showing
open, high, low,
and close prices.

The difference between a bar and a column chart is that the bars are horizonal in a bar chart and vertical in a column chart.

Candlestick charts

Candlestick charts are tailor made for illustrating movements in stock prices over the course of a day. Each "candlestick" has a "wick" at the top and bottom. The tip of the top wick indicates the high price for the day, and the tip of the wick at the bottom indicates the low price. The top of the candlestick shows the opening price, and the bottom of the candlestick indicates the closing price. If the candlestick is black, the stock's price dropped from open to close, while if it's clear (white), the stock's price increased that day (see Figure 8-7). Note that different colors may be used to indicate whether a stock's price rose or fell during the day.

Point-and-figure charts

A more obscure chart that technical analysts use is the point-and-figure chart (see Figure 8-8), which contain only Xs and Os. The Xs represent upward price trends, and the Os represent downward price trends. You use this type of chart to identify *support levels* (below which the stock price may be unlikely to drop) and *resistance levels* (above which the stock price is likely to struggle) to better judge buy and sell prices.

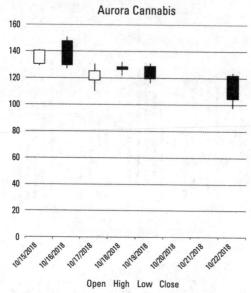

Aurora Cannabis

Open High Low Close

Image courtesy of author

FIGURE 8-7:
A sample
candlestick chart.

Resistance Level

					-	-	-	-	-			
					X		X					
			X		X	0	X	0				
			X	0	X	0	X	0				
0	X		X	0	X	0	X	0	X			
0	X	0	X	0		0	X	0	X	0		
0	X	0	X			0		0	X	0	X	0
0	X	0				0	X	0	X	0	X	0
0	X					0		0		0		0
+	+	+	+	+	+	+	+	+	+	+	+	+

Support Level

FIGURE 8-8:
A sample
point-and-
figure chart.

Image courtesy of author

Identifying chart patterns

Chart patterns are the graphical language of technical analysis, and a very interesting language at that. For technical analysts, the pattern is important because it provides a potential harbinger for what is to come. It's not 100 percent accurate, but it's usually accurate better than 50 percent of the time as odds go. In the world of trading, being right more than 50 percent of the time can be enough. Usually a proficient technician is better than that. The following sections cover common chart patterns.

Technical analysts don't deal in certainties, they deal in probabilities. Increasing the probability of success for more profitable decision-making (entering or exiting a trade) is the bottom-line mission of technical analysis.

The head and shoulders pattern

The head and shoulders pattern is essentially bearish. It's usually a signal that an uptrend has ended and the pattern is set to reverse and head downward. Technical analysts consider this to be one of the most reliable patterns.

The pattern shows three peaks and two troughs (see Figure 8-9). The three peaks break down into the tall center peak (the head) and the shorter peaks (the shoulders) that are on either side of the center peak. The two troughs form the neckline.

FIGURE 8-9:
Head and shoulders pattern.

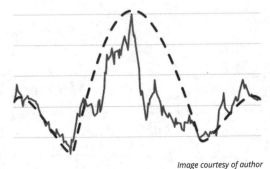

Image courtesy of author

The head and shoulders pattern tells technical analysts that the preceding trend basically ran out of gas. The selling pressures build up and overpower the buyers. Hence, the price starts to come down. The shoulder on the right is like a last effort for the bullish trend to regain its traction, but to no avail. Keep in mind that the neckline in this pattern is the support (which I discuss in the section, "Looking for resistance and support"). As support is broken, the outlook becomes bearish.

The reverse head and shoulders pattern

The reverse head and shoulders pattern signals that a downtrend has ended and is set to reverse and head upward. In this pattern, you have three troughs and two peaks. The middle trough is usually the deepest one. The small trough on the right is an interim low, which is higher than the middle trough low and typically indicates the trend is moving upward.

In this pattern, buying pressures build up and form a base from which to spring upward. Note that a bullish pattern is a series of higher highs and higher lows. In the reverse head and shoulders pattern, the neckline is resistance (see the section, "Looking for resistance and support," for details). After resistance is broken, the outlook becomes bullish.

The cup and handle pattern

This pattern is generally bullish — the price first peaks then craters into a bowl-shaped trough (the cup), as shown in Figure 8-10. It peaks again at the end with a small downward move (the handle) before it moves up. This pattern typically indicates that the stock's price took a breather to build support and then continued its bullish pattern.

FIGURE 8-10:
The cup and handle pattern.

The double top and the double bottom

Both the double top and the double bottom chart patterns indicate a trend reversal:

>> **The double top** is essentially a bearish pattern shaped like the letter M, wherein the price makes two attempts (the double top) to break through resistance but fails to do so. The bottom of the trough between the two peaks indicates support. However, the two failed attempts at the resistance level are more significant than the support at the trough, so this pattern signals a potential downturn for that stock's price.

>> **The double bottom** is the opposite reversal pattern. It's a bullish pattern shaped like the letter W, with the support level indicators stronger than the resistance (see Figure 8-11). This pattern signals a potential upturn in the

stock's price. Because this indicates a support level, bullish traders tend to look at it as a generally safe entry point to get positioned for the next potential up-move in the stock.

REMEMBER

Triple tops and triple bottoms are variations of double tops and double bottoms. These are sideways or horizontal patterns that portend a trend reversal. Don't even ask about quadruple tops and bottoms!

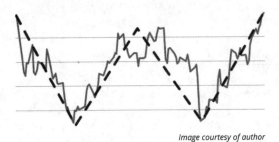

FIGURE 8-11:
The double bottom pattern.

Triangle patterns

A triangle is formed when the resistance line and the support line converge to form the triangle point that shows a general direction in the stock's price movement. The indication varies, depending on the shape or orientation of the triangle (see Figure 8–12):

» **Symmetrical** points sideways, indicating a horizontal pattern that becomes a setup for a move upward or downward when more price movement provides a bullish or bearish indicator.

» **Ascending** is a bullish pattern.

» **Descending** is bearish.

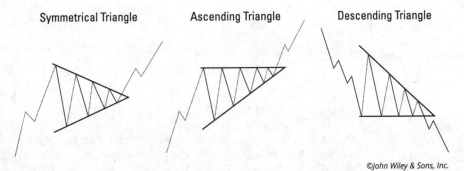

FIGURE 8-12:
Symmetrical, ascending, and descending triangle patterns.

Flags and pennants

Flags and pennants are familiar chart patterns that are short-term (usually not longer than a few weeks, see Figure 8-13). They're continuation patterns formed immediately after a sharp price movement, which is usually followed by a sideways price movement. Both the flag and the pennant are similar, except that the flag is in a channel formation, whereas the pennant pattern is triangular (see the section, "Looking for resistance and support," for more about channels).

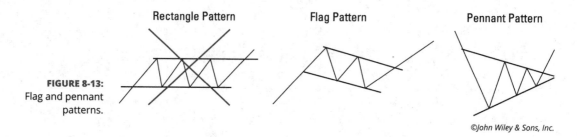

Rectangle Pattern   Flag Pattern   Pennant Pattern

FIGURE 8-13:
Flag and pennant
patterns.

©John Wiley & Sons, Inc.

Wedges

The wedge pattern (see Figure 8-14) can be either a continuation or reversal pattern. It seems to be much like a symmetrical triangle, but it slants (up or down), whereas the symmetrical triangle generally shows a sideways movement. In addition, the wedge forms over a longer period of time (typically three to six months).

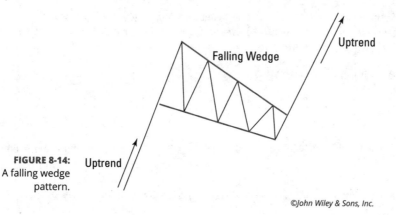

Uptrend

Falling Wedge

FIGURE 8-14:
A falling wedge
pattern.

Uptrend

©John Wiley & Sons, Inc.

Gaps

A *gap* in a chart is an empty space between two trading periods. This pattern occurs when the difference in the price between those two periods is substantial. Say that in the first period, the trading range is $10 to $15. The next trading session opens at $20. That $5 discrepancy will appear as a large gap between those two periods on the chart. These gaps are typically most noticeable on bar and candlestick charts. Gaps may happen when positive (or negative) news comes out about the company, and initial buying pressure causes the price to jump in the subsequent period as soon as markets open.

Gaps come in three flavors: breakaway, runaway, and exhaustion. The breakaway gap forms at the start of a trend, the runaway gap forms during the middle of the trend, and the exhaustion gap forms as the trend fizzles.

Interpreting Technical Indicators

An *indicator* is a mathematical calculation that can be used with the stock's price and/or volume. The end result is a value that's used to anticipate future changes in price. Technical indicators can be divided into two groups:

>> *Leading indicators* help you profit by attempting to forecast what prices will do next. These indicators provide greater rewards at the expense of increased risk. They perform best in sideways or trading markets, and work by measuring how overbought or oversold a stock is.

>> *Lagging indicators* (also called trend-following indicators) are best suited to price movements in relatively long trends. They don't warn you of any potential changes in price. Lagging indicators have you buy and sell in a mature trend, when the risk is reduced.

In the following sections, I briefly explain some of the more common technical indicators.

The Relative Strength Index

The Relative Strength Index (RSI) is a convenient metric for measuring over-bought or oversold conditions. Generally, the RSI quantifies the condition and gives you a number that acts like a barometer. On a reading of 0 to 100, the RSI becomes oversold at about the 30 level and overbought at about the 70 level.

The RSI is a metric usually calculated and quoted by most charting sources and technical analysis websites. It's generally considered a leading indicator because it forewarns of potential price movements.

For stock investors, I think the RSI is very useful for timing the purchase or sale of a particular stock. I know when I'm looking at a favorite stock that I like and notice that its RSI is below 30, that I should check to see whether anything is wrong with the stock (that is, did the fundamentals change?). If nothing is wrong and it's merely a temporary, market-driven event, I consider buying more of the stock. After all, if I loved a great stock at $40 and it's now cheaper at $35, all things being equal, I have a great buying opportunity. Conversely, if I'm not crazy about a stock and I see that it's overbought, I consider either selling it outright or at least putting a stop-loss order on the stock.

The Money Flow Index

The Money Flow Index (MFI) is like the RSI in that it measures the flow of money into and out of a security over a specified period; but unlike RSI, it accounts for trade volume, as well. MFI is useful for determining whether a security is over-bought or oversold. An MFI below 20 suggests that a security may be oversold (undervalued), and above 80 suggests that a security may be overbought (overvalued).

WARNING

No single indicator is reason enough to buy or sell a security. Check other indicators and data to confirm or challenge what one indicator is telling you.

Moving averages

A *moving average* is a series of averages of sequential subsets of data related to a security with the intent to smooth out the price data over a specified period. You're likely to encounter a 50-day moving average or a 200-day moving average, but you can specify whatever period you want to examine. Moving averages help to obscure the short-term swings in prices, so you can focus more on long-term trends. A rising moving average indicates an uptrend, whereas a declining moving average indicates a downtrend.

Moving average convergence divergence

The moving average convergence divergence (MACD) is a share price momentum indicator that describes the relationship between two moving averages of a security's price. Here are the convergence and divergence basics you need to know.

> » **Convergence:** When two moving averages converge, the trend may be coming to an end. *Convergence* is therefore an early warning. Because moving averages are always lagging indicators, measuring convergence is a way of anticipating a crossover.

REMEMBER

At a peak, one way to look at the price convergence is to say that short-term demand is faltering — traders are failing to produce new higher closes. The trend is still in place, as shown by the long-term moving average. At a price bottom, you can interpret the short-term moving average falling at a lesser pace as selling interest (supply) falters.

» **Divergence:** Conversely, when you can see a lot of daylight between two moving averages, they're *diverging,* which means the trend is safe from a crossover, at least for another few periods. In practice, abnormally wide divergence tends not to be sustainable and can be a warning of prices having reached an extreme ahead of reversing.

Bollinger Bands

The most popular volatility measure is the Bollinger Band (see Figure 8-15), invented by John Bollinger. He charted a simple 20-day moving average of the closing price with a band on either side consisting of two standard deviations of the moving average, effectively capturing about 95 percent of the variation away from the average.

FIGURE 8-15:
Bollinger Bands.

©John Wiley & Sons, Inc.

You use Bollinger Bands to display the price in the context of a norm set at the 20-day moving average, which is the number of days that Bollinger's research showed is the most effective in detecting variance in U.S. equities. The bands display *relative* highs and *relative* lows in the context of the moving average — they're adaptive to the price by the amount of the standard deviation. The bands are, so to speak, moving standard deviations.

3
Buying and Selling Cannabis Stocks, ETFs, or Mutual Funds

Deciding whether to team up with a human broker or use a discount broker, then evaluating brokers based on well-defined selection criteria.

Using screening tools to sift through and sort available cannabis investment options that meet the criteria you specify.

Getting up to speed on the various choices you need to make when buying or selling securities, so you don't get burned.

Leveraging the power of advanced trading techniques, such as buying on margin and shorting a stock, to maximize your returns and earn a profit whether the market is bullish or bearish.

IN THIS CHAPTER

cannabis

» Opting for a cannabis-friendly broker or advisor

» Saving money by trading through an online discount broker

» Choosing the right broker or advisor for you

Chapter **9**

Choosing a Broker or Advisor

Regardless of whether you buy stock in cannabis companies or invest in other industries, you must do so through a broker or a financial advisor. Think of them as salespeople in car dealerships. Just as a well-informed salesperson can help find the right vehicle for you and your family based on your needs and preferences, a broker or advisor can help you choose which investments are best for you based on your financial needs, your tolerance for risk, your financial goals, and other factors. For example, if you're young, a broker or advisor is likely to recommend an aggressive, growth-oriented approach, whereas if you're nearing retirement, she's more likely to recommend a conservative approach.

The comparison doesn't stop there. Just as you buy a new car through a dealership and not directly from the manufacturer, you buy stocks through a broker or financial advisor, not directly from a company. Even if you have a clear idea of what you want to invest in, you need a broker or advisor to process your buy and sell orders.

When choosing a broker or advisor, you basically have two options — an online discount broker or a human being (or a firm) that's licensed to place buy and sell orders. Which you choose and how you go about choosing a broker or advisor are the topics of this chapter.

Defining the Broker's Role

The broker's primary role is to serve as the vehicle through which you buy or sell stock. When I talk about "brokers," I'm referring to companies such as Charles Schwab, TD Ameritrade, E*TRADE, and many other organizations that can buy stock on your behalf. Brokers can also be individuals who work for such firms. Although you can buy some stocks directly from the company that issues them, to purchase most stocks, you still need a brokerage account with a stockbroker.

Although the primary task of brokers is the buying and selling of *securities* (stocks, bonds, and other financial instruments that hold some monetary value), they can perform other tasks for you, including the following:

» Providing financial and investment advice and access to research.

» Offering limited banking services, such as interest-bearing accounts, check writing, electronic deposits and withdrawals, and credit or debit cards.

» Brokering other securities, such as bonds, mutual funds, options, exchange traded funds (ETFs), and other investments on your behalf.

Personal stockbrokers make their money from individual investors by charging various fees, including the following:

» Brokerage commissions for buying and selling stocks and other securities.

» Service charges for performing administrative tasks and other functions.

» Margin interest charges for borrowing against your brokerage account for investment purposes, for example, for shorting stocks (see Chapter 12 for more about shorting stocks).

Financial advisors typically charge a percentage of the total value of an investor's portfolio. The rationale behind this practice is that it gives the advisor more incentive to provide quality service — the more the portfolio grows in value, the more money the financial advisor earns. However, they typically take their percentage by selling securities from the portfolio, which leaves less money to invest.

Distinguishing between Full-Service and Discount Brokers

Stockbrokers fall into two basic categories, which I discuss in the following sections:

>> **Full-service brokers** are suitable for investors who need some guidance and personal attention.

>> **Discount brokers** are better for investors who are sufficiently confident and knowledgeable about stock investing to manage with minimal help (usually in the form of self-service through the broker's website).

Before you deal with any broker (either full-service or discount), be sure the broker is listed in the Central Registration Depository and has a clean record. See the section, "Checking credentials," for details.

At your disposal: Full-service brokers

Full-service brokers are just what the name indicates. They try to provide a full range of services for investors who open accounts with them. When you open an account with a full-service broker, a representative is assigned to your account. This representative is usually called an *account executive,* a *registered representative,* or a *financial advisor* by the brokerage firm. This representative usually has a securities license (meaning she's registered with the Financial Industry Regulatory Authority [FINRA] and the SEC) and is knowledgeable about stocks in particular and investing in general.

Examples of full-service brokers are Goldman Sachs and Morgan Stanley. Of course, all brokers now have full-featured websites that provide information and self-service to varying degrees. Visit broker sites and find out as much as you can about a broker before you open your account (see the section, "Evaluating Brokers and Advisors," for details).

What they can do for you

Your account executive is responsible for assisting you, answering questions about your account and the securities in your portfolio, and transacting your buy and sell orders. Here are some of the services you can expect from full-service brokers:

>> **They offer guidance and advice.** The greatest distinction between full-service brokers and discount brokers is the personal attention you receive from your account representative. You get to be on a first-name basis with a full-service broker, and you'll disclose a lot of information about your finances and financial goals, so you want to find a representative you trust. The representative is there to make recommendations about stocks and funds that are hopefully suitable for you.

» **They provide access to research.** Full-service brokers can give you access to their investment research department to provide you with in-depth information and analysis on industries and specific companies in those industries.

» **They help you achieve your investment objectives.** A good representative gets to know you and your investment goals, and then offers advice and answers your questions about how specific investments and strategies can help you accomplish those investment goals.

» **They make investment decisions on your behalf.** Many investors don't want to be bothered when it comes to investment decisions. Full-service brokers can actually make decisions for your account with your authorization (this is referred to as a *discretionary account*, although many brokers have scaled back the use of discretion for ordinary brokerage accounts). This service is fine, but be sure to require brokers to explain their choices to you.

What to watch out for

Although full–service brokers, with their seemingly limitless assistance, can make life easy for an investor, you need to remember some important points to avoid problems:

» **Brokers and account representatives are salespeople.** No matter how well they treat you, they're still compensated based on their ability to produce revenue for the brokerage firm. They generate commissions and fees from you on behalf of the company. (In other words, they're paid to sell you things.) Whenever your representative makes a suggestion or recommendation, be sure to ask why and request a complete answer that includes the reasoning behind the recommendation. A good advisor is able to clearly explain the reasoning behind every suggestion. If you don't fully understand and agree with the advice, don't follow it.

» **Working with a full-service broker costs more than working with a discount broker.** Discount brokers are paid merely for processing your buy and sell orders. Full-service brokers do that and much more, like provide advice and guidance. Because of that, full-service brokers are more expensive (through higher brokerage commissions and advisory fees). Also, most full-service brokers expect you to invest at least $5,000 to $10,000 just to open an account, and many require higher minimums.

» **Handing over decision-making authority to your representative can be a possible negative.** Letting others make financial decisions for you is always dicey — especially when they're using your money. If they make poor investment choices that lose you money, you may not have any recourse because you authorized them to act on your behalf.

>> **Some brokers engage in an activity called churning.** *Churning* involves frequently buying and selling stocks for the sole purpose of generating commissions. Churning is great for brokers but bad for customers. If your account shows a lot of activity, ask for justification. Commissions can take a big bite out of your total portfolio value, so don't tolerate churning or other suspicious activity.

Just the basics: Discount brokers

Perhaps you don't need any hand-holding from a broker. You know what you want, and you can make your own investment decisions. All you need is a convenient way to transact your buy and sell orders. In that case, go with a discount broker. They don't offer advice or premium services — just the basics required to perform your stock transactions.

Discount brokers, as the name implies, are cheaper to engage than full-service brokers. Because you're advising yourself (or getting advice and information from third parties such as newsletters, hotlines, or independent advisors), you can save on the costs of using a full-service broker. However, without a knowledgeable broker advising you, the burden of choosing investments wisely rests entirely on your shoulders.

What they can do for you

Discount brokers offer some significant advantages over full-service brokers, such as the following.

>> **Lower cost:** This lower cost is usually the result of lower commissions, and it's the primary benefit of using discount brokers.

>> **Unbiased service:** Because they don't offer advice, discount brokers have no vested interest in trying to sell you any particular investment.

>> **Access to information:** Established discount brokers offer extensive educational materials and research tools on their websites.

What to watch out for

Of course, doing business with discount brokers also has its downsides, including the following.

>> **No guidance:** However, if you're a knowledgeable investor, the lack of advice may be welcome — no interference.

>> **No sanity check:** Sometimes a little "interference" can go a long way toward preventing you from doing something stupid, like investing in a cannabis company you haven't thoroughly vetted.

>> **Hidden fees:** Discount brokers may boast about their lower commissions, but they don't stay in business by providing everything for free. Read their statement of fees carefully *before* opening an account.

>> **Minimal customer service:** If you deal with an Internet brokerage firm, find out about its customer service capability. If you can't transact business on its website, find out where you can call for assistance with your order. Having the broker's site go down when you're wanting to buy or sell is very frustrating and could lose you money.

Deciding Whether to Fly Solo or Consult a Broker or Advisor

Back in the old days, you could find brokers or financial advisors who would tell you which stocks to buy and when to buy and sell. Not anymore. Most trading is done electronically through online discount brokers. Even if you choose to team up with a human broker or financial advisor, most of them are reluctant to advise on investing in specific industries or businesses, especially new industries like cannabis. They usually recommend a relatively conservative investment strategy and a handful of mutual funds or exchange traded funds (ETFs) to ensure that your investments are diversified, or they rely on a robo-advisor to tell them what to recommend. Regardless of how they do their jobs or which securities they recommend, they're probably not willing or able to advise you on investing in cannabis.

Because you're unlikely to find a broker or advisor who knows a great deal about the cannabis industry and can recommend potentially profitable cannabis investments, you can expect the following:

>> You're probably going to have to fly solo, regardless of whether you want to.

>> You'll probably have to do the heavy lifting in respect to finding prospective cannabis businesses and performing your own due diligence.

>> If you're like most cannabis investors, you'll be placing your buy and sell orders through an online discount broker, and not a human being.

I'm sorry to be the bearer of bad news, but that's just the way it is these days.

REMEMBER

I'm not discouraging you from working with a qualified financial advisor. A good financial advisor does much more than just recommend investments. He will work with you to reduce your taxes, increase your overall net worth, prepare for major life events that could significantly impact your finances, offer objective advice before you do something crazy, and much more.

Finding a Cannabis-Savvy Broker or Advisor

If I had a dollar for every time I've been asked to recommend a cannabis-friendly and savvy broker, I'd be a very wealthy man. The fact is, they're a rare breed. Yet, I don't recommend that you rule out the possibility entirely, and if you're seriously interested in investing in cannabis and using a human broker or advisor to do it, I encourage you to choose a broker or advisor who's at least open to the idea. Some brokers or advisors won't even consider investing in cannabis and aren't curious enough to learn about it so they can provide their clients with information and guidance in that area.

TIP

When choosing a broker or financial advisor, don't hesitate to ask them how they feel about investing in cannabis and what they know about the industry. Who knows, you could get lucky and find an advisor who's passionate about the cannabis industry, knows a lot about it, and can offer excellent guidance in that area.

The broker or advisor field is still very much a word-of-mouth business, so if you're in the market for an investment professional's guidance, start looking by asking your friends, family members, and colleagues for recommendations. Focus on the people you know who seem to be doing well financially. Find out who they would recommend (or would recommend against). After you have a list of three or four, you can schedule in-person meetings to interview your prospects.

Evaluating Brokers and Advisors

Whether you decide to place your buy or sell orders through a full-service broker or financial advisor or through an online discount broker, do your research to ensure that the person or firm is competent, reputable, trustworthy, and reliable. In the following sections, I explain what to look for in a broker and an advisor and what to watch out for.

Comparing costs

Every dollar you hand over to a broker or advisor is a dollar less you have to invest, so compare costs and value received for those costs. Insist that your broker or advisor disclose all fees, which may include one or more of the following:

>> A percentage of the total value of your portfolio (referred to as "assets under management"). For example, a full-service financial advisor may charge one or two percent of the portfolio's total value. If your investment portfolio is valued at $1 million, that's $10,000 per year, and most advisors collect that fee regardless of whether your investments earn money.

>> Hourly fees for consultations and advice.

>> A flat fee (typically $1,500 to $2,500) to create a one-time financial plan.

>> Commissions, in the form of additional compensation when an investment is bought or sold.

>> Mutual fund fees. If your advisor sells you a mutual fund, that fund will charge its own, separate fees to compensate the manager of that fund and cover other management costs.

>> Performance-based fees, if the portfolio's return exceeds that of a certain index or performance benchmark.

TIP

If you're going to pay an advisor a certain percentage of your portfolio's value, make sure that fee is tied to a performance benchmark. For example, stipulate that the fee not exceed the return on that portfolio or that your portfolio must outperform a certain index before the fee is paid.

Comparing quality and service

Don't think solely about the costs of a broker or advisor. If you can find an advisor who charges five percent of your portfolio but delivers a return of 15 percent annually, you're obviously better off than if you pay one percent and get a return of only five percent flying solo. Additionally, a qualified financial advisor can save you money in the following ways:

>> Creating a solid investment strategy that balances risk and return

>> Offering general financial advice to increase your net worth

>> Avoiding emotional decisions

>> Structuring withdrawals from accounts to minimize taxes and penalties

>> Ensuring you're sufficiently insured against personal tragedies, such as accident, illness, or death

>> Helping you navigate major financial events, such as receiving an inheritance and planning for a child's higher-level education

TIP

Bottom line: Try to estimate the dollar value a financial advisor brings to the table. If the advisor will save and earn you more money than that person charges, the person is worthy of consideration. Use this benchmark to compare advisors. Which one is most likely to deliver the most bang for your buck?

Checking credentials

Before you sign over control of any financial assets to an investment professional, check the person's credentials on Investor.gov. You can search for the person by name or by Central Registration Depository (CRD) number, as shown in Figure 9-1. If the person is a registered investment professional, the initial search result shows the person's name and CRD number, and indicates whether he's a registered investment adviser, a registered broker, or both. (By the way, Ivan Illan, whose information is shown in Figure 9-1, happens to be the author of *Success as a Financial Advisor For Dummies* [Wiley].)

FIGURE 9-1:
Look up brokers and advisors on Investor.gov.

Source: Investor.gov

You can click the Get Full Report button for additional details, including licensing information, years of experience, number of exams and licenses, and any disclosures about compensation or fees (see Figure 9-2). This is the same detailed information you'd get if you looked up the broker or advisor on FINRA's Broker-Check (brokercheck.finra.org) web page.

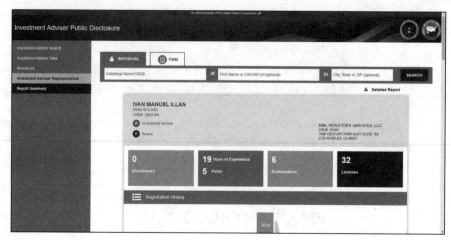

FIGURE 9-2:
You can get a full
report about any
registered broker
or advisor.

Source: U.S. Securities and Exchange Commission

Comparing online brokers

If you decide to go with an online broker, two of the most important consider-ations to make as a cannabis investor are as follows.

>> **Access and fees for over-the-counter (OTC) trades:** Most cannabis stocks in the U.S. are traded OTC, and many are penny stocks (which generally trade for less than $5 per share. You want to be sure the broker supports OTC trading and that any extra fees it charges to process OTC trades are competitive.

>> **Access and fees for trading foreign securities:** If you're interested in investing in companies that do business in countries other than the U.S. where cannabis is legal, such as Canada, be sure the broker supports trades in foreign securities and that any extra fees it charges to process those trades are competitive. (Some foreign companies have listings in the U.S. and trade like U.S. listings, without the extra fees.)

WARNING

While most online brokers advertise $0 charges for online equity trades, these free stock trades usually don't apply to OTC penny stocks and trades in foreign securi-ties. Be sure to read the fine print. Many online brokers charge an extra fee for trades of shares priced less than a certain dollar amount. Most charge extra for trades of foreign securities plus a currency conversion fee.

Here are a few online brokers you may want to compare:

>> **Charles Schwab** (www.schwab.com) enables you to trade securities in foreign markets by opening a global account. You can buy and sell OTC securities through a Schwab One brokerage account.

>> **E*TRADE** (us.etrade.com) used to offer an extensive global trading service but no longer does. Now, to trade in foreign securities, you must place your order over the phone. E*TRADE does allow the exchange of OTC securities but generally discourages OTC trading due to the heightened risks.

>> **Fidelity** (www.fidelity.com) enables all non-retirement brokerage accounts to add its international stock trading features. It also provides traders access to the OTC market. In fact, Fidelity's stock screener can search specifically for penny stocks that trade on OTC exchanges. In addition, they don't charge an additional commission on OTC trades.

>> **Interactive Brokers** (www.interactivebrokers.com) is the best choice in this list for trading on foreign exchanges, providing access to more than 200 countries and charging the lowest commissions. Where Interactive Brokers excel is with those who want to trade Canadian stocks directly, as the trades can be done online at a much lower price than that offered by competitors. Interactive Brokers also provides access to OTC markets.

>> **TD Ameritrade** (www.tdameritrade.com) offers no direct trading of foreign securities, but it does allow OTC and penny stocks to be bought and sold online for the same fees as other types of trades. Like Fidelity, TD Ameritrade's stock screener enables you to screen specifically for penny stocks.

Chapter **10**

Using Screening Tools

S tock market diversity is overwhelming, especially to first-time investors and maybe even to people like you who are looking to invest in niche markets such as cannabis. The New York Stock Exchange (the leading stock exchange in the world) lists stocks from more than 2,800 companies. Nasdaq tracks more than 3,300 stocks. Over-the-counter (OTC) indexes track another 10,000. And that's in the U.S. alone. How do you sift through all those companies to find those that meet your investment criteria and filter out the thousands of others that don't?

Fortunately, plenty of stock screeners are available to help you meet that challenge. A *stock screener* is a searchable database of companies listed on one or more stock exchanges that provides all sorts of details, analysis, and charts related to each company. It's sort of like Google or Bing, which help you find specific web pages based on search terms, but a stock screener helps you find stocks that meet your investment interests and criteria.

REMEMBER

Although commonly referred to as stock screeners, screeners are available for mutual funds, exchange traded funds, futures, indexes, and other securities.

In this chapter, I introduce you to what I think are the two best free (as of now, anyway) online stock screeners for cannabis stocks and show you how to use them. Then, I go on to explain how to use other screeners to find and choose companies to invest in, and I highlight some of the parameters (criteria) that you may find useful as you use screeners to narrow your search.

TIP

Some screeners provide more details than others, so you may use one screener to find a company (or mutual fund or ETF) that interests you and another to dig up more details about that company and its stock. What I'm saying is that the information and guidance I provide later in this chapter may come in handy when you need additional information or analysis related to a specific cannabis company.

Searching the Marijuana Stock Universe

The single best stock-screening tool for tracking down cannabis stocks to invest in is (drumroll, please!) the Marijuana Stock Universe, made available by the generous folks at The Marijuana Index. The Marijuana Stock Universe is a searchable database of all marijuana and hemp stocks listed on the following markets in the U.S. and Canada:

>> **U.S. Marijuana Index** includes cannabis stocks listed on the NYSE/AMEX, Nasdaq, OTCQX, and OTCQB markets.

>> **Canadian Marijuana Index** includes cannabis stocks listed on the TSX, TSX Venture, and CSE exchanges.

To be listed in the North American Marijuana Index, companies are required to have material involvement in the marijuana or hemp industry. This includes companies that touch the plant (such as growers, manufacturers, and dispensaries) and ancillary companies (such as fertilizer manufacturers and businesses that provide financial services to the cannabis industry). Companies must have filed financial statements in the last year and must maintain a minimum average daily trading volume of US$100.

To access the Marijuana Stock Universe, go to marijuanaindex.com and click Marijuana Stock Universe (in the menu bar near the top of the page). The Marijuana Stock Universe appears, as shown in Figure 10-1.

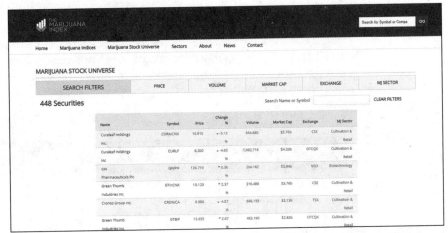

Source: Marijuana Stock Universe (marijuanaindex.com)

FIGURE 10-1:
The Marijuana
Stock Universe.

During the time of this writing, the Marijuana Stock Index listed 448 cannabis securities. You can browse through the entire list by scrolling down and using the page options at the bottom of the list to bring more securities into view. However, a more efficient approach is to use the search filters near the top of the list to narrow the list of securities. These search filters include the following:

>> **Price.** If you're looking for stocks in a specific price range, click the Price tab and drag the left and right sliders to narrow the list by price (see Figure 10-2). As you drag a slider, the list becomes shorter to show only the companies in the selected price range. You'll also see the number of securities just above the list drop.

>> **Volume.** You can filter the list of securities by daily trading volume (from zero shares traded up to one billion). Click the Volume tab and drag the left and right sliders to specify the desired range.

>> **Market Cap.** *Market capitalization* (or market cap) represents the dollar value of a company. It's calculated by multiplying the total number of shares by the current share price. To screen securities by market capitalization, click the Market Cap tab and drag the sliders to specify the desired minimum and maximum.

>> **Exchange.** By default, the Marijuana Stock Universe displays all securities regardless of the exchange or market on which they trade (see the next section for more about the different exchanges and markets). To limit the list of securities based on one or more exchanges or markets, click the Exchange tab and click the checkbox next to each exchange or market you want to include (see Figure 10-3).

>> **MJ Sector.** Probably the coolest feature of the Marijuana Stock Universe is that it enables you to screen by sector, including AgTech (agricultural technology), Biotechnology, Consumption Devices, Marijuana Products, and more. Just click the MJ Sector tab and select the sectors you want to include (see Figure 10-4).

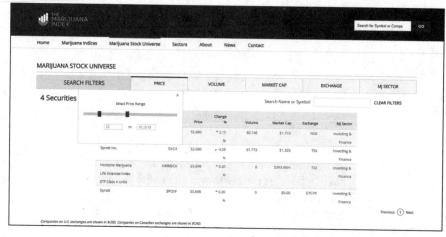

FIGURE 10-2:
Drag the sliders to screen by price.

Source: Marijuana Stock Universe (marijuanaindex.com)

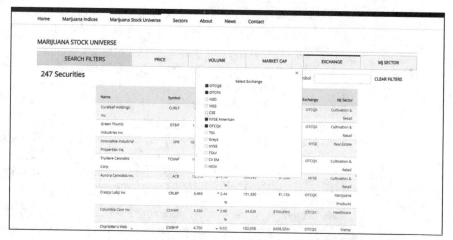

FIGURE 10-3:
Select each exchange you want to include.

Source: Marijuana Stock Universe (marijuanaindex.com)

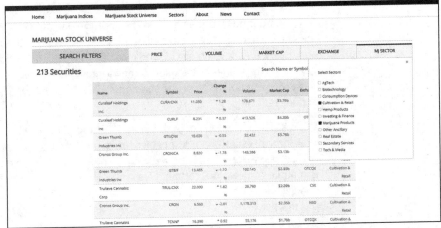

FIGURE 10-4:
Specify the
desired sectors.

REMEMBER

Filters have a cumulative effect, so if you screen by price to narrow the list and then screen by sector, the list will include only those securities that meet both your specified price range and the sectors you chose. To clear the filters and start over, click Clear Filters, in the top-right corner of the page.

Getting Up to Speed on the Different Exchanges and Markets

One of the key benefits of the Marijuana Stock Universe and the Daily Marijuana Observer's OTC database (covered in the next section) is that they cover a wide range of exchanges and markets on which cannabis stocks are traded, including over-the-counter (OTC) stocks. *OTC stocks* (many of which are *penny stocks*, meaning they sell for less than five bucks a share) are stocks that aren't listed on the major exchanges, such as the New York Stock Exchange, Nasdaq, or the Toronto Stock Exchange.

Exchanges and marketplaces covered by the Marijuana Stock Universe and Daily Marijuana Observer's OTC database include the following:

>> **OTCPK:** OTC Pink (or OTCPK) is the lowest and most speculative of the three tiers of stocks trading over the counter. Companies listed on the OTCPK market don't have to meet any disclosure requirements or financial standards and could include companies in default or financial distress. I recommend steering clear of these stocks at least until you've built a track record of success trading OTC stocks in the higher tiers.

>> **OTCQB:** Commonly referred to as "The Venture Market," OTCQB is the middle tier of stocks trading over the counter. Companies listed in this market are early-stage and developing U.S. and international companies that don't yet qualify for the higher OTCQX tier. To be included in this market, companies must meet minimum reporting standards, pass a bid test, and undergo annual verification.

>> **OTCQX:** This is the top tier of the three OTC stocks and includes blue-chip (well-known, established) companies that aren't listed on the more traditional exchanges (such as NYSE and Nasdaq). To qualify to be listed on the OTCQX, companies must follow certain rules and criteria and are subject to Securities and Exchange Commission (SEC) regulation. Penny stocks are excluded from this market.

>> **CV EM:** Short for *caveat emptor*, which is Latin for "buyer beware," CV EM is a special designation for OTC stocks to warn investors to take special care and perform thorough due diligence before buying shares in the company.

>> **Grays:** The term "grays" refers to Gray Sheet stocks, which are usually shares in startups or spin-offs that are sold publicly but before they're officially available for trading on a stock exchange or other financial market. You could find some great deals here or some real lemons.

>> **NYSE American:** Formerly known as the American Stock Exchange (AMEX) and more recently as NYSE MKT, NYSE American is similar to the NYSE, but it deals mainly in small- and mid-cap stocks and derivatives, so it's likely to offer a wider variety of cannabis stocks than what's listed on the NYSE.

>> **CSE:** Short for Canadian Securities Exchange, CSE is an alternative stock exchange in Canada that offers simplified reporting requirements and reduced barriers to listing for Canadian companies. This makes it easier for small cannabis companies to get listed.

>> **TSX:** The Toronto Stock Exchange (TSX) is one of the largest stock exchanges in North America (listing more than 1,500 companies) and the eighth largest in the world (based on the market capitalization of the companies listed). TSX leans toward listing larger, more established Canadian companies.

>> **TSXV:** Short for TSX Venture Exchange, TSXV lists smaller Canadian companies that don't qualify to be listed on the TSX. TSXV is the Canadian equivalent to OTC markets.

>> **NSD:** Nasdaq is one of the big, formal U.S. stock exchanges. You'll find stocks for some of the biggest U.S. players in the cannabis space listed on this exchange, but your choice of cannabis stocks will likely be very limited.

>> **NYSE:** The New York Stock Exchange (NYSE) is the largest stock exchange in the world (in terms of market capitalization of its listed companies). As with the Nasdaq, you'll find stocks for some of the biggest cannabis companies in the U.S., but smaller companies are underrepresented.

REMEMBER

Many stock screeners don't display OTC stocks, which include a vast majority of cannabis stocks, so when you're choosing a stock screener, make sure it lists stocks traded on OTC markets; otherwise, your selection of stocks will be severely restricted.

Browsing through the Daily Marijuana Observer's List of OTC Cannabis Stocks

The Daily Marijuana Observer's OTC-Listed Cannabis Stocks Database is another excellent resource for tracking down over-the-counter cannabis stocks. You can search for stocks by name or ticker symbol or use the filters listed off to the side of the page to browse stocks by country, exchange, or sector (see Figure 10-5).

FIGURE 10-5:
The Daily Marijuana Observer's OTC-Listed Cannabis Stocks Database.

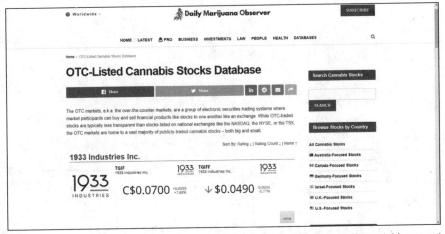

Source: Daily Marijuana Observer (mjobserver.com)

To access the OTC-Listed Cannabis Stocks Database, go to mjobserver.com, select Databases (from the menu bar at the top), click Cannabis Stocks, and under Browse a List of All Cannabis Stocks, click Visit Database. You can then browse and search the database in the following ways:

» Click in the text box below "Search Cannabis Stocks," type a company name or ticker symbol, and click the Search button.

» Scroll down the list and use the Next button at the bottom of the list to view additional listings.

>> Use the filters on the right side of the page to narrow the list by country, exchange, or sector. For example, under Browse Stocks by Country, you can choose to view All Cannabis Stocks or only those from certain countries: Australia, Canada, Germany, Israel, the U.K., or the U.S.

>> Use the Sort By options above the list (and off to the right) to sort the list by rating, rating count, or company name. (Click the Sort By option again to flip the order of the list, if desired.)

>> When you find a company or stock that interests you, click the View button (in the lower-right corner of the company's listing) to view charts and details about that company or stock (see Figure 10-6).

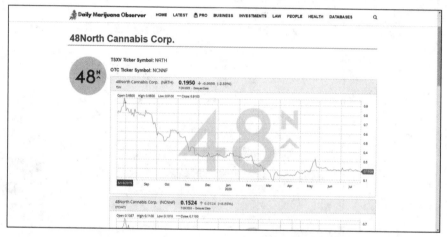

FIGURE 10-6:
Details about the selected company or stock.

Source: Daily Marijuana Observer (mjobserver.com)

Checking Out Other Stock Screeners

You can find plenty of other stock screeners on the web. I introduced a few of them in Chapter 6. Some screeners are free, but the better ones typically require a subscription. Here are a few that you may want to check out (the first two offer features specifically for people interested in investing in cannabis):

>> **Trade Ideas** (www.trade-ideas.com) is a powerful stock screener that includes a Marijuana Channel dedicated exclusively to marijuana stocks, including those listed on OTC markets. It's also one of the more expensive services, charging about $3 per day or $6.50 per day (for premium trade ideas) when priced at annual subscription rates. Another excellent feature of

Trade Ideas is that it interfaces with most popular online brokerages, so when you find a stock you want to buy, you can execute your order from the Trade Ideas website.

>> **Barchart** (www.barchart.com) provides a free list of cannabis stocks, but it's a short list. To access the list, go to the Barchart website, open the Stocks menu (in the top-left corner of the page), and under Stock Market Ideas, click Cannabis Stocks. Barchart's list of cannabis stocks appears, as shown in Figure 10-7.

>> **Yahoo! Finance Stock Screener** (finance.yahoo.com/screener) is a great all-purpose stock screener. To use it, go to the Yahoo! Finance screener web page and click Equity Screener (in the toolbar near the top of the page). You can then build a screener by adding various filters, including Region, Market Cap, Price, Sector, and Industry. Where this screener falls short (for cannabis investors) is that it doesn't provide a sector or industry option specifically for cannabis.

TIP

Yahoo! does provide a curated watchlist of about 20 cannabis stocks (see Figure 10-8). To access it, go to finance.yahoo.com, click Watchlists (in the menu bar near the top of the page), scroll down the page, and click Cannabis Stocks.

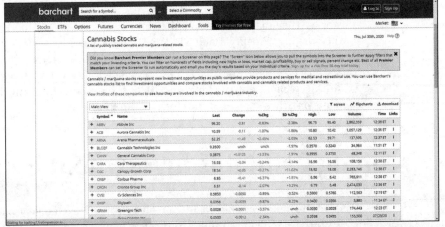

FIGURE 10-7:
Barchart's list of cannabis stocks.

Source: barchart.com

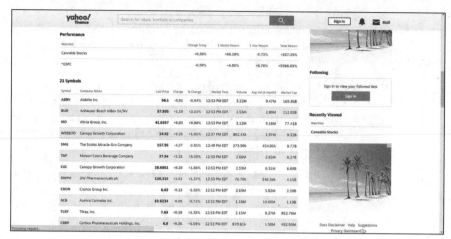

FIGURE 10-8:
Yahoo! Finance's
Cannabis Stocks
watchlist.

Unfortunately, most stock screeners lack the ability to pull up a comprehensive list of publicly traded cannabis stocks. Usually, the best you can hope for is a stock screener that lets you pull up a list of OTC stocks or a limited list of only those cannabis stocks that trade on the major exchanges.

TIP

If you're using an online broker, most (if not all) of them feature a stock screener. Unfortunately, like most of the general stock screeners available online, those offered by online brokers don't provide an option to pull up a list of cannabis stocks. They may also offer limited access, if any, to OTC markets. At the time of this writing, Fidelity's and TD Ameritrade's stock screeners were the only two that supposedly provided information about OTC stocks. (I say "supposedly" because I couldn't find an OTC option in Fidelity's stock screener.) However, these stock screeners may provide valuable information about a stock if you know the name or ticker symbol of the stock you're interested in.

Screening Cannabis Investment Funds

If you're more interested in cannabis-focused exchange traded funds (ETFs), venture capitalist (VC) funds, or private equity (PE) funds, than you are in individual cannabis stocks, you can find the best tools for tracking down cannabis funds at the Daily Marijuana Observer:

1. **Go to mjobserver.com and click Databases (in the menu bar in the top-right corner of the page).**

This displays a list of different collections of databases, including Cannabis Stocks, Cannabis ETFs, and Cannabis Funds (which includes ETFs and VC and PE funds).

2. **Click the desired group.**

   A list of additional options appears, allowing you to choose a specific database in the selected group.

3. **Click the Visit Database option for the database you want to access.**

   A list of investment options appears that are relevant to the database you choose. For example, if you choose to view the All Cannabis ETFs Database, its listings appear, as shown in Figure 10-9.

4. **Click the View button, to the lower right of fund that interests you, to view details about it.**

FIGURE 10-9: A list of indexed cannabis ETFs.

Source: Daily Marijuana Observer (mjobserver.com)

REMEMBER

Most websites and online brokers that feature stock screeners also include an ETF screener, but they rarely include screeners specifically for cannabis ETFs or for VC or PE funds, which makes the Daily Marijuana Observer's investment fund databases so unique and so useful to you as a cannabis investor.

WARNING

Before you invest in any fund, research the fund manager as thoroughly as you would research the founders and managers of a business. Make sure the person knows the cannabis industry inside and out. A fund's return depends directly on the people who are choosing where to invest the fund's capital.

What to Screen for

Screeners typically feature a variety of filters that enable you to focus on securities based on different parameters, such as region or country, market capitalization, price, sector, and industry. You set the parameters and execute your search, and the screener displays a list of only those securities that match the specified parameters.

In this section, I explain some of the most important parameters to use as you screen companies and securities.

REMEMBER

Not all screeners use the same parameters. In fact, the two screeners covered in this chapter that are most useful for identifying cannabis investment opportunities support very few of the parameters I describe next. However, if you use one screener to find a stock and another to dig up more details about it, having an understanding of these parameters will help. In the following section, I use the Equity Screener at Yahoo! Finance as an example.

First up: The major categories

When you first access a market screener, you usually enter some general parameters first to start the process of narrowing your list of candidates. For example, if you go to Yahoo! Finance (`finance.yahoo.com`), click Screeners in the menu at the top, and click Equity Screener, you're prompted to specify the following parameters (see Figure 10-10):

>> **Region:** Here you enter data about your chosen country to refine your search. If you're looking for U.S. stocks, the choice, of course, is "United States." For cannabis stocks, you probably want to focus on the U.S. and Canada, and perhaps Australia, Germany, and Israel.

>> **Market Cap:** In the Market Cap category, you choose the size of the company — Small Cap, Mid Cap, Large Cap, or Mega Cap.

Looking for growth potential? Go for small cap or mid cap. Looking for more safety? Go to large cap or mega cap.

TIP

>> **Price:** In the Price field, enter a minimum and maximum. For example, if you're interested specifically in penny stocks, you can enter a maximum of $5.

>> **Sector and Industry:** A sector is a group of interrelated industries. For example, the healthcare sector has varied industries such as hospitals, medical device manufacturers, pharmaceuticals, drug retailers, and so on. After choosing a sector, you can narrow your search more by specifying an

industry within that sector; for example, if you choose Healthcare as the sector, you can then choose Biotechnology or Drug Manufacturers as the industry.

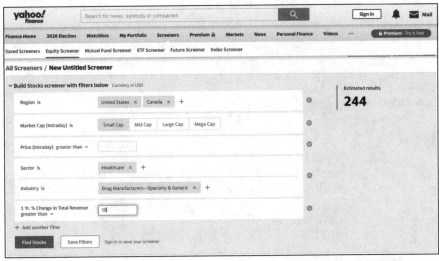

Source: Yahoo! Finance (finance.yahoo.com)

The main event: Specific filters

After specifying your preferences, you can click + Add Another Filter to display a pop-up menu containing many additional filters broken into several groups, including Fair Value, Share Statistics, Balance Sheet, Income, and Valuation Measures (see Figure 10-11). Using these filters, you can further narrow the list of stocks. I don't cover all the filters here because there are too many to cover, but in the following sections, I briefly touch on the most relevant ones. Every screener has a different way to access these filters, and some may not offer certain filters that I mention.

Share statistics

The group of filters labeled Share Statistics contains over 40 stock-related criteria ranging from share price action (the 52-week high or low) to fundamentals such as total assets or total liabilities. One area I like to focus on is the price-to-earnings (P/E) ratio. This ratio is one of the most widely followed ratios, and I consider it the most important valuation ratio (it can be considered a profitability ratio as well). It ties a company's current stock price to the company's net earnings. The net earnings are the heart and soul of the company, so always check this ratio.

Choose filters to screen Stocks	Q Find filters	✕

Fair Value 🔒

☐ Earnings Consistency	☐ Est. EPS Growth (%)	☐ Est. Revenue Growth (%)
☐ Revenue Consistency	☐ Est. Rate of Return (%)	☐ Valuation
☐ Years of Consecutive Positive EPS		

Share Statistics

☐ Altman Z Score	☐ Avg Vol (3 month)	☐ Basic Weighted Average Shares Outstanding (LTM)
☐ Beta (3Y Monthly)	☐ Beta - 1 Year (LTM)	☐ Volume (Intraday)
☐ Diluted Weighted Average Shares Outstanding (LTM)	☐ ECS Total Common Shares Outstanding (LTM)	☐ ECS Total Shares Outstanding on Filing Date (LTM)
	☐ Price (End of Day)	☐ Volume (End of Day)
☐ 52 Week Price % Change	☑ Price (Intraday)	☐ Price Change (Intraday)
☐ 52 Week Price High	☐ 52 Week Price Low	☐ Last Close BS Shout (LTM)
☐ Last Close Indicated Dividend / Stock Price (LTM)	☐ Market Cap (Last Close)	☐ Last Close Market Cap / EBT Excl. Unusual Items (LTM)
☐ Last Close Price (LTM)	☐ Price / Earnings (P/E)	☐ Long Term Debt / Equity (LT D/E) %

Close

Source: Yahoo! Finance (finance.yahoo.com)

All things considered, I generally prefer low ratios (under 15 is good, and under 25 is acceptable). If I'm considering a growth stock, I definitely want a ratio under 40 (unless there are extenuating circumstances that I like and that aren't reflected in the P/E ratio).

REMEMBER

Cannabis stocks tend to have much lower P/Es than those of well-established companies in well-established industries, because the cannabis industry isn't mature yet. More private companies have earnings at this point than do publicly traded companies.

REMEMBER

Make sure your search parameters have a minimum P/E of, say, 1 and a maximum of between 15 (for large cap, stable, dividend-paying stocks) and 40 (for growth stocks) so that you have some measure of safety (and sanity!).

If you want to speculate and find stocks to go short on (see Chapter 12), two approaches apply:

» You can put in a minimum P/E of, say, 100 and an unlimited maximum (or 9,999 if a number is needed) to get very pricey stocks that are vulnerable to a correction.

» You can put in a maximum P/E of 0, which would indicate that you're searching for companies with losses (earnings under zero).

Income

The Income group offers some important filters tied to sales and profits. Keep in mind that income in terms of sales and profits is one of your most important screening criteria.

Sales revenue (called Total Revenue in the Yahoo! Equity Screener) may be expressed in absolute numbers or percentages. In some stock screeners, ranges may be described as something like "under $1 million in sales" up to "over $1 billion in sales." On a percentage basis, some stock screeners may have a minimum and a maximum. An example of this is if you were searching for companies that increased their sales by at least 10 percent. You'd enter 10 in the minimum percentage and either leave the maximum blank or plug in a high number such as 999. Another twist is that you may find a stock screener that shows sales revenue with an average percentage over three or five years so that you can see more consistency over an extended period.

Profit margin (called Net Income Margin % in the Yahoo! Equity Screener) is basically the percent of sales representing the company's net profit. If a company has $1 million in sales and $200,000 in net profit, the profit margin is 20 percent ($200,000 divided by $1,000,000). For this metric, you'd enter a minimum of 20 percent and a maximum of 100 percent because that's the highest possible (but improbable) profit margin you can reach.

REMEMBER

Keep in mind that the data you can sift through isn't just for the most recent year; some stock screeners give you a summary of three years or longer, such as what a company's profit margin has been over a three-year period, so you can get a better view of the company's consistent profitability. The only thing better than a solid profit in the current year is a solid profit year after year (three consecutive years or more).

Valuation measures

For value investors (who embrace fundamental analysis, as discussed in Chapter 7), the following parameters are important to help home in on the right values. In Yahoo! Equity Screener, all of these are in the group labeled Valuation Measures.

>> **Price-to-sales ratio:** A price-to-sales ratio (PSR) close to 1 is positive. When market capitalization greatly exceeds the sales number, the stock leans to the pricey side. In the stock screener's PSR field, consider entering a minimum of 0, or leave it blank. A good maximum value is 3.

>> **P/E/G ratio:** You obtain the P/E/G (price/earnings to growth) ratio when you divide the stock's P/E ratio by its year-over-year earnings growth rate. Typically, the lower the P/E/G, the better the value of the stock. A P/E/G ratio over 1 suggests that the stock is overvalued, and a ratio under 1 is considered undervalued. Therefore, when you use the P/E/G ratio in a stock-screening tool, leave the minimum blank (or at 0), and use a maximum of 1.

» **Price/Book Value (P/B):** This ratio compares a company's market value (share price multiplied by number of outstanding shares) to its book value (net assets of the company). Anything under 1.0 is considered a great P/B value because it indicates a potentially undervalued stock. A P/B value of 3.0 or less is good.

Financial Highlights

In the Financial Highlights group, Return On Equity % is a useful filter. ROE is a good measure of how wisely a company uses its equity (original investment plus any money it borrowed) to generate profits. Because this is an average (in percentage terms) over five years, do a search for a minimum of 10 percent and an unlimited maximum (or just plug in 999 percent). If you do get one that's anywhere near 999 percent, by the way, call me and let me know!

A Few Final Points to Keep in Mind

Listen: Don't go nuts with all the parameters and search criteria because you want to find the "perfect stock." Your best approach is to use criteria that focus on the key fundamentals.

» **Market leadership:** Determine whether the company ranks among the best in its industry.

» **Profit:** Make sure the company is consistently profitable or at least has a good chance of becoming profitable.

» **Sales:** Make sure the company has growing sales.

» **A good balance sheet:** Ensure that assets are greater than liabilities (in other words, the company has low debt).

Chapter **11**

Placing Buy and Sell Orders for Cannabis Stocks and ETFs

You've found a cannabis company you want to invest in, you've opened a brokerage account, and now you're ready to start buying and selling cannabis stocks. If you're already familiar with the process of buying and selling shares in publicly traded companies, feel free to skip this chapter. If you're not familiar with the process or you need a refresher session on how to place trades and understand the choices that control how and when the trade is executed, read on.

Trading shares of stock and exchange traded funds (ETFs) is as easy as placing an order at a fast-food restaurant, which may sound easy until you pull into the drive-through of an unfamiliar restaurant and try to figure out what you want, reading the menu while cars are lining up behind you and the order taker is waiting impatiently for your order. Then, it gets a little challenging. It's even worse when you try to place a stock order. At least at the fast food restaurant, the menu items make sense. Stock orders, on the other hand, can be difficult to decipher — market order, limit order, stop order, stop-loss order, buy stop order huh?!

In this chapter, I explain the process of buying and selling stocks and ETFs, decipher the items on the menu in plain English, and provide guidance on when and how to enter settings that control how and when your order is executed.

REMEMBER

Before you can start trading securities, you need to open and fund a brokerage account. The process of opening a brokerage account varies from broker to broker, but it usually involves completing a new account application online and supplying identifying information, such as your Social Security number and driver's license number, and choosing an account type — for example, an individual retirement account (IRA) or a standard brokerage account. See Chapter 9 for more about stockbrokers.

Understanding the Bid-Ask Spread

Before you get into the nitty gritty of the different choices you have when placing an order to buy or sell shares in a company, you should be familiar with the concept of the bid-ask spread. The *bid-ask spread* is the difference between the price a buyer is willing to pay for shares and the price a seller is willing to accept. This difference is the *transaction cost* — what the brokers and other market makers earn as a commission for executing the order.

Several factors impact the bid-ask spread, including the following.

>> **Liquidity:** How quick and easy it is to buy and sell shares, which is related to the daily volume of shares exchanged. Stocks that trade in large volumes tend to have a lower bid-ask spread.

>> **Volatility:** Swings in share prices. When share prices are volatile, the bid-ask spread tends to widen.

>> **Share price:** Lower share prices tend to widen the bid-ask spread, mostly because stocks with low share prices are in less demand.

>> **Supply and demand:** Stocks in high demand and low supply have a narrow bid-ask spread. Stocks in high supply and low demand have a wider bid-ask spread.

When you view a detailed stock quote or choose to buy or sell shares online, the online broker typically displays the bid and ask price, as shown in Figure 11-1. Here, the bid for Organigram Holdings, Inc. (OGI) is $1.22 and the ask is $1.31, which means the spread is $0.09, which is nearly 7 percent — a high price to pay for simply buying or selling one share.

FIGURE 11-1:
Details about an investment security typically include the bid and ask prices.

Source: Fidelity (fidelity.com)

REMEMBER

The bid-ask spread is a hidden cost to investors, but it's not all that hidden. Perhaps more importantly, the spread can help you gauge the supply and demand for a stock and its liquidity. A large spread may be cause for concern. Unless demand increases, selling your shares later may be difficult or expensive.

Placing an Order to Buy or Sell Shares

Placing a buy or sell order is easy. All you do is call your broker or log on to your online brokerage account and specify the name of the company you want to invest in (or its ticker symbol) and the number of shares you want to buy or sell. It gets more complicated when you start adding conditions and a timeframe for the sale, as explained in the sections that follow. Here are the steps for entering a basic buy or sell order through an online brokerage:

1. **Find the company or stock you want to buy or sell.**

If you're selling shares, the stock is included in your list of investments.

2. **Click the company's link to access details about it.**

3. **Click the Buy or Sell button, as shown in Figure 11-2.**

A dialog box appears, prompting you to specify details about the trade.

The dialog box includes general information about your account, the company name, the ticker symbol, and settings that enable you to specify the action, order type, and time the order remains in force.

FIGURE 11-2:
Click the Buy or
Sell button.

4. **Enter your preferences, as explained in the rest of this chapter, and click the Preview Order button.**

A preview window appears, as shown in Figure 11-3, which enables you to verify the details and then place the order or go back to edit it.

WARNING

Note that the order shown in Figure 11-4 includes an Estimated Foreign Settlement Fee of $50. Why? Because this order is being placed through a U.S. brokerage for shares in a Canadian company — Fire & Flower Holdings Corp. (FFLWF).

5. **When you're ready to place your order, click the Place Order button (see Figure 11-4).**

A confirmation dialog box appears, indicating that your order has been received.

FIGURE 11-3:
Enter your
preferences and
click the Preview
Order button.

Source: Fidelity (fidelity.com)

FIGURE 11-4:
After verifying the
details, click the
Place Order
button.

Source: Fidelity (fidelity.com)

Choosing an Action

When trading stocks, your first choice is obvious: you can buy shares, sell a specified number of shares, or sell all shares. In the following sections, I show you what to expect when you choose each action.

REMEMBER

Whether you choose to buy, sell, or sell all shares, after choosing the action, you must specify the order type (see the later section, "Understanding the Different Order Types") and the time the order is to remain in force (see the later section, "Specifying a Timeframe").

Buy

When you choose to buy, you must specify the name or ticker symbol of the company or fund and the number of shares or the dollar amount you want to invest. If you're buying stocks, bonds, or ETFs, you specify the number of bonds or shares. If you're investing in a mutual fund, you specify a dollar amount; at the end of the day, the broker calculates the share price and divides that number into the total dollar amount you chose to invest to determine the number of shares.

TIP

Most online brokers feature a calculator next to the Buy option that enables you to specify a dollar amount and calculate the number of shares you can purchase for that amount based on the current share price.

Sell

To sell shares or bonds, you typically access the screen that shows a list of all your investments, click the link for the company's name or symbol in the list, and then click the Sell button. The Sell screen appears, prompting you to specify the number of shares you want to sell, the order type, and the time the order is to remain in force. Enter the desired number of shares, and then skip to the later section, "Understanding the Different Order Types," to continue.

REMEMBER

If you held some shares for one year or less and other shares for more than one year, you probably want to choose the option to sell specific shares, so you can sell the shares you held for longer than a year first. Long-term capital gains are taxed at a lower rate than short-term capital gains.

CHOOSING AN EXIT STRATEGY

Before buying a security, you're wise to have an exit strategy already in place for selling it. Here are a few exit strategies you may want to consider.

- **Support and resistance:** You identify the support and resistance levels, as explained in Chapter 8. You can then place a stop-loss order near the support level to sell shares and minimize your loss if the share price drops below that level. You can set an alert when the price nears the resistance level, to let you know that you need to re-evaluate your position — you may want to sell your shares and take your profit or hold onto your shares if you think the price will break through the resistance level. (See the next section for more about stop-loss orders.)

- **The one percent rule:** This strategy involves setting your maximum loss for any security at one percent of the total you have available to invest. For example, if you have $50,000 in savings, you exit your position before you lose any more than $500 on any single investment.

- **The time exit strategy:** With this strategy, you decide an amount of time to hold an investment before selling it or at least re-evaluating it. This strategy is useful for when you notice that a security isn't performing as you had hoped. You can then decide that if its performance doesn't improve in a certain amount of time, you'll exit your position.

Sell all shares

When you're ready to exit a position, you simply sell all the shares you're holding. To sell all shares, you typically access the screen that shows a list of all your investments, click the link for the company's name or symbol in the list, and then click the Sell button. The Sell screen appears, prompting you to specify the number of shares you want to sell, the order type, and the time the order is to remain in force. Choose the option to Sell All Shares, and then skip to the later section, "Understanding the Different Order Types," to continue.

Understanding the Different Order Types

Whenever you place an order for a security, you must specify the order type. The order type specifies conditions that define how the trade is executed. For example, a market order tells the broker to buy or sell shares at the best available price. A limit order, on the other hand, tells the broker to buy or sell at a certain price or better, but no worse than the specified price.

Order types enable you to buy stocks at a lower price, to sell at a higher price, and to minimize potential losses. When stock markets become bearish or uncertain, these conditions become even more important. For example, a limit order that specifies "Buy Sky High Cannabis at $45" may result in buying some shares at $45, or $44, or $43, but not $46, $50, or $55.

Market orders

The simplest type of order is a *market order* — an order to buy or sell a stock at the market's current best available price. Orders don't get any more basic than that. For example, suppose Sky High Cannabis is selling at $10 per share. You place a market order for 1,000 shares. Because the share price can fluctuate in the time it takes to execute that trade, you could end up paying more or less than $10 per share, and you may pay different prices for different shares — for instance, you could get 500 shares at $10 per share, 300 shares at $10.15 per share, and the remaining 200 shares at $9.63 per share.

The advantage of a market order is that the transaction is processed immediately and in full, and you get your stock or your money without worrying whether your trade will be executed. In contrast, if you use a limit order and specify a price, the trade may or may not execute if your desired price (or better) isn't reached. The disadvantage of a market order is that you can't control the price at which you buy or sell shares, which could result in losses if the change in price is not in your favor.

REMEMBER

Market orders for shares in a given company get finalized in the order in which they're placed, so the actual price may be higher or lower than the price when you placed your order.

Limit orders

A *limit order* tells the brokerage to buy (or sell) only at a specified price or better. Limit orders are generally more useful when buying than selling shares, but here's how they work in each instance.

>> **When you're buying:** Just because you like a particular company and you want its stock doesn't mean you're willing to pay whatever the market price happens to be. Maybe you want to buy shares in Sky High Cannabis, but you think the current market price of $20 per share is too high. You prefer to buy it at $16 because you think that price reflects its true market value. What do you do? You tell your broker, "Buy Sky High with a limit order at $16" (or you can enter a limit order on the broker's website). You then have to specify how long your order is to remain in effect (see the later section, "Specifying a Timeframe").

What happens if the share price drops to $16.01? Nothing, because that's a penny more than the $16 you specified. What if it drops to $15.75? Assuming enough shares are available to fill your order and you're first in line to have your order filled, you get all your shares at $15.75. But suppose you ordered 1,000 shares at $16 and only 500 shares are available — then, you get 500 shares at $16 and the rest at the next price that's $16 or less. If the price suddenly jumps to $17 and keeps climbing, your order may expire before you get any more shares.

>> **When you're selling:** You may want to use a limit order when you're selling to avoid the possibility of selling shares at too low a price. For example, suppose the market price of shares in Sky High Cannabis is $20 and you want to sell 1,000 shares for at least $19.75 per share. You enter a limit order and specify that price. If the price drops to $19.85, and one or more investors have bid $19.85 and collectively want 1,000 shares or more, all your shares are sold at $19.85. If only 200 shares sell at $19.95 and the share price jumps to $21, additional shares are sold at $21. If only 200 shares sell at $21 before the share price changes, only 200 shares are sold at $21. As the price fluctuates, more shares are sold as long as the price doesn't drop below $19.75.

TIP

Consider using a limit order to sell when the share price increases to a certain level. For example, suppose you buy shares in Sky High Cannabis for $20, expecting it to rise to $30 in the next couple of months and then drop after that. You place a limit order for $30 and specify that the order is "good till cancelled," meaning the order remains in effect until you cancel it or all your shares (or the number you chose to sell) are sold for $30 or higher per share.

Stop orders

Stop orders are useful to protect a profit or prevent an excessive loss if the share price changes suddenly and dramatically before your trade can be executed. Stop orders can be divided into two types: stop loss and stop limit.

Stop loss

You typically use a *stop-loss* order to protect a profit on shares that have increased in price since you bought them. (This type of order is often called a "sell stop" order.) For example, suppose you buy 1,000 shares in Sky High Cannabis for $10 per share and the price rises to $20 per share. You're happy to keep the shares as long as the share price is in the $18 to $20 range or higher, but if the share price takes a dive, you don't want to lose that entire $10 per share profit. You could live with making about $7 per share. So, you place a stop-loss order and set the price at $18.

As long as the share price stays above $18, nothing happens. As soon as the share price drops to $18 or below, the stop-loss order becomes a market order, and the broker sells all shares (or the number specified) at the market price, which you're hoping is $17 per share or better. However, if the share price drops below $17 before all the shares are sold, the broker will continue to sell shares at the lower prices until the order is filled.

If you're shorting a stock (see Chapter 12), you want to buy shares when the price is high and sell when the price is low. When buying a stock you want to short, you can use a "buy stop" order to set an order price *above* the current market price. The order will execute as soon as the share price rises to that level.

Stop limit

With a *stop-limit* order, you specify two prices: a stop price that triggers the trade and a limit price to specify a lower or upper limit on the price you're willing to sell or the price you're willing to pay. Consider the example from the previous section: you bought 1,000 shares of Sky High Cannabis at $10 per share, and the share price has risen to $20. You want to earn at least $7 per share, so you place a stop order to trigger a sale when the stock price drops to $18. However, you want to make sure you're not selling shares at a ridiculously low price, so you enter a stop of $18 and a limit of $16.

Now, suppose the share price drops to $17.75. That triggers a market order, and the broker starts selling your shares at $17.75. Maybe it sells 300 shares. Then the price suddenly drops to $15 per share. The broker stops selling your shares because $15 is less than your limit price of $16. If the share price then bounces up to $16.50, the broker sells more shares. As long as the share price is between $16 and $18, the broker will sell shares until the number of shares you want to sell are sold.

Trailing stop orders

Trailing stop orders are stop orders (see the previous section) with a twist. Instead of setting a fixed share price to trigger an action, you specify a dollar amount or percentage the stock price must rise or fall to trigger that action. The broker automatically buys or sells the security as soon as its price jumps or drops by the specified dollar amount or percentage. Trailing stop orders can be trailing stop-loss or trailing stop-limit orders:

>> With a *trailing stop-loss order*, as the price of the security moves in a favorable direction, the trailing stop price adjusts automatically, but as soon as the price turns in an unfavorable direction by the dollar amount or percentage specified, the trade is triggered as a market order.

>> With a *trailing stop-limit order,* as the price of the security moves in a favorable direction, the trailing limit price adjusts automatically, but as soon as the price turns in an unfavorable direction by the dollar amount or percentage specified, the trade is triggered and will be executed at the trailing limit price or better.

A stop-loss order guarantees execution (that the number of shares specified will be bought or sold), but it doesn't guarantee a certain share price. A stop-limit order guarantees the specified price (or better), but doesn't guarantee execution; it's possible that none or only some of the desired number of shares will be bought or sold.

Imagine you bought stock in Sterling Cannabis (SC) for $30 a share. You place a trailing stop order and specify 10 percent and that the order is good till canceled. At $30 per share, the trailing stop is $27. If the share price increases to $40, your trailing stop automatically increases to $36. If it continues to rise to $50, your trailing stop automatically adjusts to $45. Now, suppose the share price starts to drop. The trailing stop remains fixed at $45, and if the price reaches $45, the broker sells the number of shares specified at the market price.

A trailing stop isn't a "set it and forget it" technique. Monitoring your investment is critical, especially if you set stops using dollar amounts (instead of percentages). For example, if the share price increases substantially, you may want to increase the dollar amount accordingly.

Specifying a Timeframe

Regardless of the order type, you must specify a timeframe for executing the order. Your timeframe choices may vary depending on the broker, but they usually range from immediate to Good Till Canceled, which is usually 90 or 180 days (three or six months), after which time, if the order isn't filled, it's canceled.

In this section, I explain the timeframe options most brokers offer.

Day

Choosing Day as the timeframe means the order is effective from the time you place it until the end of the day. If it's not filled by the end of the day, it's automatically cancelled. Day orders can be useful if you decide you'd be happy with a certain share price today but aren't sure you'd be happy with that same price tomorrow. For example, suppose you're thinking of selling a stock at $40 per share, but now it's selling at $37. You think, "If I can get $40 a share today, I'll be happy." By the end of the day, the share price has risen to $39. Now, you're not so sure $40 is high enough.

Good till canceled

Good-till-canceled (GTC) keeps your order in effect until you cancel it. However, brokers usually have their own time limits on GTC orders, so GTC usually means that the order is good until 1) it's filled, 2) you cancel it, or 3) 90 days pass, whichever happens first.

REMEMBER

GTC orders are always coupled with a condition (see the previous section on different order types). For example, suppose you think Cannabis Cures Inc. would make a great addition to your portfolio but the current price of $24 is too high. You've done your homework and concluded that a share price of $20 would be more in line with the company's value. You could place a limit order for 500 shares at $20 per share good till cancelled. That way, if the share price drops to $20 or less over the next 90 days, the order is executed automatically — you don't have to constantly monitor the price.

Fill or kill

Fill or kill (FOK) is an all-or-nothing proposition. It specifies that the order be filled immediately (usually within a few seconds) in its entirety or canceled. FOK is a good choice when you spot a bargain and want to jump on it but you're not willing to accept a partial order or haggle over price.

WARNING

Most FOK orders are killed (canceled), so be prepared for that possibility. For example, if you're trying to buy 1,000 shares at $25 per share and the broker can find only 900 shares selling at the price or lower really quickly, you won't get those 900 shares.

Immediate or cancel

Immediate or cancel (IOC) instructs the broker to buy or sell as many shares as possible at the specified price immediately (usually within a few seconds) and then cancel the rest of the order. Unlike FOK, IOC is not an all-or-nothing proposition, so if you choose to buy 1,000 shares at $25 per share, and the broker can find only 900 shares at that price, you get 900 shares at $25 each, and the broker cancels the rest of the order.

Market on open

Market on open (MOO), often simply called "on open," instructs the broker to execute a market order as soon as the market opens. Keep in mind, though, that with a market order, you may not get the share price you specified. It could be significantly higher or lower. The broker will try to buy or sell the number of shares specified at the best possible price.

WARNING

"On open" doesn't mean the previous day's closing price. News and after-hour trading activity can increase or decrease demand for shares, which impacts the share's opening price.

Market on close

Market on close (MOC), often called "at the close" or "on close," instructs the broker to execute the order at the closing share price or as close to that price as possible. Investors usually place MOC orders in anticipation of the movement of a stock's price the following day.

WARNING

A lot can happen before the end of the day, so be careful placing an MOC order, especially early in the day. The price could move significantly over that time, causing you to sell at a much lower price than you wanted or buy at a much higher price than you wanted.

Chapter 12

Exploring Advanced Trading Techniques

When you have a good handle on placing standard brokerage orders, as explained in Chapter 11, you may want to consider a couple more advanced trading options that can possibly increase your return on investment and enable you to profit when share prices are falling instead of rising.

In this chapter, I explain two advanced trading techniques: buying on margin (with some borrowed money to increase your leverage) and selling short (betting that a stock's price will tank).

WARNING

Both techniques explained in this chapter are risky. If the stock price doesn't move in a favorable direction for you, you could lose a lot of money buying on margin (and much more money trying to short a stock). Don't try these techniques unless you're an experienced investor, you fully understand the risks, and you're investing with money you can afford to lose.

Buying on Margin

Buying on margin means buying securities, such as stocks, with funds you borrow from your broker. It's similar to buying a house with a mortgage. For example, you buy a house for $200,000 with a down payment of $20,000 and a mortgage loan of $180,000. Two years later, you sell the house for $240,000, thereby earning a $20,000 profit. In other words, you doubled your money, meaning you earned a 100-percent return on your investment!

Buying on margin is an example of using leverage to maximize your gain when prices rise. Leverage is simply using borrowed money when you purchase an asset to increase your investment and your potential profit. In this example, you were able to add $180,000 to the $20,000 you had in savings to buy a much more expensive house. Over two years, the price of the house increased by 20 percent (to $240,000), and you earned $20,000 (a 100-percent profit). Had you bought a $20,000 house and its value increased by 20 percent (to $24,000), you would have earned a mere 20-percent profit, equivalent to just $4,000.

WARNING

Buying on margin is great in a favorable (bull) market, but it works against you in an unfavorable (bear) market. For example, if the price of that $200,000 house were to drop to $180,000 in two years and you had to sell it, you would lose your entire $20,000 investment, and if the price dropped to $160,000 and you had to sell, you would lose *another* $20,000.

Registering to buy on margin

You need approval from your brokerage firm before you can buy on margin, which typically involves nothing more than signing a margin agreement and ensuring you have a minimum account balance of $2,000 or more.

When you sign the margin agreement, you're typically allowed to borrow up to 50 percent of the purchase price of marginal investments. For example, if you want to buy $6,000 worth of shares in a company, you can borrow only up to $3,000 for that purchase. The other $3,000 needs to be cash from your account.

If your stake in the investment drops below a certain percentage (typically 30 or 35 percent), you receive a *margin call*, requiring that you deposit additional funds (cash or securities) to bring your stake up to the minimum. For example, if you invest $3,000 cash and borrow $3,000 more to buy shares in a company, and the total investment value drops to $4,000, your stake is only $1,000 ($4,000 minus the $3,000 you borrowed), which is only 25 percent. If the minimum is 35 percent, your minimum stake would be ($4,000 x 0.35 = $1,400), so you would need to deposit an additional $400 in cash or securities into your account.

Check with your broker because each firm has different requirements, rules, and minimums. In the following sections, I describe the potential outcomes (good and bad) of buying on margin, explain how to maintain a balance, and provide some pointers for successfully buying on margin.

Examining marginal outcomes

Suppose you think that the stock for the company Sativa Grass, currently at $5 per share, will increase in value. You want to buy 1,000 shares, but you have only $2,500. What can you do? If you're intent on buying 1,000 shares (versus simply buying the 500 shares that you have cash for), you can borrow the additional $2,500 from your broker on margin. Suppose you do just that. What are the potential outcomes? In the following sections, I answer that question.

If the stock price goes up

Obviously, this is the desired outcome. If Sativa Grass rises to $10 per share, your investment is worth $10,000, and your outstanding margin loan is $2,500. If you sell all your shares, the total proceeds will pay off the loan and leave you with a $7,500 net profit. This really illustrates the power of leverage. While the share price doubled, the $2,500 you invested tripled. You just earned a 200 percent return on your investment! (For the sake of this example, I omitted any charges, such as commissions and interest paid on the margin loan.) Another way to look at it is that if you had invested only the $2,500 you had in your account, you would have a profit of only $1,500. However, by leveraging the power of other people's money, that same $2,500 investment earned you a profit of $5,000!

REMEMBER

Leverage can be very profitable, but it's risky. It's still debt, so you must pay it off eventually with interest, regardless of the stock's performance.

If the stock price stagnates or drops

If the stock goes nowhere, you still have to pay interest on that margin loan. If the stock pays dividends, that money can help defray the interest paid on the loan. In fact, if the dividends exceed the interest payments, you may even earn a profit by holding onto the stock, even if its share price stagnates or drops temporarily.

However, buying on margin can work against you if the price drops and you have to sell. For example, what if Sativa Grass stock dropped to $3 per share? Now, those 1,000 shares are worth only $3,000, and if you had to sell, you'd lose $2,000 (after paying back the $2,500 loan, you'd have only $500). If you don't have to sell, you're not exactly looking at disaster at this point, because there's a chance the share price will recover. However, at this point, your stake in the investment is only $500, which represents about 17 percent ($500 divided by $3,000), in which case you'd get the dreaded margin call. To bring your stake up to 35 percent (or $1,050), you'd need to deposit another $550 into your account (in cash or securities). See the next section for information about appropriate debt-to-equity ratios on margin loans.

Striving for success on margin

Margin, as you can see from the previous sections, can escalate your profits on the upside but magnify your losses on the downside. If your stock plummets, you can end up with a margin loan that exceeds the market value of the stock you used the loan to purchase. In 2008, margin debt hit very high levels, and that subsequently resulted in tumbling stock prices. In 2015, total margin debt again hit record highs by midyear, and it contributed to the stock market's down moves during late 2015 and early 2016 as selling pressures forced the sale of stocks tied to margin loans (with margin calls to boot!). In December 2018, one of the worst months in recent memory, excessive exposure of margin debt again exacerbated the losses as many investors were forced to sell and pay back the margin debt. Ugh!

If you buy stock on margin, use a disciplined approach. Be extra careful when using leverage, such as a margin loan, because it can backfire. Keep the following points in mind:

TIP

>> **Have ample reserves of cash or marginable securities in your account.** Try to maintain a stake of at least 40 percent in all investments you buy on margin.

>> **If you're a beginner, consider using margin to buy stocks in large companies that have relatively stable prices and pay good dividends.** Some people buy income stocks with dividend yields that exceed the margin interest rate, meaning the stock ends up paying the interest on the margin loan and still yielding a profit while share prices (hopefully) rise.

You may want to combine margin buying with a stop-loss order, as I describe in Chapter 11, so that you don't lose your shirt if the share price tanks and doesn't have time to recover before you need to sell.

>> **Closely monitor your stocks.** If the market turns against you, the result can be especially painful if you don't have the cash to cover the margin calls and you don't have the time to wait for a market recovery.

>> **Have a payback plan for your margin debt.** Taking margin loans against your investments involves paying interest and eventually paying off the loan. Be sure to include this cost of investing when calculating the expected return on your investment.

Shorting a Stock

The vast majority of stock investors are familiar with buying a stock and holding onto it for a while in the hope that the share price increases. This kind of thinking is called *going long*, and investors who go long are considered to be *long on stocks*. Going long essentially means that you're bullish and planning to profit from rising prices. However, astute investors also profit in the market when stock prices fall. *Going short* on a stock (also called *shorting a stock, selling short,* or *doing a short sale*) is a common technique for profiting from a stock price decline. A short sale is essentially a bet that a particular stock's price will drop. Investors have made big profits during bear markets by going short.

Most people easily understand making money by going long. It boils down to "buying low and selling high." Piece of cake. Conversely, going short means making money by selling high and then buying low. Huh? Thinking in reverse isn't a piece of cake. Although the concept of selling high and then buying low may tax the mind, the mechanics of going short are really simple. Consider an example that uses a fictitious company called Sativa Grass. The company has a P/E ratio of 60, revenue has flattened, it has lots of debt, and it's losing market share. Worse yet, news is out that the cannabis industry will face hard times for the foreseeable future. Sativa Grass stock looks like an ideal candidate for shorting. The future may be bleak for Sativa Grass, but it's promising for savvy investors. The following sections provide the full scoop on going short, but first, a few words to lay the groundwork.

REMEMBER

To go short, you have to be deemed (by your broker) creditworthy — your account needs to be approved for short selling, which usually means your account needs to maintain a certain balance, you must have a certain amount of cash available to cover your position, or both. When you're approved for margin trading, you're probably approved to sell short, too. Talk to your broker (or check the broker's website for information) about any account limitations that may prevent you from shorting stocks. (See Chapter 9 for information on working with brokers.)

Note that if the stock generates any dividends, they're paid to the stock's owner, not to the person who borrows the shares to go short.

WARNING

When you go long on stocks, the most you can lose is your entire investment. When you go short, you can lose far more money than you have invested, especially if you're not paying attention or you're not using a buy-stop order to protect yourself in the event that the stock price continues to rise (more about that in the later section, "Taking a hit when the stock price keeps rising"). Because of the risk, I strongly discourage novice investors from trying to short stocks.

Setting up a short sale

To execute a short sale, borrow shares from another investor and sell them immediately, then you wait for the price to drop, buy the shares back at the lower price, return the shares to the other investor, and pocket the difference between the price you sold the shares for and the price you paid to buy them back.

For example, suppose you think Sativa Grass is the right stock to short — you're pretty sure its share price is going to tank. With Sativa Grass at $15, you instruct your broker to "go short 400 shares on Sativa Grass." (It doesn't have to be 400 shares; I'm just using that as an example.) Here's what happens next:

1. Your broker borrows 400 shares of Sativa Grass stock, either from his own inventory or from another client or broker.

That's right. The stock can be borrowed from a client, no permission necessary. The broker guarantees the transaction, and the client/stock owner never has to be informed about it because he never loses legal and beneficial right to the stock. You borrow 400 shares, and you'll return 400 shares when it's time to complete the transaction.

2. Your broker immediately sells the borrowed shares and puts the money in your account.

Your account is credited with $6,000 (400 shares multiplied by $15) in cash — the money gained from selling the borrowed stock. This cash acts like a loan on which you're charged interest.

3. You wait for the stock price to drop.

This is the nerve-wracking part, because the share price could rise or fall, and you need to decide on the right time to buy back the 400 shares you borrowed. The lower the share price drops, the bigger your profit, but if the share price rises, you stand to lose money.

4. You buy the shares back (hopefully at a significantly lower price) and return them to their rightful owner.

When it's time to close the transaction (because either you want to close it or the owner of the shares wants to sell them, so you have to return them), you must return the number of shares you borrowed (in this case, 400 shares). If you buy back the 400 shares at $5 per share (a total of $2,000), and you return those shares to their owner, you earn a $4,000 profit. (To keep the example tidy, I don't include brokerage commissions.)

Taking a hit when the stock price keeps rising

Now for the dark side of short selling. Suppose you were wrong about Sativa Grass and the stock price skyrockets, from $15 to $35. Now what? You still have to return the 400 shares you borrowed, but with the share price at $35, you'd have to pay $14,000 for those 400 shares. Ouch! How do you pay for it? Well, you have that original $6,000 in your account from when you initially went short on the stock. But where do you get the other $8,000 ($14,000 less the original $6,000)? You guessed it — your pocket! You have to cough up the difference. If the stock continues to rise, that's a lot of coughing.

How much money do you lose if the stock goes to $60 or more? A heck of a lot. As a matter of fact, there's no limit to how much you can lose.

TIP

Because the potential for loss is unlimited when you short a stock, I suggest that you use a buy-stop order to limit the loss. Better yet, make it a good-till-cancelled (GTC) order, as explained in Chapter 11. For example, using a buy-stop order, GTC, you could specify a sell price of $20. If the share price hits $20, you'd sell the 400 shares for a total of $8,000 and end up losing only $2,000. That's still a significant loss, but it's a lot less than if you were to wait until the share price rose to $35 or more.

THE UPTICK RULE

For many years, the stock market had something called the *uptick rule*. This rule stated that you could enter into a short sale only when the stock had just completed an uptick. "Tick" in this case means a price movement; an uptick is a move up, and a downtick is a move down. The amount of the tick doesn't matter. So, if you short a stock at the price of $40, the immediate prior price must have been $39.99 or lower. The reason for this rule (a Federal Reserve regulation) is that short selling can aggravate declining stock prices in a rapidly falling market. In practice, going short on a stock whose price is already declining can make the stock price drop even more. Excessive short selling can make the stock more volatile than it would be otherwise.

In 2007, however, the uptick rule was removed. This action contributed to the increased volatility that investors saw during 2007–2008. Investors had to adapt accordingly. It meant getting used to wider swings in stock price movements on days of heavy trading activity.

Responding when you feel the squeeze

When a lot of people are short on a particular stock and its price starts to rise, they scramble to buy back the stock before they lose too much money. The increased demand for shares hastens the stock's ascent and puts pressure (called a *short squeeze*) on investors who've been shorting the stock.

Now, suppose the investor you borrowed the shares from wants to sell them and doesn't have them to sell (because you sold them to someone else). What happens then? Now is when you feel the short squeeze. Your broker demands that you return the borrowed shares, so you have no option but to buy shares at the market price and return them. You can no longer wait for the share price to drop.

WARNING

Going short can be a great maneuver in a declining (bear) market, but it can be brutal if the share price rises. If you're a beginner, stay away from short selling until you have enough experience (and money) to risk it.

Recognizing the ups and downs of shorting cannabis stocks

The year 2019 was a brutal one for cannabis stocks in Canada and the U.S., but it was a stellar year for short sellers, who harvested nearly $1 billion from shorting the top 20 cannabis companies.

The sector had entered 2019 with big promises and fat valuations, but one quarter after another, a string of companies reported disappointing quarterly results, failing to meet the expectations they had set for themselves and for investors. All this bad news sent cannabis stock prices plunging.

The Horizons Marijuana Life Sciences Index ETF (HMMJ) dropped 43 percent, and the ETFMG Alternative Harvest ETF (MJ) dropped 36 percent, while the S&P 500 index gained 32 percent over the same period. Shorting Aurora Cannabis Inc. (ACB) through 2019 yielded the most profit for investors — a total of $264.8 million. Those who shorted Chronos Group Inc. (CRON) came in second with a total net profit of about $271 million, and investors in Tilray, Inc. netted a profit of just over $174.3 million.

Among the major licensed producers in Canada, only Aphria Inc. (APHA) generated a total loss for short sellers in 2019, in the amount of $65 million. Organigram Holdings Inc. (OGI) also generated a net loss for short sellers, but just barely, in the amount of nearly $600,000.

All this positive news about shorting cannabis stocks tends to encourage investors to jump on the bandwagon. But be careful. Even if you're successful in selling high and buying low, the costs of shorting a stock could take a big chunk out of any profit. As I write this, investors looking to jump into a short position are having to pay handsomely to do so. The average cost to borrow stock across the entire sector is 26.5 percent, and 30.5 percent among the top 20 names, costing investors about $2.8 million a day or $1.01 billion annually at those rates. The top 20 names make up nearly 90 percent of all the weed stocks that investors are borrowing to short.

Cannabis short sellers got off to a hot start in 2020 after netting slightly more than $1 billion in profits in 2019. However, cannabis stocks have caught fire in recent weeks, and short sellers' 2020 profits are now up in smoke.

According to S3 Partners analyst Ihor Dusaniwsky, the last major rally in mid-April 2020 generated a $123 million loss for short sellers and brought year-to-date 2020 short seller returns into negative territory at a $119 million loss. He said S3's portfolio of 240 U.S.- and Canada-listed cannabis stocks currently has $2.81 billion in total short interest. In the past month, short sellers have added $147 million to their positions.

The silver lining for cannabis short sellers in 2020 is that borrow fees have been dropping, down 5.1 percent year-to-date for the top 20 most shorted cannabis stocks. Despite the decline in fees, cannabis short sellers are still paying more than $1.46 million daily to maintain their positions.

Shorting cannabis stocks is likely to continue into 2021, but I predict that the short sellers will be in dire straits when the economy returns to pre-pandemic levels, so be especially careful betting against the industry. If you get burned short-selling, you stand to suffer more than just your profits going up in smoke.

4

Exploring Cannabis Investment Strategies

Checking out different cannabis investment strategies to determine which ones are best for you at any given time.

Following the money in an attempt to ride the waves created by other cannabis investors.

Choosing to invest in cannabis companies that operate only in countries where cannabis is legal.

Exploring various investment strategies that may help to minimize your risks while maximizing your gains.

Chapter **13**

Following the Money: Momentum Investing (aka Speculating)

The traditional approach to investing in stocks is to "buy low and sell high," but some investment professionals recommend a different strategy: *buy high and sell higher*. After all, you earn a profit either way.

This strategy, referred to as *momentum investing*, is based on the premise that stock prices are driven more by emotion than logic, and if you've been following the stock markets lately, that seems abundantly clear. Fear fuels momentum — both fear of losing money when the stock market tanks, and fear of missing out (FOMO) when prices are soaring. Investors often succumb to *herd mentality* — doing whatever they observe everyone else doing (or what they *think* everyone else is doing). If everyone's buying marijuana stocks, investing in marijuana must be a good idea, right? And if everyone's selling their shares, then maybe it's time to dump your marijuana stocks. Well, maybe, maybe not, but that's the general idea behind momentum investing.

Based on these observations of the human tendency to follow the crowd, momentum investors generally buy a stock when it's performing well, hold it for as long as the price continues to rise, and sell it just before or not too long after the positive momentum shifts to negative momentum. They decide whether to buy or sell based on the belief that the current trend in either direction will continue for some time.

REMEMBER

Momentum investing does have some data to back it up. A 1993 study published in the *Journal of Finance* showed the performance of a stock over a 3- to 12-month timeframe typically reflected how the stock would perform over the following 3- to 12-month timeframe. This same study claimed that "an investor using a momentum-based system would have produced returns substantially better than the overall U.S. market between 1965 and 1989." What they mean by "substantially" is anyone's guess, but what's important is that momentum investors earned more money on their investments than investors who used other strategies.

WARNING

Although this strategy is popularly called "momentum investing," it's not technically investing — it's short-term *speculating*. Investing is primarily about fundamentals and a long-term holding period, preferably 5 years or longer, but definitely far more than 12 months. In contrast, momentum investing . . . I mean speculating . . . relies almost exclusively on technical analysis (see Chapter 8) and typically has a time frame of 12 months or less. To traditional investors, "momentum investing" is a sly oxymoron.

I am not encouraging you to engage in this speculative strategy. I write about it only to inform you concerning how it works and caution you about the risks. During the Internet stock mania days 20 years ago — the dotcom era — "momentum investing" gained lots of advocates, until they racked up huge losses as their high-flying dotcom stocks went bankrupt. Value investors referred to "momentum investing" as "the greater fool theory" — the fantasy that you can make money buying overvalued securities because you can always find a greater fool to sell them for at an even higher price.

In this chapter, I explain how to use momentum investing to (hopefully) profit from investing in cannabis stocks.

Spotting Opportunities to Buy: Upward Momentum

Momentum investors (speculators) lean toward technical analysis (see Chapter 8) instead of fundamental analysis (see Chapter 7) when choosing which stocks to buy, when to buy, and when to sell. As I explain in Chapter 8, investors who rely on technical analysis spend most of their time looking at charts to spot patterns in an attempt to predict the future movement of a stock's price. With momentum investing, you basically want to buy stocks that show sustainable upward momentum and sell them before the price starts to trend downward.

The key word here is *sustainable,* which means you're looking for a pattern that you have reason to believe will continue for the foreseeable future. One way to identify a stock with sustainable upward momentum is to look at its 50-day and 100-day simple moving averages in relation to one another.

A *simple moving average (SMA)* shows the change in a stock's *average* price over a certain number of days. For example, to calculate the 5-day SMA of a stock for a given day, you total the stock's closing prices over the past 5 days and divide by 5. To calculate the 50-day moving average, you total the stock's closing prices over the past 50 days and divide by 50. To create an SMA chart, you calculate the SMA for the desired period (for example, for each of the past 50 days) and plot those points on a chart, as shown in Figure 13-1. You end up with a line or curve that smooths out the daily fluctuations in the share price (which reduces the "noise") to make the stock's overall momentum clearer and easier to visualize and understand.

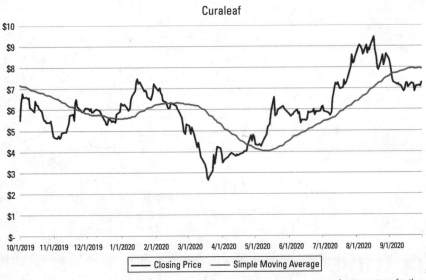

FIGURE 13-1:
A 50-day moving average chart for Curaleaf.

Image courtesy of author

REMEMBER

The good news is that you don't have to calculate simple moving averages and chart them. Nearly every online broker features moving average charts as part of its service. I explained how to calculate the SMA and create a chart just so you would have a clearer understanding of how this investment strategy works.

TIP

As a momentum investor, you look for times when the short-term upward trend is strong enough to trigger a positive shift in the long-term trend. The most common way to spot such a shift is to chart a stock's 50-day and 100-day moving averages and look for points where the two lines cross. When the 50-day SMA line moves from below to above the 100-day SMA line (see Figure 13-2), this is a sign that the short-term trend *may be* strong enough to trigger an upward shift in the long-term momentum — a buy signal.

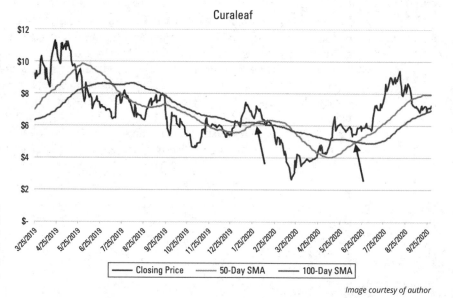

Curaleaf

FIGURE 13-2:
Look for points where the 50-day SMA moves above the 100-day SMA.

Image courtesy of author

However, if you look at enough of these moving averages charts, you start to notice that this technique doesn't always work. You'll notice plenty of instances where the 50-day SMA line moves from below to above the 100-day SMA line that corresponds with a sell-off. Likewise, you'll notice plenty of instances where the 50-day SMA line dives down below the 100-day SMA line corresponds to an upward shift in share price. In other words, don't blindly follow this technique.

Momentum investors may examine the SMA over longer periods or use other types of charts to gauge a stock's momentum and identify buy and sell opportunities, but this basic method enables you to wrap your head around the concept and try it if you so desire.

WARNING

Be careful buying into an apparent rally, because short sellers can quickly inflate a stock's price when they exit their positions in anticipation that the stock price will soon tank. See the later section, "Watching out for the short squeeze," for details.

Watching for Signals to Sell: Downward Momentum

After buying a cannabis stock with upward momentum, your next decision is when to sell it. At this point, monitoring the stock's SMA is even more important, because at any time in the future, the trend can flip from upward to downward. You want to sell your stock as close to the stock's peak as possible, and as you feel comfortable doing. As is commonly said among investors, "Pigs get fat, and hogs get slaughtered." Don't be too greedy when deciding the right time to sell.

TIP

If you're unsure whether a stock has peaked, consider cashing out your principle (the initial amount you invested) and riding to the top with your gains (the remaining shares). As you become more familiar with cannabis stocks, you may want to consider taking bigger risks. Deciding when and how much to sell depends on your personal risk tolerance and how much you can afford to and want to gamble.

Now, instead of looking for points where the 50-day SMA moves from below to above the line for the 100-day SMA, you want to watch for when that 50-day line crosses down from above to below the 100-day line (see Figure 13-3). How far that 50-day line dives down before you pull the trigger is up to you, but if you want to remain true to this strategy, the sooner you sell, the better.

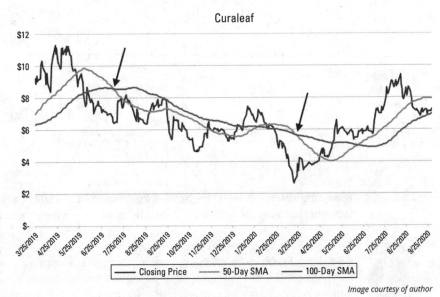

FIGURE 13-3:
Sell when the 50-day SMA drops below the 100-day SMA.

Curaleaf

Image courtesy of author

Following the Smart Money

Smart money is capital controlled by institutional investors, savvy private investors, central banks, mutual and exchange traded fund (ETF) managers, and other financial professionals. Smart money investors buy and sell shares in bulk, so a sudden spike in a stock's trading volume on a given day is a good sign that one or more smart money investors have purchased or sold a large volume of shares.

By examining trading volume side-by-side with a simple moving average chart, you can often spot instances where a spike in volume coincides with a shift in a stock's momentum (see Figure 13-4):

» A large volume bought often predicts a shift to an upward trend.

» A large volume sold often predicts a shift to a downward trend.

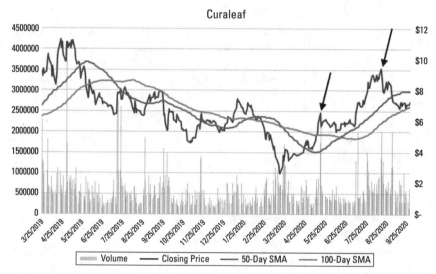

FIGURE 13-4: Smart money moves may help to predict a shift in momentum.

Image courtesy of author

Following smart money investors is usually a smart move, because other, smaller investors are likely to follow their lead (remember the herd mentality?).

REMEMBER For a few days after the smart money investors buy or sell a bunch of shares, you may notice a short-term shift in momentum that contradicts what you would normally expect. For example, suppose an institutional investor buys a large volume of shares. You expect the share price to rise, but it drops. This is usually a short-term deviation caused by smaller investors not paying attention to what's going on. Within a few days, the herd catches on and shifts in the direction you'd expect. (Of course, we need to qualify this by saying "usually" — usually the herd follows the smart money, and sometimes the smart money isn't so smart.)

Avoiding Some of the Risks Inherent in Momentum Investing

Investing always carries some risks, but momentum investing has some unique risks you should be aware of before trying it. In this section, I explain some of the risks and provide guidance on how to avoid them. (Most of the time, just knowing of the potential threat is all you need to avoid it.)

TIP

Before adopting any investment strategy with real money, try it with fake money. Numerous financial websites feature sample investment portfolios or simulators, such as Investopedia's Stock Market Game (www.investopedia.com/simulator) and the MarketWatch Virtual Stock Exchange (www.marketwatch.com/game). Most of these simulators are set up as games in which you compete against other investors.

Watching out for the short squeeze

A *short squeeze* is a spike in a stock's price that forces a large number of short sellers to close their positions, which pushes the price higher. *Short selling* is a strategy for profiting from a stock when its price *drops* (see Chapter 12). A short seller borrows shares from another investor, immediately sells them, then waits for the stock price to drop. When it goes as low as the short seller thinks it will go, he buys shares at the lower price, returns them to the lender of the shares, and pockets the difference.

If a short seller buys stock expecting the price to drop and, instead, the price rises, the more it rises, the more money the short seller stands to lose when he ultimately decides (or is forced) to close his position. At any time, the lender of the shares can demand their return. When or even before that happens, the short seller may close his position (buy shares and return them to the lender to cut his losses), further driving up the stock's price and trading volume.

As a momentum investor looking at a simple moving average chart and the trading volume, you may believe that this surge in price reflects the popularity of the stock when the increase is really due mostly to short sellers panicking.

Stock exchanges release short interest data every month (or more often), and you can usually obtain this data by visiting the stock exchange's website. For example, to obtain short interest data from Nasdaq, you can take the following steps:

1. **Open your web browser and go to www.nasdaq.com.**

2. **Type the stock's symbol or the company name in the Find a Symbol box, then click the stock in the drop-down list that appears.**

3. **In the navigation bar on the left, click Short Interest. A list appears, showing the number of shares being shorted, average daily share volume, and days to cover (see Figure 13-5).**

DATE	SHORT INTEREST	% CHANGE	AVG. DAILY SHARE VOL	DAYS TO COVER
9/15/2020	1,603,668	−24.54	1,345,622	1.19
8/31/2020	2,125,259	−6.89	1,614,383	1.32
8/14/2020	2,282,499	3.78	1,015,962	2.25
7/31/2020	2,199,331	−12.56	1,145,182	1.92
7/15/2020	2,515,336	50.41	999,620	2.52
6/30/2020	1,672,369	2.25	515,231	3.25
6/15/2020	1,635,548	−2.94	728,918	2.24
5/29/2020	1,685,114	−7.25	1,453,325	1.16
5/15/2020	1,816,768	6.04	658,652	2.76
4/30/2020	1,713,210	−4.61	854,551	2

FIGURE 13-5: Short interest data.

Image courtesy of author

The higher the number of days to cover, the greater the short interest, and the stronger the belief among short sellers that the stock price will drop. If you're thinking of buying on the upward momentum, you may want to reconsider. However, some investors, known as *contrarians*, will buy when short interest is high, thinking that if the share price continues to rise, short sellers will be forced to buy even more, which will drive the price higher. In other words, their strategy is to make money specifically on the spike in price caused by the short squeeze.

Steering clear of pump-and-dump scams

Many cannabis stocks are *penny stocks*, meaning they're cheap, which makes them easier to use in pump-and-dump scams; con artists buy lots of shares, then they get lots of suckers to buy them, which drives up the price. As soon as the price is high enough for their greedy, cheating minds, they dump their shares, taking their profit while the other investors lose a ton of money. See Chapter 4 for more about pump-and-dump scams and how to avoid them.

Avoiding cannabis stock and industry bubbles

Investors often pour money into "sexy" companies, including just about all companies in the cannabis sector. All this money drives stock valuations sky high, which creates a bubble, and all bubbles eventually burst. During the dot-com boom of the 1990s, speculators drove the value of the Nasdaq composite index higher than 100 times its forward earnings, with some companies valued at 300 times their forward earnings. When the dot-com bubble burst over the course of March of 2000 to February of 2003, the Nasdaq composite index lost 70 percent of its value.

WARNING

The moral of this story is to check a company's fundamentals before investing in it, even if you're doing momentum investing. Pulling up a company's price-to-earnings (P/E) ratio takes only a few seconds and serves as a valuable "sanity check." Sure, already inflated stock prices can continue to rise, but they almost always drop, and when they do, you can lose a lot of money trying to buy high and sell higher. (See Chapters 7 and 10 for details on how to check a company's P/E ratio and other fundamentals.)

Knowing when momentum investing works and when it doesn't

Momentum investing typically delivers better results during periods when markets are relatively stable. During periods of significant volatility, other investment strategies may be more effective, such as diversification (which is always a good idea), investing in value stocks, and holding onto some cash.

REMEMBER

Volatility is fluctuation in the price or value of individual stocks, sectors, or the stock market overall. You can gauge the volatility of a stock by looking at its *standard deviation* — the average amount a stock's price has differed from the mean (average) over a period of time. Instead of getting into the math, just pull up a chart of the stock's price over the desired period of time that shows Bollinger Bands, which consist of three lines: a line showing the simple moving average (SMA), a line showing the standard deviation above the SMA, and a line showing the standard deviation below the SMA (see Figure 13-6). The greater the distances between standard deviation lines and the SMA line (that is, the wider the band), the greater the volatility.

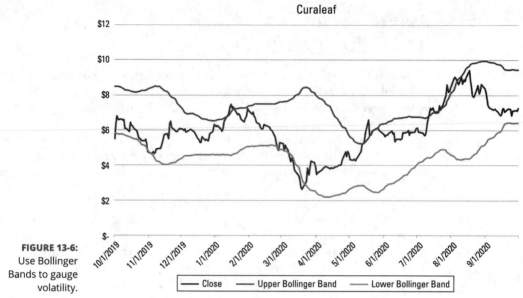

FIGURE 13-6:
Use Bollinger
Bands to gauge
volatility.

Image courtesy of author

Chapter **14**

Investing in Canadian Cannabis Companies

B ay Street is the Wall Street of cannabis. (Bay Street is a major thoroughfare in Toronto, Ontario, Canada and the center of Toronto's financial district.) I call it the Wall Street of cannabis because the U.S. ceded its domination over the cannabis industry (from a finance and regulatory standpoint) to Canada by being slow to respond to public opinion, science, and the change in cultural and social norms around marijuana products.

Canada is now the global leader in terms of cannabis financing. It boasts the most publicly traded cannabis companies and also serves as the leading case study in the economic and social value of ending marijuana prohibition. Cannabis is legal across Canada for both adult-recreational and medical use, and now Canada is home to the four largest publicly traded cannabis companies:

» Canopy Growth Corporation

» Cronos Group Inc.

>> Aurora Cannabis Inc.

>> Aphria Inc.

In this chapter, I introduce you to these global leaders, but first, I examine the big question of whether Canadian or U.S. cannabis companies have more potential for investors.

Deciding Whether to Invest in Canadian or U.S. Cannabis Businesses

Canada and the United States are the two biggest markets for cannabis. Canadian companies have the advantage of operating in the only developed country where adult use (recreational) marijuana is legal nationally. On the other hand, U.S. companies are operating in the largest marijuana market in the world based on annual sales. The big question is which country has the better investment opportunities.

The bottom line is that both markets have advantages and disadvantages. If you're going to take an asset allocation approach to building a portfolio of cannabis stocks, I think that investing in both markets is prudent.

In the following sections, I present the pros and cons of each market.

The pros and cons of the Canadian cannabis market

Canada's big advantage is that it is one of the few countries in the world where both medical and adult-use (recreational) cannabis is legal nationally. However, Canadian marijuana businesses have been plagued by cumbersome regulatory issues. Health Canada, which oversees the Canadian weed industry, has been slow to review cultivation and sales license applications, and was responsible for delaying the launch of high-margin derivatives by two months. Products, such as edibles, infused beverages, vapes, topicals, and concentrates, finally began hitting dispensary shelves in Canada in mid-December 2019.

REMEMBER

Even though Canada is a much smaller consumer market than the U.S. (a bit smaller than California), it's still a respectable market. According to the "Cannabis Market Data: Overview" page on the Canada.ca government website (www.canada.ca/en/health-canada/services/drugs-medication/cannabis/research-data/market.html):

» In total, 8,622,543 packaged units of cannabis were sold across Canada for medical and non-medical purposes.

- Dried cannabis sales represent 73 percent of total sales, with 6,272,755 packaged units sold.

- Cannabis extracts sales represent 14 percent of total sales, with 1,223,252 packaged units sold.

- Edible cannabis sales represent 13 percent of total sales, with 1,113,054 packaged units sold.

» Nationally, 44,965,769 packaged units of cannabis products were held in inventory by cultivators, processors, distributors, and retailers.

- Distributors and retailers hold 40 percent of the total inventory of packaged units of cannabis products.

- The total inventory of packaged units of dried cannabis held by cultivators, processors, distributors, and retailers represents 4.4 times total sales. Likewise, total inventory of packaged units of cannabis extracts represents 8.0 times total sales.

» The total licensed indoor and outdoor cultivation area held by license holders stood at 1,965,436 m² and 487 hectares (4,870,000 m²), respectively.

» The number of unpackaged plants held by federal license holders stood at 6,759,317 at the end of June 2020.

REMEMBER

Bottom line: The Canadian cannabis consumer market, though heavily regulated, is still a significant market in terms of consumption. As such, certain consumer-based opportunities in retail operations (such as dispensaries) and in cultivation make sense.

TIP

For additional reports and data relevant to Canada's cannabis industry, visit www.cannabisbenchmarks.com/report-category/canada.

A BRIEF HISTORY OF CANADA'S CANNABIS LEGALIZATION

Canada's march to full legalization of marijuana began in the late 1990s when public opinion polls showed that more and more Canadians believed that consuming marijuana shouldn't be a criminal offense. In 2000, the Ontario Court of Appeal ruled that cannabis prohibition was unconstitutional in a case that involved a Canadian who was consuming cannabis to help with his epilepsy.

In 2001, Canada introduced the Marihuana Medical Access Regulations Act (MMAR), which allowed a patient to possess a dried flower/bud with a government-issued license approved by a physician. With the passage of MMAR, Canada became the first country to legalize cannabis for medical use. In 2014, the Marihuana for Medical Purposes Regulations (MMPR) replaced the MMAR, making it no longer necessary to obtain a government license for medical use (a prescription was still necessary).

In 2015, Canada's current Prime Minister, Justin Trudeau, led the Liberal Party to a majority government victory, thanks, in part, to making the legalization of adult-use (recreational) cannabis a major part of his platform. In 2017, the Government of Canada introduced the Cannabis Act to legalize recreational use for anyone 18 years or older and possession of up to 30 grams.

After several revisions, the Cannabis Act came into effect on October 17, 2018, making Canada the second country in the world, after Uruguay, to formally legalize the cultivation, possession, acquisition, and consumption of cannabis and its by-products for medical and adult use. Canada is the first G7 and G20 nation to do so.

For more about Canada's cannabis laws and regulations, visit www.canada.ca/en/health-canada/services/drugs-medication/cannabis/laws-regulations.html.

The pros and cons of the U.S. cannabis market

The big advantage U.S. cannabis businesses have is that they're operating in the biggest cannabis marketplace. With the understanding that analyst estimates are really all over the place, most analysts are counting on Canada to generate in the neighborhood of $5 billion in sales by 2024. The U.S., by comparison, is expected to reach $30 billion by 2024, according to the *State of Legal Cannabis Markets* report, released in 2019 by Arcview Market Research and BDSA.

The two big drawbacks in the U.S. are that marijuana is still illegal on a national level and, in states where cannabis is legal, high tax rates and licensing delays are taking their toll. For example, California is expected to be the largest marijuana market in the world by annual sales, but prohibitively high taxes get passed along to the consumer, making it virtually impossible for legal producers to compete with black-market product.

Growing pains will continue for all North American marijuana stocks, but the ramp-up in sales and the push toward profitability will be considerably easier for U.S. cannabis companies than for their Canadian counterparts. Canadian marijuana sales have stagnated badly since August 2020, while new state-level legalizations and organic growth continue to add nicely to the total revenue being generated from marijuana in the United States.

Scoping Out the Four Leading Canadian Cannabis Companies

If you're interested in investing in Canadian cannabis companies, you should be familiar with the four companies that were dominating the market during the writing of this book. I'm not advising that you invest in these companies, but by taking a closer look at them, you can begin to understand some of the key factors to consider before investing in Canadian cannabis.

REMEMBER

I begin each section with the market capitalization of the company. *Market Cap* indicates what a company is worth on the open market, as well as the market's perception of its future prospects (by reflecting what investors are willing to pay for its stock). This enables you to understand the relative size of one company versus another.

Canopy Growth Corporation

Market Cap: US$8.88 billion

Canopy Growth Corporation (CGC) is an Ontario-based company that has the distinction of having been the first federally regulated and licensed, publicly traded cannabis grower in North America. Now, thanks in part to an investment of close to US$4 billion by Constellation Brands in August of 2018, Canopy Growth is the largest marijuana company in existence as of this writing and per market capitalization.

REMEMBER

This investment by Constellation Brands indicates that Canopy Growth's strategy, financials, and management team have been fully vetted by a reputable investment group. Constellation Brands has a rigorous due diligence process in place.

CGC reported its final-quarter results from 2019 early in the new year, and the figures boast some impressive accomplishments. The company made a whopping C$90.5 million in the first fiscal quarter of 2020 and is positioning itself to bring cannabidiol (CBD) products to the U.S. market by the end of the fiscal year. With increased harvests and demand for medical cannabis, Canopy Growth is staying busy: to date, it has a portfolio of 111 patents and 270 applications.

Cronos Group

Market Cap: US$2.52 billion

Cronos Group's (CRON's) reach is impressive — the cannabinoid company is already boasting international production and distribution across five continents, building products from hemp-derived CBD to vape pens. While the company's stock has experienced some volatility due to a class action suit filed against the company, its overall rise in value suggests that its cannabis sales and deliveries may be on the rise.

According to the company, Cronos Group generated C$7.64 million in revenue in the third fiscal quarter of 2019 due to the opening of the adult-recreational-use market in Canada. This represents a significant year-over-year increase.

Aurora Cannabis

Market Cap: US$1.27 billion

Headquartered in Edmonton, Aurora Cannabis (ACB) is a major cannabis producer and a licensed distributor. Aurora boasts a strong international presence, having purchased Berlin-based Pedanios GmbH and having received a supply agreement for the Italian cannabis market (through a subsidiary called Pedanios). It also purchased MedReleaf and CanniMed in 2018.

Aurora's financials for its 2019 fourth quarter were quite strong compared with previous quarters as well, generating net revenue of roughly C$95 million. In fact, net revenue increased by 61 percent from the previous quarter.

Aphria

Market Cap: US$1.76 billion

Founded in 2014, Aphria (APHA) is a relatively new entrant into the legal cannabis space. It focuses on medical cannabis, having first received a license to produce and sell medical products. For the last fiscal quarter of 2019, Aphria reported a net revenue of C$128.6 million.

TIP

In recent months, in an effort to expand into the U.S. market, Aphria has engaged in high-profile (and sometimes highly controversial) acquisitions. To determine whether an acquisition makes sense and is likely to benefit a company, answer the following two questions:

» **Will the acquisition boost the company's revenue immediately?** The answer to this question should be yes. If the acquisition won't boost the acquiring company's revenue, it's unlikely to increase the intrinsic value of the acquiring company.

» **Does the acquisition create vertical integration for the company?** Vertical integration enables companies to operate more efficiently and cost-effectively. For example, if a brand portfolio buys a cultivation asset to increase its Earnings Before Interest, Taxes, Depreciation, and Amortization (EBITDA) margins for its brands, that's a move that makes sense.

Chapter **15**

Investing in Countries Where Marijuana Is Legal

Not many countries around the world have legalized cannabis to any meaningful extent, but those that do may provide investors with additional opportunities. They also pose new challenges to investors, especially with respect to the legal and regulatory environment in which cannabis businesses operate in those countries.

Before investing in cannabis companies outside the U.S. and Canada, doing your proverbial homework is even more important. In this chapter, I list the countries in which cannabis is legal to some degree and briefly describe the legal and regulatory climate in each of those countries at the time I was writing this book (although by the time you read it, that climate may have changed).

TIP

If you decide to invest in cannabis in one of the countries covered in this chapter, I encourage you to hire an attorney in that country who's knowledgeable about the cannabis business to advise and guide you. A qualified attorney can help you gauge the risk and steer you clear of any shady operations.

Argentina

When Argentina first legalized medical cannabis in 2017, the news made major headlines, but local activists and patients complained that the law failed to address patients' needs. For example, this early law limited medical cannabis use to children with epilepsy. As a result, patients continued to rely on the black market.

In the summer of 2020, Argentina's health minister met with stakeholders in the country to draft regulations to relax restrictions on the use of medical cannabis and clear up confusion caused by the previous legislation. The new measures were expected to usher in the following changes:

>> Expand the list of medical conditions cannabis can be used to treat.

>> Allow patients, researchers, or individual users who register with the country's national cannabis program (REPROCANN) to grow the plant.

>> Allow patients to purchase medical cannabis through a growth network.

>> Allow participating pharmacies to produce cannabis creams and topicals, and users who aren't registered with REPROCANN to obtain medical cannabis from a pharmacy with a doctor's prescription.

>> Guarantee access to medical cannabis to all patients free of charge, regardless of their health coverage.

In addition, the government would begin drafting a plan for large-scale cultivation and production.

Argentina's neighbors, including Brazil, Colombia, and Uruguay, have robust cannabis markets, so now is a great time for Argentina to tap into its own market and provide cannabis to its citizens. Soon, Argentina may be able to catch up with surrounding countries when it comes to their cannabis economy. This should make Argentina an attractive market for foreign investments.

Bottom line: Argentina is a market to watch. With a population of nearly 45 million, Argentina is a sizeable consumer market. In terms of the market being open and ready for investment tracking to a decent return on investment (ROI) and rate of return, I think it's too soon. I say track the market but wait until the regulators ease restrictions on consumers and wait for adult use to take hold.

Australia

In January 2020, the Australian Capital Territory (ACT) passed new legislation to relax the restrictions on growing and possessing marijuana. Under the new laws,

>> residents of the territory 18 years and older are each allowed to grow a maximum of two plants at home;

>> the total number of plants that can be grown at home is four;

>> residents 18 years and older are allowed to be in possession of up to 50 grams of dried cannabis; and

>> the commercial sale of cannabis via retail outlets or coffee shops remains prohibited.

As in the U.S., the new law contradicts a federal ban on cannabis growth and possession, so it's not likely to open a huge market for cannabis across the country.

What is interesting about Australia is that it's well positioned to become a major player in the global export market, which is expected to be worth $55 billion by 2025. Australia already has a thriving agricultural sector in place and has plenty of experience in the agri-pharma business. It's currently responsible for about 50 percent of the world's legal poppy supply, used by pharmaceutical companies to produce medical-grade opiates including codeine and morphine.

However, several obstacles stand in the way of Australia's progress toward dominating the global cannabis export market, including the following:

>> Heavy financing requirements

>> An overly complex and stringent licensing system

>> Medical professionals who are reluctant to prescribe cannabis to patients

>> Additional freight costs for shipping cannabis to the largest markets — in North America and Europe

Even with these obstacles, Australia is a country to watch as a supplier of premier products to growing markets in the U.S., Canada, and Europe. Large companies, including AusCann, Althea, and the Cann Group, are already building strong reputations in foreign markets.

Bottom line: Australia is poised to be a major player in the cannabis market, but it's too soon to invest in my opinion. Until Australia is able to be a major supplier to the U.S., the return and rate of investment in the Australian market remains spurious at best.

Brazil

Unlike its neighbors Colombia and Uruguay, Brazil has been slow to relax its prohibition of cannabis, possibly due to its long history of violence related to the illegal drug trade. However, Brazil leads the world in several commodities markets, and pressure from its farms to expand into growing hemp may push politicians to fast-track legislation on growing and exporting cannabis. Otherwise, Brazil risks losing market share to other more progressive countries.

To give you some idea of how restrictive Brazil's cannabis laws currently are, as I was writing this, the country permitted cannabis only for medical use and offered patients only three ways to obtain it legally:

» By purchasing registered products — cannabis-based medications, such as Mevatyl oral spray (internationally known as Sativex)

» By purchasing products with "sanitary authorization" — cannabis medications manufactured in Brazil or imported in bulk by companies that obtained "sanitary authorization" from the government to do so

» By asking to import on an individual basis

Legal cannabis use in Brazil is restricted to medical use, and most of that is limited to cannabidiol (CBD) oil. However, because of Brazil's size, it's a country that investors may want to keep an eye on for future opportunities.

Bottom line: Brazil is a tremendous market, but the regulatory environment is just too restrictive to invest safely. The current administration is not friendly to the business. Wait for a more liberal government to take charge before revisiting Brazil as a cannabis investment option.

Chile

Chile legalized medicinal marijuana back in 2015, and it now has the highest cannabis consumption rate per capita in Latin America. It has a population of 18 million people and is relatively stable politically and economically, so many firms see it as a good base for their South American operations. Khron and AusKann are among the cannabis producers setting up shop in Chile. Along with Mexico, the country is tipped to be the key driver of medical marijuana growth in Latin America.

Bottom line: Chile is a growing market with the highest per capita cannabis consumption in Latin America. It's a small market, with a population of less than 19 million, but a worthy market. I think Chile is a good market to explore for investment, provided you work with qualified local attorneys and have the ability to conduct thorough and transparent due diligence on your prospect.

Colombia

International cannabis companies are rushing to Colombia, attracted by the country's relatively advanced regulations, beefed-up security, perfect weather conditions, and cheap production costs (while a gram of cannabis flower costs about US$2.10 to produce in Canada, it costs between US$0.50 and US$0.80 in Colombia). Exports of medical cannabis in particular are expected to grow significantly over the next five years.

Unlike many countries in the region that only recently approved the clinical use of cannabis (like Peru), Colombia is further along the track. It approved its regulatory framework in July 2016, which sets rules for the production, distribution, sale, and export of seeds as well as derivative cannabis products.

However, stiff regulations have complicated the production and export of cannabis products. The export approval process has been described by investors as "tortuous," and the permit approval process is convoluted, leading to long delays for obtaining permits. Regulation requires growers to get licenses from government offices ranging from the Justice Ministry to the National Food and Drug Surveillance Institute, INVIMA. Companies are required to obtain licenses for the manufacture of cannabis by-products, the use of seeds for planting, growing plants, and a separate license for growing psychoactive cannabis plants.

Another problem is the massive volume of license applications, which has required increasing government staff to process them.

REMEMBER

Colombia offers many opportunities for cannabis investors, but this is a market in which you will definitely need a local attorney and consultant before investing.

Bottom line: Colombia is one of the safer bets when it comes to investing in foreign markets, but it still requires local partners and support to navigate the cumbersome bureaucracy that characterizes the permit process. Colombia is poised to be a major export market in the coming years.

Czech Republic

The Czech Republic legalized cannabis for medical use in 2013, but the country's medical marijuana program has been stunted by a number of problems, including the following:

>> Supply shortages

>> A highly bureaucratic process for obtaining prescriptions

>> A very limited number of qualifying conditions for medical marijuana use

>> A limited number of physicians permitted to prescribe medical marijuana — in 2018, only 57 doctors could prescribe medical marijuana to patients in a country with a population of nearly 11 million, and only 41 pharmacies were allowed to sell it

In May of 2020, the Czech government approved an amendment to the country's medical cannabis legislation that could expand the number of growers and increase access to marijuana-based treatments. The amendment will come into effect starting July 2021 if it secures approval from both parliament and the country's president. If the amendment fails to make way for smaller growers to join the industry, allowing home cultivation for patients could become an option.

Initially, cannabis was imported from foreign countries, before Elkoplast Slušovice was granted the sole domestic license to cultivate the plant for medical use. Elkoplast Slušovice cultivates a single strain of cannabis with a THC content of about 20 percent.

Recently, the Czech Ministry of Health announced that medical marijuana will be covered by health insurance companies, which could lead to more interest and investment in the market.

Bottom line: Hold off on investing in cannabis in the Czech Republic. The business market isn't sufficient to justify an investment at this point, and regulatory change will take some time. Keep an eye on this market, but don't invest right now.

Ecuador

Ecuador has legalized the cultivation of hemp and removed it from its list of substances subject to the regulations of the country's penal code, so the plant is now under the jurisdiction of Ecuador's Ministry of Agriculture and Livestock. Plants are restricted to those grown for industrial purposes (such as textiles, paper, and plastics) and non-psychoactive cannabis (for pharmaceuticals and cosmetics).

Cannabis companies are interested in Ecuador for two big reasons: First, the country's climate is ideal for growing cannabis. Second, labor costs are highly competitive.

As an investor, realize that the market for cannabis in Ecuador is limited to medical use, and even that is limited to CBD. Also, in a country that has a perfect climate for growing cannabis, even if recreational use were legalized, the people growing it for themselves and the black market would probably significantly limit demand from commercial operations.

Bottom line: Ecuador is a minor player that would make a good export market but is too restricted at the moment for that kind of business. I suggest watching the market, but I don't recommend investing in the cannabis sector in Ecuador at this time.

Germany

Germany is Europe's economic powerhouse and has the most potential among European countries for becoming a major market for cannabis. The country legalized medical cannabis in March 2017, and since that time has become Europe's largest market for medical cannabis, but only for the seriously ill who have a doctor's prescription. In Germany, the consumption of narcotics is not legal but is considered to be a form of non-punishable self-harm.

During the first half of 2020, Germany's pharmacies imported 4,126 kilograms (9,096 pounds) of medical cannabis flower, which represents a 60 percent increase over the same period in 2019. However, a small portion of that may have been exported to Italy, the Czech Republic, Luxembourg, Malta, Poland, and other European countries.

Bottom line: Germany will eventually be a major player in the cannabis market. It has the largest consumer base in Europe at the moment and boasts the largest medical cannabis market in Europe. The market is limited due to the regulatory environment, but the potential is huge. I would invest in the German market, but make sure you have adequate legal support.

Greece

In 2017, Greece became the sixth European country to legalize medical cannabis. Adult recreational-use cannabis remains illegal. The country has downgraded cannabis from a class A to a class B drug, thus acknowledging its medical value. However, patients can access cannabis medication only with a prescription and only for specified medical conditions, including epilepsy, muscle spasms, post-traumatic stress disorder (PTSD), HIV/AIDS, chronic pain, and cancer.

To meet the growing demand for medical marijuana, Greek authorities made cannabis production facilities legal, which has attracted interest from Canadian and Israeli investors. When Greece issued its first 14 cannabis growing licenses, companies in Greece and in 30 foreign countries applied. The authorities expected the licenses to produce around 1,400 jobs and revenue of around 159 million euros. In 2019, analysts believed that future cannabis investments could create up to 7,000 jobs and produce revenue of up to 1.5 billion euros for Greece.

Greece is well positioned to become one of Europe's largest cannabis producers, because it has a favorable climate for growing cannabis and is one of the first European countries to legalize the cultivation of medical marijuana. However, the medical cannabis market is focused almost exclusively on CBD. Production, sales, and consumption are limited to products with tetrahydrocannabinol (THC) levels lower than 0.2 percent, and CBD sellers and producers are not allowed to advertise their products as health supplements.

Bottom line: Greece is an emerging market that should be monitored for investment. It has a lot of potential, but it's not fully matured yet. Any cannabis investor in Greece will need local legal and consultative support.

Ireland

As a cannabis investor, forget about Ireland for now. The country has taken a tough stance against marijuana, and laws and sentiment remain mostly conservative, so Ireland is attracting little interest from cannabis companies or investors.

The one glimmer of hope is that in June 2019, Ireland's Minister of Health signed off on a program that will facilitate access to medical cannabis products for five years. CBD is also legal for limited use, but recreational cannabis remains illegal.

Bottom line: Ireland is closed for business as far as cannabis is concerned. It's not even a market to watch.

Israel

Outside of Canada, Israel is one of the most cannabis-friendly countries and one of the most attractive countries for cannabis investors. Medical marijuana has been legal here since the early 1990s for patients with cancer; pain-related illnesses such as Parkinson's, multiple sclerosis, and Crohn's disease; and PTSD. In addition:

>> Companies in Israel can legally grow and export cannabis.

>> Israel is one of only three countries in the world where cannabis research is sponsored by the government, so many firms are relocating their research operations to Israel. At least 15 U.S. companies have moved all of their research and development operations onto Israeli soil.

>> Israel continues to relax its anti-cannabis laws. For example, in June 2020, Israel's legislature advanced two cannabis-related bills — one focused on decriminalization and the second on legalizing cannabis for individuals 21 or older. If passed, these bills would pave the way for the legalization of adult-use (recreational) cannabis.

Bottom line: Israel is a leading cannabis market and has dominated the technology space in cannabis for years. It's a prime market for international investment replete with potential for export business and leading brands. Major cannabis portfolios are well served, accruing assets in the Israeli cannabis market.

Italy

Cannabis in Italy is legal but strictly regulated for medical and industrial use, and decriminalized for adult recreational use. Licensed growers (for medical and industrial cannabis) are permitted to grow cannabis containing THC levels below 0.2 percent and above that level when authorized (but only through the use of certified seeds). Italians are free to grow their own cannabis for personal consumption, but that could change at any time with a change in government, as can any future legalization of products with higher THC concentrations.

In the wake of the coronavirus, Italy is hard at work trying to rebalance itself and reboot its economy, so marijuana legalization isn't exactly a top priority for the country. However, as soon as Italy emerges from the pandemic, it's sure to revisit the issue.

Bottom line: Italy, like Germany and the U.K., has a big consumer market, both legal and illegal. It is an emerging market from a regulatory standpoint. Take a wait-and-see approach on investing in cannabis in Italy right now. It will become a major player when adult recreational use is legalized.

Jamaica

You can't help but associate Jamaica with cannabis. Many people consider it the unofficial capital of cannabis. One of the big draws for some tourists is that they can buy pre-rolled joints on the streets of Jamaica and law enforcement will pretty much ignore any public consumption. However, until relatively recently, possession of even a small amount of marijuana could result in arrest and jail time.

In 2015, Jamaica passed a series of amendments to its Dangerous Drugs Act, decriminalizing marijuana and introducing licenses for its cultivation and sale. Initially, only three business licenses were awarded, but by 2020 that number rose to more than 150 licenses.

Government officials, recognizing the importance of marijuana as part of the country's brand and its potential for generating revenue, have created an entire framework for exporting cannabis. Jamaica is well positioned to become a leading exporter of cannabis around the world.

Bottom line: Jamaica is poised to be a major player in the export cannabis market. The country's long tradition and association with marijuana makes it a prime market for genetics and branded strains. Definitely consider an investment in the Jamaican cannabis market, but be sure to have proper legal support on the ground and the right partners to help you avoid being scammed and to assist in navigating the local bureaucracy.

The Netherlands

Like any college age student who's been to Amsterdam, I too rushed straight to the first "coffee shop" I could find to sample the local fare. Cannabis has been available for recreational use in coffee shops since 1976 (if you want coffee, you go to a *koffiehuis* or *café*). Except for some laws governing medical use, cannabis in the Netherlands is illegal, but decriminalized for personal use, so recreational use is tolerated.

Late in 2019, the Dutch government passed the Controlled Cannabis Supply Chain Experiment Act to initiate the development and implementation of a four-year pilot program in 10 cities where 79 coffee shops would be supplied exclusively by government-selected and monitored cultivators and producers of cannabis flower and hash. The purpose of this experiment is to see how a lawful supply chain would play out in the Netherlands.

The experiment is a good start, but it isn't ideal for several reasons:

>> Four of the biggest markets — Amsterdam, Rotterdam, The Hague, and Utrecht — aren't participating.

>> No imports are allowed, so product selection is limited.

>> The 79 participating coffee shops constitute a small group that may not represent the diversity of coffee shops across the country.

As in the U.S., participation is limited to certain growers who meet the specified criteria, including but not limited to the following:

>> Being a resident of the Netherlands with a company in the Netherlands or a legal entity with a Dutch address

>> Passing background checks

>> Submitting a comprehensive business plan, including a financial plan, which details record keeping, testing, meeting coffee shop demand, complying with quality assurance standards, and more

Based on the information provided during the application process, the Minister for Healthcare and the Minister for Justice and Security will select five to ten growers to supply the coffee shops participating in the program.

Bottom line: The Netherlands is an emerging market but still too immature to support a robust export market and too tightly regulated and small to support a consumer market. Take a wait-and-see approach to the Dutch market at this time.

New Zealand

On October 17, 2020, New Zealand was scheduled to vote on a cannabis referendum regarding the proposed legal framework outlined in the Cannabis Legalisation and Control Bill, which addressed the following controls:

>> A consumption age of 20 years old

>> Limits on THC potency

>> A levy to boost health services

>> A ban on smoking a joint anywhere except at home or in licensed premises

The bill would have also allowed companies to manufacture medical cannabis products for domestic and international markets and also removed CBD as a controlled drug, instead making it a prescription medication.

Despite the Public Health Association of New Zealand (PHANZ) urging a "yes" vote, it appears at the time of this printing that the referendum narrowly lost. At least for now, cannabis won't be legalized in New Zealand.

Bottom line: For now, investors need to take a wait-and-see approach and not jump into this market just yet.

Norway

Norway was the first Scandinavian country to decriminalize drugs, but that doesn't make Norway a cannabis-friendly country or a place of interest to cannabis investors.

Only very restricted medical use is legal. Patients looking for treatment can legally buy Sativex and Bedrocan if they have a prescription. Doctors are allowed to prescribe cannabis treatments if they work as specialists in a hospital, but they need special approval from the Norwegian Ministry of Health to prescribe cannabis products with a THC concentration higher than one percent. Other than that, production, processing, distribution, sale, purchase, and possession of drugs, including cannabis, are illegal.

Bottom line: Norway is not far enough along to consider investing in its cannabis market. The restrictions are too stringent to provide investors with a meaningful ROI or rate of return.

Peru

Peru legalized medical cannabis in 2017, when it also decriminalized its possession for personal consumption in quantities not exceeding eight grams of dried marijuana or two grams of derivatives. Business licenses for medical cannabis are available for research, wholesale import and commercialization, retail commercialization, and production.

By allowing for medical cannabis, the Peruvian government has opened the country to new investment opportunities, increasing imports from other countries, increasing the availability of cannabis products, and expanding opportunities for medical cannabis suppliers.

Bottom line: Peru is an emerging market but still not mature enough to justify investing in. Take a wait-and-see approach until Peru can prove to be a worthy export market.

Poland

Selling or possessing cannabis or using it recreationally is illegal in Poland, but medical marijuana (CBD) has been legal since 2017. International cannabis companies have invested in CBD production in Poland for medical products as a way to expand production and distribution efforts through the European Union. Some analysts think that Poland could become a leader in the medical cannabis market in the EU.

Bottom line: It's too soon to invest in the Polish cannabis market at this time. For Poland to become a real player, the regulatory environment will need to change dramatically. Likewise, Poland's position within the EU has come under pressure as a result of the country's draconian LGBTQ+ laws. If Poland leaves the EU, its position in respect to Europe's cannabis market will suffer a serious setback.

Portugal

Portugal's cannabis laws are regarded as among the most progressive in the world. In 2001, the government decriminalized personal cannabis use, focusing on treatment rather than punishment. As such, overall numbers of drug users in the country have dropped. However, it wasn't until 2018 that medicinal cannabis was legalized.

CBD is legal for medicinal purposes. It can also be purchased and consumed without a prescription, as long as the THC content (the substance responsible for the "high") is below 0.2 percent.

Bottom line: Portugal is an emerging cannabis market that is not yet ripe for major investment. Take a wait-and-see approach with respect to this market.

Switzerland

While it is illegal to consume, produce, possess, or sell cannabis flowers or cannabis products that contain more than one percent of THC in Switzerland, the plant itself is not illegal — the focus is on THC. Products such as CBD creams, oils, and tinctures are completely legal as long as the concentration of THC is less than one percent. In contrast, other European countries have thresholds ranging from 0.05 to 0.3 percent.

Doctors who hold an exceptional license granted by the Federal Office of Public Health can prescribe medications with higher THC concentrations. Additionally, doctors can prescribe magistral formulas that are based on THC-containing marijuana.

Bottom line: Switzerland is not mature enough to justify an investment into the cannabis market at this time.

Thailand

Although Thailand has a deep cultural connection with cannabis through its use in traditional medicine, the government just recently recognized its medical benefits and legalized its use in the treatment of certain medical conditions. Legalization of medical marijuana caused a spike in its adult recreational use, but it's still illegal. Possession and use are permitted only with the appropriate license or a doctor's prescription. For now, only a few government sectors, along with patients, agriculturalists, and other people granted official permission, have access to the plant.

Unfortunately, the lack of regulatory specifications inhibited the development of sufficient supply infrastructure. This lack of infrastructure, coupled with increasing demand, has resulted in a cannabis shortage. Only 18 cultivation licenses were issued by February 2020, due to stringent regulations by the government. However, the Thai government has already drafted amendments to current laws and regulations, attempting to promote marijuana as an economic crop.

Bottom line: Thailand, like Ireland, is not really open for business. Steer clear of cannabis investments in the Thai market at this time.

United Kingdom

Cannabis is used widely throughout the United Kingdom (U.K.), by people of all ages and from all socio-economic backgrounds. The U.K. legalized medical marijuana for the treatment of certain conditions, but recreational use remains illegal.

Since the legalization of medical marijuana in 2018, the U.K.'s medical cannabis market has barely gotten off the ground. A two-tier system has formed, in which few patients access products through legal channels while most resort to illicit suppliers. Looking ahead, however, some industry insiders are hopeful that recently implemented import rules could boost the number of legal medical cannabis prescriptions from the currently low level.

Bottom line: The U.K. is an emerging cannabis market but very restrictive and bureaucratic. Take a wait-and-see approach to the British cannabis market. The U.K.'s consumer market has a lot of potential, but the country's cannabis laws would need to become much less restrictive to allow for any real business to develop.

Zambia

Zambia is following the lead of other African nations by relaxing their laws on cannabis and instituting cannabis cultivation. Unlike other countries that took more time organizing rights to use it within their own borders, Zambia has skipped steps to get to market as fast as possible. As a result, Zambia has legalized cannabis for treating certain medical conditions and for export to other countries, but recreational use remains illegal.

How this approach will play out remains to be seen. It could be great for the economy, but awful for locals. It could provide more jobs and income, or it could generate more criminal activity. One thing is certain: the green rush of Africa is just beginning, and Zambia is leading the way.

Bottom line: Zambia is definitely a market to watch when considering an investment in export markets, but wait to see how international cannabis export markets develop and how Zambia stacks up against markets such as Colombia and Ecuador.

the industry

» **Knowing what you're buying**

» **Keeping your investment capital close to home**

» **Spreading your wealth**

» **Cutting your losses and taking your profits**

Chapter **16**

Minimizing Risks While Maximizing Gains

E very investor's dream is to minimize risks while maximizing gains. Unfortunately, as every investor knows, that's a pipe dream. To win big, you have to bet big. You must take risks. The greater the risk, the greater the potential profit. You can't have one without the other, right?

Well, generally that's true, all other factors being equal, but when you're investing in a young industry with so much uncertainty, you *can* minimize risks and maximize gains — mostly by remaining well informed and not doing anything stupid. Investors who lose their shirts investing in cannabis are usually those whose greed outstrips their intelligence.

In this chapter, I provide guidance on how to become a savvier cannabis investor, reduce your exposure to risk, and (hopefully) make more profitable investment decisions.

Staying Plugged in to the Industry

Investors who know the industry have a huge advantage over those who don't — including some managers of cannabis ETFs. When you know the industry, you're more like an inside trader (but not really, because insider trading is illegal). However, when you know the movers and the shakers in the industry; when you can tell the difference between people in the industry who know what they're doing and those who don't; when you clearly understand the environment in which cannabis companies operate, and you have an inside track on acquisitions, mergers, and other deals in the works, you have a big advantage over casual cannabis investors who base their investment decisions on hot stock tips or whichever cannabis company gets the most press or has the biggest social media profile.

Becoming knowledgeable about an industry, any industry, is challenging and time consuming and requires a lot of reading, even for seasoned investors, but that's exactly why being plugged into the industry is so valuable. All the time and effort required to stay connected and informed creates a large barrier to entry — it's something casual investors won't do, which enables you to profit from their ignorance.

Plenty of great online resources are available to help you get up to speed on the industry, including websites, online publications, email newsletters, apps, and discussion forums (see Chapter 6 for details). Even better, get involved in the culture and the industry to increase your exposure to people who work in the business and have lots of connections with other people in that field. Get a job with a cannabis company or volunteer with a group that's working to legalize cannabis in your state. The more you know, the better.

WARNING

When you're establishing relationships with people in the industry, you're more susceptible to falling for too-good-to-be-true business and investment opportunities, so be extra vigilant.

TIP

Staying abreast of everything that's going on in an entire industry can become overwhelming and exhausting, so consider focusing your research on one specific business type, such as any of the following:

>> Cultivation operations (growers)

>> Extraction and cannabis-infused products, such as vape pens and edibles

>> Consumer brands

>> Lab testing

>> Pharmaceuticals

» Dispensaries (cannabis retailers)

» Cannabis delivery operations

» Supply-chain software developers

» Cannabis real estate

You can always broaden your knowledge by expanding into other areas of the industry, but deep knowledge in one area usually produces better results than a shallow understanding of the industry as a whole. See Chapter 5 for more about different types of cannabis businesses and investment opportunities.

Investing in the People, Not the Plant

Casual cannabis investors invest in cannabis. Savvy cannabis investors invest in people. The people running the cannabis operation and formulating the strategy for success in a highly competitive industry will make or break the company . . . and your investment in it. Before investing in a company, research its management team to ensure that the individuals on the team have a proven track record of building successful businesses and delivering value to shareholders.

TIP

Also review the management's team's stake in the company and how managers are compensated. Managers who are material owners in the company have a greater incentive to make the company successful.

WARNING

Many cannabis entrepreneurs got their start in the black market, which attracts a very particular personality type — people who tend to adopt a less conventional code of ethics. If you are investing in a private company, look closely at the management team and ask to meet the key managers in person. Likewise, run background checks on all the key players when evaluating your investment. (See Chapter 7 for more about researching the management team.)

Performing Your Due Diligence

Casual investors, especially those who invest in cannabis, tend to have a herd mentality, investing in companies they've heard most about or those with the biggest and most recent gains in the stock market. As a result, they're susceptible to overpaying for high-flying stocks, thereby increasing their exposure to risk while reducing their potential for profit. Savvy investors, on the other hand, invest in people and companies that have value and a realistic potential for turning a profit.

I strongly encourage you to vet any cannabis company and its management team thoroughly before investing in it. See Chapter 7 for details.

REMEMBER

In Chapters 8 and 13, I explain how to use technical analysis to profit from cannabis stocks by identifying patterns in the movement of stock prices. Even if you choose to use this strategy to identify companies with potential, you should perform your due diligence as a way of conducting a "sanity check" before investing any money. Using fundamental analysis (Chapter 7) and technical analysis (Chapter 8) in tandem provides the best of both strategies.

Trading Cannabis Stocks on Private Markets

The decision of whether to trade cannabis stocks on the public exchanges or private markets is a clear trade-off between risk and reward. Buying stocks on public exchanges carries less risk, because these exchanges perform some of your due diligence for you, by requiring that companies be transparent about their finances and operations. This transparency enables you to access a lot of information about a company before you invest. In addition, publicly traded stocks are more liquid, meaning you have a better chance of being able to sell the stock when you decide to cash out.

Private markets carry more risks, because they have fewer restrictions in place and less stringent accounting and reporting rules and enforcement. It's more like the Wild West, where investors are responsible for their own protection. The trade-off is that private markets enable you to buy in at a lower level for the possibility of earning bigger returns.

REMEMBER

To minimize your risk while maximizing your gain, invest in private companies but only after thoroughly vetting promising cannabis businesses to ensure that they have a solid management team in place and a great strategy for turning a profit. Having industry knowledge and connections can help you gain the transparency needed to make less risky investment decisions when trading shares on private markets.

Investing in the Biggest Markets

Five countries account for most of the cannabis production in the world, so focus on investing in companies that operate in the five biggest markets. According to "The State of Legal Cannabis Markets," a report released by Arcview Market Research and BDSA, these are the five countries expected to account for most of the world's cannabis sales by 2024:

>> United States with $30.1 billion

>> Canada with $5.18 billion

>> Germany with $1.35 billion

>> Mexico with $1.02 billion

>> United Kingdom with $546.9 million

As you can see, the U.S. is the leader by far, which is why I recommend that U.S. investors keep their investment capital close to home. Canada is also a great choice because although it's running a distant second, it has the big advantage over the U.S. of being a country where cannabis is federally legal.

TIP

Cannabis companies in countries where marijuana is federally legal have the advantage of being able to export to other countries, so even though Canada's market is running a distant second to that of the U.S., its cannabis companies can legally export to other countries. For example, Canadian companies Aurora Cannabis, Tilray, Canopy Growth, and Aphria have all earned European Union Good Manufacturing Practices (EU GMP) certification to export their products to countries in the EU. If you visit Aphria Inc.'s Global Operations web page at `aphriainc.com/global-operations`, you can see its global distribution.

Diversifying Inside and Outside the Industry

WARNING

You've heard it before and are about to hear it again: don't put all your eggs in one basket. When you find a great cannabis company to invest in, betting all your money on that company is understandably very tempting. After all, if the company's stock soars, you can earn a handsome profit in a short period of time. However, if the stock tanks, you lose a significant portion of your investment capital, in which case you have little to no capital to work with to recover from your losses.

REMEMBER

Even if you have a high tolerance of risk, think about the possibility of not having any capital to work with if your latest stock pick goes belly up. That should be enough to convince you not to put all your eggs in one basket.

The cannabis industry itself provides numerous opportunities to diversify. You can invest in multiple types of cannabis businesses — cultivation, extraction, brands, and so on — or invest in ancillary businesses. Ancillary businesses can include equipment and fertilizer manufacturers that supply cultivation operations, software companies that serve the cannabis industry, pharmaceutical companies investing in cannabis research, and beverage companies seeking growth opportunities via cannabis.

Also consider diversifying into different sectors of the economy — healthcare, information technology, financials, consumer staples, and so on — that won't be impacted if the cannabis sector takes a hit.

Investing in Multi-state Operators

Multi-state operators (MSOs) are cannabis companies that have operations in multiple legal cannabis states, usually in the most highly populated, affluent markets for medical and adult recreational cannabis use. They're often structured as holding companies with state subsidiaries licensed to do business in their respective states. During the writing of this book, these were some of the biggest MSOs with subsidiaries operating in several states in the U.S.:

>> 4Front Ventures

>> Acreage Holdings (ACRG.U), (ACRGF)

>> Cresco Labs (CL.CN), (CRLBF)

>> Curaleaf (CURA.CN), (CURLF)

>> Golden Leaf (GLH.CN), (GLDFF)

>> Grassroots (Private)

>> Green Thumb Industries (GTII.CN), (GTBIF)

>> Harvest Health & Recreation Inc. (HARV.CN), (HRVSF)

>> iAnthus (IAN.CN), (ITHUF)

>> MedMen (MMEN.CN), (MMNFF)

>> TerraTech (TRTC)

>> Trulieve (TRUL.CN), (TCNNF)

WARNING

The fact that I mention a company by name in this book doesn't mean I'm recommending that you invest in it. Stock values of many of the companies on this list tanked over the course of 2019 to 2020, and nobody knows whether those stock prices will ever recover.

Keep an Eye on the ETFs

Even if you choose to invest in individual cannabis companies instead of exchange traded funds (ETFs), check the big cannabis ETF portfolios or holdings to see which companies they're investing in. For example, go to Yahoo! Finance at `finance.yahoo.com`, type **MJ** in the search box, and click the ETFMG Alternative Harvest ETF entry. In the toolbar for the ETF's listing, click Holdings, then scroll down to the section, "Top 10 Holdings," to view the list of the ten cannabis companies that represent the highest percentages of the fund's assets (see Figure 16-1).

WARNING

Cannabis ETF holdings are just one piece of the puzzle when you're deciding which cannabis companies to invest in. Pull up the fund's prospectus to find out who's managing it and research the management. You can access the fund's prospectus through your online broker or by searching online for the fund's name or ticker symbol followed by "prospectus," clicking the link to the fund's home page, and then clicking the link to the fund's prospectus. The prospectus contains the names of the fund's managers, but probably not much more than that. Research the managers to be sure they have experience and knowledge of the industry. Fund managers who know the cannabis industry are generally better than those whose experience is limited to financial analysis.

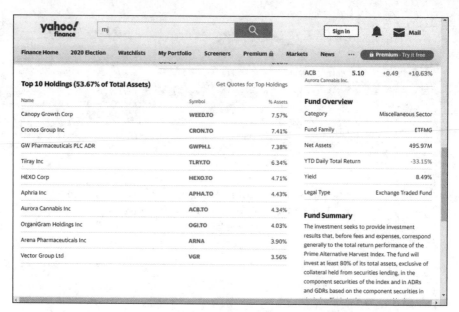

FIGURE 16-1:
ETFMG
Alternative
Harvest ETF's Top
10 Holdings.

Source: Yahoo! Finance (finance.yahoo.com)

Invest in Innovative Companies

When cannabis is booming, many cannabis companies will do well. However, as the market matures, the most innovative companies will thrive, while less innovative companies will fall by the wayside. Look for companies with the leading brands and products that are growing their market share, and look past companies that are losing market share.

TIP

Spend some time exploring `Leafly.com` — a website geared to cannabis consumers — to find out what's hot and what's not and get a feel for the community. In Chapter 6, I mention several cannabis-industry and investment news websites, but when you're looking for innovative companies, sometimes the best approach is to tap consumers for leads. The News page is particularly helpful; just click the menu icon in the upper-left corner of the home page and click News.

Use Different Stock Order Types to Your Advantage

You can often protect against potential losses and even profit when the market drops by using different stock order types strategically. For example, when placing an order for shares of a stock, you can specify a limit order, so that you don't pay a far higher price than you intended. A limit order to buy is filled only if the price is at or below the maximum price you specify. A limit order to sell is filled only at the price you specified or higher. You can also use stop loss orders and trailing stop orders to gain more control over the prices you pay for shares and how much you sell them for.

One order type not discussed in Chapter 11 is the *put option*, which is a bet that a stock or exchange-traded fund (ETF) will fall in price. If you see a cannabis company about to go down the tubes, for example, you can use a put option to bet against the company. Put options are speculative. You're not investing in a company; you're taking an educated gamble — you're speculating.

You can also use a put as an insurance policy to protect against loss if you expect share prices to drop. For example, if you're holding a stock for the long term but you're concerned about it in the short term, consider using a put option on that stock. You're not hoping the share price drops; you're merely protecting you holdings. If the share price drops, the put option will increase in value. If the share price rises, you only lose the cost of the put option (the premium you paid for the insurance).

Here's how it works: Suppose you own 200 shares of a Canopy Growth at $50 per share, and you think the share price will drop dramatically over the next three months. You buy a put option that enables you to sell your shares for $50 (the strike price) within three months even if the share price drops. Your broker charges you $2 per share, so you pay $400 for the put option. Lucky for you, two months later, the share price drops to $30. You exercise your put option and rake in a profit of $20 per share. You have 200 shares, so your profit is $4,000 minus the $400 you paid for the put option, which leaves you with $3,600. It's a little more complicated than that, but this gives you a general idea of how put options work.

If the share price drops as you expected it to, you can use the proceeds from the put option to buy more shares at a lower price.

For additional details on how to use options and other advanced investment strategies, check out *High-Level Investing For Dummies*, by Paul Mladjenovic (Wiley).

Don't Get Greedy

Everyone dreams of getting rich in the stock market, and nothing's wrong with that, but greed can override good sense and lead investors to make common mistakes, such as the following:

>> **Investing in get-rich-quick schemes.** Remember, if it sounds too good to be true, it probably is. Con artists prey on greedy investors, because they know that these investors will believe whatever they *want* to believe, even when they see something that would otherwise make them skeptical.

>> **Buying in too late.** When you see a stock's price soaring, greed often makes you believe that the price will continue to rise, even when the company's data is waving red flags, warning investors to steer clear of the stock.

>> **Ignoring the facts.** Greed causes you to believe what you *want* to believe, convincing you to invest in companies that you *want* to perform well instead of companies you *think* will perform well, based on solid data such as the company's P/E ratio or news about mergers, acquisitions, or changes in management.

5
The Part of Tens

Ten ways to earn a profit even when the cannabis industry goes south, including buying value stocks and shorting bad stocks.

Ten reasons that may convince you not to invest in marijuana stocks right now, especially if you're on the fence.

Ten important criteria to look for in a company before buying stocks or bonds in that company.

Ten common mistakes to avoid while you're trying to earn a bundle investing in cannabis companies.

» **Invest more in businesses with solid fundamentals**

» **Short sell overvalued stocks**

» **Head to a different market sector**

» **Use options to your advantage**

Chapter **17**

Ten Ways to Profit When the Market Drops

Whenever an industry is hot, like cannabis, all that most investors see is what they want to see — the upside of investing in the industry. As long as investment capital is pouring in and stock prices are rising, everyone's happy. But what goes up must come down, and even in its infancy, the cannabis industry has already experienced the downside.

What do you do when share prices drop? This depends on several factors, including why prices are dropping, whether you're a long-term or short-term investor, where you think the cannabis industry or a specific company you invested in is heading, and your own investment strategy.

In this chapter, I present ten possible courses of action to profit or lessen your losses when the cannabis industry or a specific company's stock value heads south.

Be Patient, But Vigilant

What goes up must come down, but usually what comes down goes up, too. Cannabis acceptance and the push for legalization are gaining momentum, so the long-term outlook for the industry is positive. The industry as a whole is likely to continue to grow.

REMEMBER

However, that doesn't necessarily mean that every cannabis business will eventually be successful, so remain vigilant. Keep in touch with what's going on in the industry and what's happening at the businesses you're invested in. If a business you're invested in schedules a conference call with investors and analysts, be sure to listen in on that call to find out what the business is doing to improve its competitive position.

Review Your Portfolio

You should be reviewing your investment portfolio on a regular basis with your broker or financial advisor, but if you haven't done that lately, use the drop in share prices as an opportunity to review your holdings.

What you're looking for are quality cannabis companies. Head back to Chapter 7, which covers fundamental analysis, and check to be sure that each cannabis business you're invested in is financially sound and has a great management team in place.

Cut Your Losses

If you don't expect your investments to recover (or recover in the timeframe you need them to), one option is to cut your losses by selling your shares. Cutting your losses is never easy because you never know for sure what will happen after you sell — prices could rebound the next day — but if they don't, your investments will continue to bleed, while at the same time the capital remaining in those investments could be used to buy shares in other companies that are performing better.

Buy More Shares

If you're invested in a solid cannabis company you believe in, a drop in share price could be the perfect opportunity to buy more shares at a discount. Keep one eye on the share price and the other on the direction of key financial indicators, such as the company's sales, revenue, and price-to-earnings ratio. If the share price is dropping while the company is doing better than ever, that could be a signal to buy more shares.

Focus on Value Stocks

When the stock market takes a dive or a particular industry takes a hit, the investors who suffer most are the speculators who put their money in companies whose stock price vastly exceeded the company's profit potential. Shifting to a value-investing strategy can help protect your investments from some of the wildest swings in share prices and ensure that your money is with businesses built on a firm foundation. (*Value investing* involves choosing stocks that appear to be undervalued in respect to what the company is actually worth.)

Short Bad Stocks

Short selling is an investment strategy that enables you to profit from a drop in share prices. You borrow shares from another investor and immediately sell those shares. When the share price drops to the level you desire, you buy back the shares and return them to the lender. The difference between the price you sold the shares for and the price you paid to buy them back is your profit.

Timing is crucial when shorting stocks. You want to borrow and sell shares as their price peaks and then buy the shares back to return them to the investor from which you borrowed them as soon as you believe the share price has bottomed out (or you've gained the desired profit). See Chapter 12 for more about short-selling.

WARNING

Short selling is a risky venture. If you borrow shares from an investor and the share price continues to rise, you stand to lose more than your initial investment. What if the price never drops and the person you borrowed the shares from demands that you return them? In addition, as long as you hold those borrowed shares, you may be charged interest and other fees.

Find Potential Treasures
with Bond Ratings

One sign of a company's health is its bond rating, which reflects its ability to pay off its debt. Businesses that borrow heavily without achieving corresponding increases in revenues and profits are at risk of defaulting on their loans. Bond rating agencies, including Moody's and Standard & Poor's, assign bond ratings to companies. Companies with ratings of AAA, AA, and A are considered investment grade.

TIP

Before buying shares of a company, check its credit rating, which is especially important in a market or industry in which share prices are trending downward. Also, steer clear of companies with poor credit ratings.

Rotate Sectors

Although this book is about investing in cannabis, it's a market sector just like other market sectors — energy, materials, financials, information technology, consumer staples, and so on. Often, when one sector is doing poorly, another sector is doing well. Sometimes, being invested heavily in the cannabis sector may not be to your benefit. Shifting money from cannabis investments to investments in other sectors may be a good move to ride out a downturn in cannabis.

REMEMBER

Cannabis is more of a subset of other sectors — an industry within a sector or a subset of a set of industries. For example, medical cannabis is a subset of pharmaceuticals, which is a subset of the Healthcare sector. Adult-use marijuana companies are a subset of the consumer-discretionary sector. However, cannabis companies span a broad range of sectors, including AgTech, Biotechnology, Consumption Devices, Cultivation and Retail, Real Estate, and Tech and Media.

Buy a Call Option

If you have reason to believe that the share price of a certain cannabis company will increase significantly in the near future, but you're afraid of suffering a big loss if it heads in the opposite direction, consider buying a call option. A *call option* gives you the right, but doesn't obligate you, to buy a stock or other investment security at a specified price (referred to as the *strike price*) within a set period of time.

For example, if a stock is selling at $250 a share, you might be able to buy a call option at one dollar a share. Suppose you're interested in buying 100 shares. Instead of paying $25,000 to buy 100 shares at $250 per share, you pay $100 for the right to buy those shares for $250 per share within two months. Suppose the stock price shoots up $50 per share to $300. You can buy the shares at $250 per share plus your $100 (for the call option), which equals a total investment of $25,100. You sell the shares for a total of $30,000, earning a profit of $30,000 − $25,100 = $4,900.

However, the real beauty of the call option is that it protects you from a big drop in share price. For example, if instead of rising $50 over that two-month period, suppose the share price dropped $50. If you had bought 100 shares, you'd be out $5,000. On the other hand, by buying a call option, you'd be out only $100.

Write a Covered Call Option

With a covered call option, you're the seller instead of the buyer of the call option. With a covered call option, you can earn money in a market that's trending downward by selling call options on securities you own, but you must have enough securities to cover the option if the buyer exercises the option to buy.

TIP

Covered call options are useful if you're a long-term investor who wants to hold on to your stocks in a certain company but are confident that for the short term the share price is likely to fall, so anyone buying the call option is unlikely to exercise it. Regardless of whether the investor exercises the call option, you keep the money she paid for it.

WARNING

Ideally, a covered call is best just before a drop in share price, so you get to keep your shares *and* the money the other investor paid to buy the call option. However, selling call options has two downsides. First, it limits your potential profit from the stock if the price goes up, because the buyer of the call option will probably execute it, meaning you'll have to sell them your shares at the agreed-upon share price. Second, if the share price drops, you still have to hold on to the shares just in case the buyer of the call option decides to execute her option to buy.

Chapter **18**

Ten Reasons Not to Invest in Marijuana Stocks

You're going to invest in cannabis. You bought this book, you're reading this book, you're already personally invested, so you're going to invest in cannabis. Nothing I can say will keep you from it. And that's okay. I just want to keep drilling it into you that investing in cannabis is risky business. Many people who invested years ago got the jitters, sold their shares, and lost a lot of money. Some people lost money to con artists or well-intentioned friends or family members. Others lost out because they invested in cannabis businesses that didn't make it. However, as long as you're well aware of the risks, if you decide to move forward, I applaud your bold initiative, and I hope you receive ample compensation for your risk-taking. People like you are the ones who drive innovation and fuel the success of new industries such as cannabis.

Still, I'm going to take this last opportunity to caution you in the hopes that the risks persuade you to tread carefully — to do your homework and perform your due diligence. Savvy investors stand to earn handsome returns on their investments as long as they make smart investments. Those who rush in and are clueless and careless will lose their shirts.

In this chapter, I present ten reasons for not investing in cannabis. Keep these reasons in mind as you seek your fortune in the green rush.

Marijuana Is Still Federally Illegal in the U.S.

Although momentum seems in favor of federal legalization of marijuana sometime in the future, nobody has a crystal ball that can tell them for sure what will happen. A new study might come out revealing some currently unknown harmful effect that makes legislators who are already against legalization dig in their heels. Or, some other unforeseen event or change in culture or beliefs could cause voters to become less accepting of marijuana use. Who knows?

Until marijuana is federally legal, the federal laws against it will restrict growth in the industry in several ways, including the following:

>> Increase the cost of doing business

>> Continue to fuel the black market for cannabis

>> Complicate and increase the cost of expanding businesses across state lines and into foreign markets

>> Make banking and other financial services less available for cannabis businesses

When you invest in cannabis, to a certain degree, you're betting that it will ultimately become legal on a federal level. I believe that will happen eventually, but it's not a sure thing, and even if it were, nobody knows when it will happen.

Marijuana Investment Scams Are Rampant

Con artists profit on the human desire to have a better life. Some would call that greed, but I really think most people just want to have enough money to pursue their dreams. Many people see cannabis as the next gold rush. In fact, the recent boom in legal cannabis companies has been described as a "green rush." Everyone wants to get in on the action and not to miss out on the opportunity to profit from this exciting new industry. And that's exactly what makes people vulnerable to scams — that and the fact that people generally trust others.

Con artists know that people are eager to invest in cannabis, so whenever someone expresses this eagerness, they become a target. Of course, the threat of a scam isn't reason enough to avoid investing in cannabis, but it is a good reason to remain skeptical of opportunities that seem too good to be true. See Chapter 4 for more about popular scams and schemes to watch out for.

Earning a Profit as a Cannabis Business Is a Huge Challenge

As an investor, you're wise to invest in profitable businesses or at least those that have a good chance of being highly profitable. Unfortunately, cannabis is a heavily taxed and regulated industry, which increases the costs and complexities of doing business. It's not like selling bottled water. Here are a few line items that take a huge bite out of cannabis business profits:

>> **Taxes.** Cannabis businesses are prohibited from claiming business deductions on their federal taxes. Also, the high sales and excise taxes on cannabis products reduce demand and steer sales to the black market.

>> **Application and licensing fees.** Application and licensing fees for legitimate cannabis businesses can be exorbitant in some states; for example, Connecticut charges a $25,000 application fee and a cultivation licensing fee of $75,000. In addition, businesses often must hire a lawyer to navigate the process.

>> **Capital requirements.** Many states require cannabis businesses to hold a certain minimum in liquid assets (typically hundreds of thousands of dollars) to obtain and keep their license.

>> **Compliance costs.** Companies often incur high legal costs and must purchase specialized software to remain compliant because most states require tracking cannabis "from seed to sale."

I could go on, but the point is that earning a profit in cannabis isn't easy, and until it becomes easier, cannabis businesses will have a tough time proving their value to investors.

Illegal Operations Undermine Demand for Legal Products

In many areas where cannabis is legal, the black market continues to thrive because 1) cannabis is often cheaper on the black market where businesses don't pay taxes or application and licensing fees and don't incur the costs of attorneys and compliance, and 2) the cannabis community is sort of anti-establishment, so many consumers prefer to buy from unlicensed growers and dealers.

In addition, in many states in which cannabis is legal, people are allowed to grow a certain number of cannabis plants of their own. They need to buy seeds, fertilizer, and maybe the equipment to set up a grow room, which gives suppliers of those items additional business, but it decreases demand from commercial growers, manufacturers, and dispensaries.

The Industry Is Very Fragmented

The cannabis industry consists mostly of small businesses competing against one another, which means businesses will come and go. Some will fail, and some will succeed. Eventually, as cannabis legalization grows, large national companies will step in and either buy up competing companies or drive them out of business. People who invest in cannabis now, when the industry is fragmented, are likely to experience losses as some of the companies they "bet on" fall to the competition.

REMEMBER

The take-home message here is that if you're accustomed to trading in companies listed on the major stock exchanges, such as the NYSE and Nasdaq, now may not be the best time to invest in cannabis. You may want to wait until the industry starts to consolidate; then, you'll have an easier time predicting winners and losers.

Oversupply Is More Likely Than Not

Many states in which cannabis is legal face problems with oversupply — too many growers growing more cannabis than the consumers in the state want or need. Oversupply drives down prices and profits and makes companies less attractive to investors.

REMEMBER

Oversupply is another problem that's at least partially due to the fact that cannabis is illegal on a federal level. If cannabis were legal federally, or if growers could at least ship their products over state lines, they'd have a larger market in which to sell and compete. As it is now, states must deal with the problem of oversupply internally, which usually means issuing fewer licenses to cultivators or charging significantly more for applications and licenses.

Bad News Is Just Around the Corner

To a large degree, rumors and news drive the stock market. In fact, some investment gurus advise to "buy on the rumor and sell on the news." With cannabis, the opportunity for bad news is pretty high. In 2018, good news (mostly a combination of hype and hope) drove share prices in cannabis companies sky high. Shortly thereafter, the bad news (mostly poor earnings reports from some of the major players) led to a massive selloff.

This boom-to-bust cycle is likely to continue because hype and hope continue to motivate investors in this industry. In addition, because cannabis is a drug, both good news about its benefits and bad news about its side effects are likely to contribute to the volatility.

REMEMBER

There is money to be made by investing in cannabis, but I urge you to invest with your head and not your heart. Carefully research each company's fundamentals (see Chapter 7) and be sure the share price is supported by those fundamentals.

Marijuana Laws Are Slow to Change

As long as marijuana remains illegal at the federal level, many states are going to drag their feet over legalization, and local jurisdictions are going to use the federal law as an excuse to pass their own restrictions on its sale and use. When the federal prohibition of marijuana will end is anybody's guess. I think it's likely to happen the next time the Democrats control the White House and Congress, which might happen before this book is published, four years later, or maybe even a much longer time from now.

Company Shares Are Being Diluted

As I explain in Chapter 5, companies can secure financing through debt (borrowing) or equity (selling shares in the company), which is true of all companies. What's different about cannabis companies is that they have trouble securing loans from banks, so they have to rely more on equity. When they get in a financial pinch, if they can't get a loan, they need to sell more shares, and the more shares they sell, the more diluted the price of existing shares becomes. Unfortunately, investors have little control over decisions to issue more shares, even though that decision impacts the value of their investment.

REMEMBER

Shares can be diluted in any sector, any industry, and any company, but the possibility is higher among cannabis companies.

Demand Is Unpredictable

Several states that have legalized marijuana are finding that demand can be unpredictable for a variety of reasons, including the following:

» Cross-border sales may increase demand for marijuana in legal states surrounded by illegal states. However, when bordering states legalize it, cross-border sales decline.

» Any black-market sales reduce demand for legal cannabis.

» Any bad news about negative side effects reduces demand, although the drop in demand is usually short-lived.

REMEMBER

Whether demand for cannabis will increase or decrease with its legalization is hotly debated. I think demand is almost certain to rise with legalization, but others think it could fall as marijuana loses its appeal as a "forbidden fruit."

Chapter **19**

Ten (Plus One) Criteria for Choosing a Cannabis Investment

You'll find no shortage of investing strategies and schemes online for earning a fortune trading stocks, but no magic formula exists. If such a formula did exist, the person who discovered it probably wouldn't be so eager to share it or to try to make money selling the "foolproof" technique. You can also find plenty of investment gurus online touting the best cannabis companies or stocks to invest in or predicting what will be the next big thing in cannabis, but can you really trust them?

The most profitable and safest way to invest in cannabis is no secret: put your money in the best companies. While that certainly sounds easy enough, how do you know which cannabis companies are best? How do you really know that a company will be successful and that you'll earn a good return on your investment?

The answer is, you don't. However, you can increase your odds by investing in profitable businesses, or businesses that have what it takes to be profitable. In this chapter, I present ten criteria for choosing a business to invest in.

REMEMBER

A business doesn't have to meet all ten criteria to be a good investment. For example, if a business has a great management team, the fact that the business isn't profitable yet may be less important. However, you should consider all these criteria before investing in any cannabis business.

Experienced and Successful Management Team

I cannot stress enough the importance of vetting the people who are running the business. These are the folks who will make or break the business (and your investment), so you want to be sure they're knowledgeable and experienced in both cannabis and running a business, and that they don't have a history of failed business ventures. Here's what to look for:

>> Any past criminal activity that could be a warning sign that the business is not legitimate, such as past Securities and Exchange Commission (SEC) violations

>> Cannabis knowledge and experience

>> Business management knowledge and experience

>> No long track record of failed business ventures

>> A positive reputation — respected in the cannabis industry or in business circles

REMEMBER

An individual rarely has all the qualities needed to run a successful cannabis business. For example, someone with loads of cannabis knowledge and experience may not have business or people management expertise. However, the management team as a group should have all the knowledge, skills, and experience required.

Steady Revenue Growth

Revenue growth is a good indicator of a business's success, showing whether sales are increasing or decreasing. If revenue growth is steady or negative, the business is failing to remain competitive. Check the business's revenue from month to month and from quarter to quarter. If the company has been in business for several years, look at its annual revenue from one year to the next. You can find a company's revenue on its income statement.

TIP

To compare revenue growth between two or more businesses, convert the dollar values to percentages. Start with this year's revenue, subtract the revenue from the same period last year, divide the result by last year's revenue, and then multiply by 100. Note that you don't need to know the revenue for an entire year to make this calculation. For example, suppose it's July, so the business only has revenue from the first six months of this year. This year, the company had $10 million in revenue. For the first half of last year, the company had $8 million in revenue. Its revenue growth as a percentage is:

($10 million − $8 million)/$8 million x 100 = 25%

Consistent Profit Growth

Profit is total revenue minus total expenses. A positive result means the business has earned more than it has spent. A well-run business shows growth not only in revenue but also in net profit. Negative or declining profit growth with rising revenue growth could be a sign that a business's operational efficiency is dropping — that revenue isn't keeping up with increases in expenses to operate the business.

REMEMBER

A negative profit margin (revenue minus expenses) is not necessarily bad. Successful businesses often operate at a loss when they're investing toward future growth. If profit growth is negative or declining, dig deeper to find out what the business is investing in, how it's getting the money to continue operating, and, if it is borrowing money, whether it has the means to make the loan payments.

Comparatively Low Price-to-Earnings Ratio

Price-to-earnings ratio is a stock's share price divided by its *earnings per share*, which is the company's total profits divided by the number of shares. Suppose a stock's share price is $10, its annual profit is $1 million, and the total number of shares is 500,000. Earnings per share is $1 million divided by 500,000, which equals $2 per share. The P/E ratio is $2 divided by $10, which is a ratio of 5 to 1.

By itself, the P/E ratio doesn't tell you much, but when you compare it to the P/E ratios of other companies in the same business, it's a good indicator of whether a stock's price reflects the company's value. A comparatively low P/E ratio may indicate a good value for your investment.

WARNING

Don't consider the P/E ratio in a vacuum. A company that's growing fast and investing heavily in that growth may have a high P/E ratio but be a better investment than a company that's more profitable now but is losing market share.

Positive Money Flow Indicator

One way to gauge a company's value is to check the *money flow index (MFI)*, which measures the momentum of a security by looking at movements of trading volume and price. If investment dollars are flowing toward one company and away from another, this trend could be a sign that the company drawing more investor interest is on its way up, while the other company is on its way down.

REMEMBER

The MFI falls into the realm of technical analysis (see Chapter 8), and it may not be the best indicator of a company's health. A rising share price could be an indicator of a pump-and-dump scheme or simply that the company's name was mentioned in a news article that shed a positive light on it. It's more an indicator of investor sentiment than the health and vitality of the business.

Expanding Free Cash Flow

When a company has a *positive cash flow* (is earning more than it's spending), it has money to reinvest in the business, settle debts, pay expenses, build a buffer against future financial setbacks, and even share its profits with investors. Generally speaking, you want to invest in companies that demonstrate an increasingly positive cash flow.

REMEMBER

In a young industry like cannabis, in which businesses are just getting started, fewer businesses are likely to have a positive cash flow, let alone an expanding free cash flow. They're more focused on getting started and growing. In addition, too much free cash flow could be a sign that the business isn't spending enough money for growth or isn't leveraging the money it has as optimally as possible.

Operations in Other States or Countries

Due to laws prohibiting the sale and transportation of marijuana across borders, cannabis businesses often struggle to survive in their own jurisdictions and face even greater challenges establishing operations in other states and countries.

However, those that are successful in increasing their reach tend to be impacted less by challenges or setbacks in individual markets. In addition, they're better positioned to expand into other markets as marijuana laws are relaxed.

Growing Market

Markets for certain products expand and contract. For example, the market for vape products in the cannabis industry is huge, because many consumers want a similar experience to smoking it without the smoke. However, when people started getting sick from black market vaping products, the vape market took a huge hit. It has since recovered, but this example shows how industries can be affected by new products (vapes) and news.

Before investing in a company, consider how well it caters to current consumer demand and how well it adjusts to changes in consumer demand. In many ways, the cannabis industry is like the smartphone industry — to be successful, a cannabis company must be able to stay ahead of the curve on consumer demand.

Increasing Market Share

The cannabis industry is highly competitive, and demand for product isn't unlimited. To grow, businesses must increase their share of the pie; they can't simply make more pie (increase demand), and the ability to grow by expanding into different markets is often restricted by legal and regulatory issues. So, when investing in cannabis, look for companies with increasing market share.

You may be able to find out a cannabis company's market share by researching on cannabis business news sites (see Chapter 6 for online resources). Or, you can search these same sites to find out the total revenue for the industry in the country or state in which the company operates and then divide the company's revenue by the industry's revenue for that same period.

Positive Reputation in the Industry

As you immerse yourself in the cannabis industry and read cannabis newsletters and other publications, you'll begin to notice the names of companies and people appearing again and again. Pay close attention to which companies and people seem to be leading the industry. Which people are renowned authorities in the industry? Which companies and people seem to be the most highly respected? Then, research these companies and individuals to find out what they're doing and what they're saying about other businesses and individuals in the industry.

As you begin to identify the movers and the shakers in the industry, you'll develop a better sense of where to invest your money. Who's partnering with whom? Where are cannabis companies going to buy the products and services they need? You can often tell a lot about a company by looking at its business associates.

Manageable Debt

Plenty of companies, including cannabis companies, struggle with solvency. Excessive debt is a key issue in today's economy. When domestic energy became a hot industry a few years ago, many of those companies ultimately went bankrupt due to unsustainable debt. Imagine if you didn't have enough income to cover your mortgage, utility bills, and credit card payments — the same thing can happen to businesses. Managing debt is a critical success factor especially for cannabis (or any) companies that are not yet profitable.

You also want to look at the debt holder. Some companies, particularly those that seek aged debt, are toxic lenders. Avoid any company that has debt holders with convertible notes or aged debt — it's a killer.

» Making data-driven investment decisions

» Being realistic about what's likely to happen in the industry

» Avoiding the lure of deals that seem too good to be true

» Considering the costs of doing business

Chapter **20**

Ten Mistakes to Avoid

To a large degree, successful investing depends on avoiding expensive mistakes, such as being seduced by a deal that's too good to be true, not properly vetting a business before investing in it, or having an overly optimistic view of a company's or an industry's prospects. When you make a mistake as an investor, you take a double-hit — you lose money, and you have less capital to invest in other potentially profitable ventures (a loss referred to as an *opportunity cost*).

However, chances are good that you'll make mistakes, and that's not all bad — you benefit from these learning opportunities. The key is to avoid making big, dumb mistakes. In this chapter, I highlight some common and expensive mistakes that novice cannabis investors make, and I offer guidance on how to avoid them.

Failing to Diversify Sufficiently

At some time in your life, you've probably been advised not to put all your eggs in one basket — not to bet everything on the potential success of one venture. Maybe you've even given that advice yourself. It's certainly wise advice when you're investing in cannabis. Don't get so focused on the industry or on a specific company that you ignore this standard practice.

TIP

Spread out your investment capital by investing not only in different businesses, but also in different sectors and types of investment securities (for example, bonds as well as stocks). One easy way to diversify is to buy mutual funds or exchange traded funds (ETFs), but I don't recommend buying cannabis mutual funds or ETFs, because I think you can make better decisions about which stocks to hold in your portfolio. Just be sure to spread your investment capital across different cannabis companies involved in different aspects of the business — for example, growers, manufacturers, distributors, and even ancillary businesses, such as software companies that serve the industry — in addition to diversifying in other ways.

Relying Solely on Online Information

WARNING

Since the advent of the Internet, false and misleading information has never been easier to spread, so don't rely exclusively on online information to make your investment decisions. Be especially skeptical of any unsolicited information you receive through e-mail messages, social media posts, or pop-up advertisements.

Balance the information you find online with offline information. If possible, schedule a visit to the company's physical location, meet with the business owner or senior management, hire a private investigator to perform background checks on the owner and managers, and examine the company's balance sheet and other financial reports. What's most important is to determine whether the company is a legitimate business and whether management is competent, reputable, and committed to the success of the business and not just their own bank accounts. See Chapter 7 for guidance on how to fully vet a cannabis company and its management team.

Not Performing Due Diligence

The cannabis industry is subject to a lot of hype, both formal and informal, making investors eager to participate and to get in at the bottom level of an industry that's about to take off. Unfortunately, many investors get so eager that they invest in marijuana businesses without first finding out what they're worth. As a result, investors rush into the sector, driving up the price of cannabis stocks far beyond what's reasonable, and months later these same stocks crash.

Before investing in cannabis, perform your due diligence as explained in Chapter 7. Also, keep your eye on the industry and on external factors, such as legislation, that impact the industry. In short, don't buy the hype. Make well-informed investment decisions.

Believing Federal Legalization Will Happen Soon

As soon as marijuana is legalized in the United States, the cannabis industry will take off, but nobody knows when or even whether that will happen. I believe it will, but until it does, base your investment decisions on the current environment in which cannabis businesses are operating. Don't base your investment decisions on what you expect will happen or, even worse, what you hope will happen. As long as you're investing in well-managed cannabis companies, you'll reap the benefits regardless of whether or when federal legalization happens.

Failing to Account for Regulations

In the cannabis industry, compliance is expensive, while non-compliance can destroy a business. Before investing in any cannabis business, be sure it's licensed and is complying with all the rules and regulations that govern its operation in the relevant jurisdictions.

Regulators are notoriously stringent when it comes compliance. I worked on the acquisition of a dispensary in Los Angeles in 2013 where the operator was one day late submitting his annual finger printing requirement. One day late. The regulator in Los Angeles found him "uncompliant," and he lost his license to operate his dispensary. Needless to say, the deal fell apart.

Failing to Consider the Possibility of Bad News

News and rumors drive stock prices, especially for stocks in companies that are closely scrutinized, such as tobacco, pharmaceuticals, and cannabis, so be prepared for the repercussions of any bad news. Such news may involve negative reports about a company's owners or managers, new research findings about the dangers of cannabis use, changes in cannabis legislation or enforcement of existing laws that create new hurdles for businesses, product recalls, and more. In short, expect the unexpected and prepare for the worst.

Buying or Selling Too Late or Too Early

In the world of investing, timing is everything. If you wait too long to invest in a growing industry or business, you stand to miss out on a lucrative opportunity. Buy too early, and you could be in for a rocky ride before you reap any profit, and in the meantime you miss out on other opportunities. Sell too early or in a panic when the share price drops, and you stand to lose money, but if you sell too late, you could lose even more money.

Trying to time the market is often a fool's game, but that doesn't mean you should ignore what's going on or delay investment decisions arbitrarily. Stay informed about the industry and the businesses you're invested in and keep an eye on investor sentiment. Base your investment decisions, and your timing, on the best information currently available.

Ignoring Business Fundamentals

Investors who are overly eager about investing in cannabis often overlook that it's a business like any other business — the goal is to be profitable. Before investing in a business, evaluate its current financial status and its potential for growing its revenue and profits. Here are a few fundamentals to check:

>> Revenue growth

>> Earnings (net profit)

>> Debt-to-equity ratio

>> Price-to-earnings ratio

>> Competitiveness (relative strength in the industry)

>> Management

See Chapter 7 for more about evaluating a company's fundamentals.

Expecting All Marijuana Stocks to Be Winners

The marijuana industry is highly competitive, and in this environment winners and losers are continuously emerging. When the industry is hot, you may think that you can't possibly go wrong by investing in a cannabis business — any cannabis business — but that's a common misconception. You're better off assuming that every marijuana stock will be a loser and then examining the company's fundamentals to give them a chance to prove you wrong.

Buying a Stock Just Because It's Cheap

Irish poet and playwright Oscar Wilde defined a cynic as someone who "knows the price of everything and the value of nothing." While he was referring to people who pinch pennies at the expense of benefits, the same can be true of investors who focus too much on share price and overlook a company's profit potential. Just because a stock is less than a dollar or less than five dollars or ten dollars or whatever you consider "cheap" doesn't mean it's a good deal. Likewise, just because a stock's price is high doesn't mean it's overpriced.

WARNING

Low-priced stocks are often attractive to con artists who run pump-and-dump schemes, because they can buy lots of shares for a relatively low initial investment, artificially inflate the price by hyping it on the web and through social media, and then dump their shares to earn a tidy profit. Before investing in any penny stocks, do your homework.

Index

A

Access to an Expert tool (Cannabis Stock Trades), 91
account executive. *See* brokers
Acreage Holdings, 242
actions, choosing, 182–183
activism, 50–51
adult-use cannabis, 24, 25, 48
advertising firms, 35–36
advisors. *See* brokers
AdvisorShares Pure Cannabis ETF (YOLO), 85
AdvisorShares Vice ETF (ACT), 86
Amendment 64 (Colorado), 47
American Growth Fund Series II E (MUTF: AMREX), 86
AMEX, 78
Amplify Seymour Cannabis ETF (CNBS), 86
analyst coverage, following, 119–120
Ancient Strains, 101
ancillary businesses
    about, 13, 24, 31–32
    advertising firms, 35–36
    banking, 32–33
    biotech companies, 36–37
    blockchain, 34
    breweries, 32
    cash management, 32–33
    delivery services, 34–35
    grow equipment manufacturers/suppliers, 35
    investing in, 81–82
    marketing firms, 35–36
    payroll, 32–33
    pharmaceutical companies, 36–37
    professional employer organizations (PEOs), 36
    public relations firms, 35–36
    real estate, 37
    security equipment suppliers, 38
    security services, 38
    software companies, 38
ancillary investing, 11
angel investing, 15, 76
Aphria Inc. (APHA), 198, 214, 219, 241
application fees, 257
apps
    for finding investment opportunities, 17
    online investment, 90–96
Argentina, 222
ascending triangle pattern, 141
assets under management, 156
attitudes
    differences in, 48
    evolution of, 48–49
Aurora Cannabis Inc. (NYSE: ACB), 83, 84–85, 198, 214, 218, 241
Australia, 223
Azer, Viven, 119

B

background check, 17
bad news, considerations for, 269–270
Baker (blog), 97
balance sheets, 111
Bank Secrecy Act (BSA, 1970), 42
banking services, 32–33, 65
bankruptcy protections, 42
bar charts, 136–137
Barchart, 94, 169
Barr, William, 63
BDSA, 97
bearish trend, 132
Belichick, Bill, 52–53
bid-ask spread, 178–179
biotech companies, 36–37
blockchain, 34

blogs, 97–99
Bollinger, John, 145
Bollinger Bands, 145–146
bond ratings, 252
book value, 19
boom-to-bust cycle, 259
bought deal financing, 62
brands, 23
Brazil, 224
breweries, 32
BrokerCheck, 157
brokers
  checking credentials for, 157–158
  choosing, 149–159
  compared with going it alone, 154–155
  defined, 21
  evaluating, 155–159
  finding, 155
  for finding investment opportunities, 17
  full-service compared with discount, 150–154
  getting investment leads from, 102
  online, 158–159
  role of, 150
budroom, 49
bullish trend, 131
burn rate, 111
business
  evaluating strategies for, 112–114
  fundamentals of, 270
  starting your own, 12–13, 82
business failure, as a risk, 67
business land occupation taxes, 55
Business Resources (Marijuana Business Daily), 97
business types
  about, 23–24, 26
  adult-use, 24, 25
  advertising firms, 35–36
  ancillary businesses, 31–38
  banking, 32–33
  biotech companies, 36–37
  blockchain, 34
  breweries, 32

  cash management services, 32–33
  cultivation, 27
  delivery services, 34–35
  device makers, 31
  dispensaries, 30–31
  grow equipment manufacturers/suppliers, 35
  manufacturing, 28–30
  marketing firms, 35–36
  medical-use, 24–25
  payroll, 32–33
  pharmaceutical companies, 36–37
  processed product brand, 30
  professional employer organizations, 36
  public relations firms, 35–36
  real estate, 37
  retailers, 30–31
  security equipment suppliers, 38
  security services, 38
  software companies, 38
  vertical integration, 27
Buy action, 182
buying. *See also* trading
  call options, 252–253
  exchange traded notes (ETNs), 86
  exchange-traded funds (ETFs), 84–86
  insider, 116–117
  on margin, 191–192
  mutual funds, 86–87
  over-the-counter (OTC) stocks, 84
  shares of Canadian cannabis companies, 87
  stocks, 14, 83–87
  too late/early, 270

C

call options
  buying, 252–253
  covered, 253
Cambria Cannabis ETF (TOKE), 85
Canada
  buying and selling shares of companies in, 87
  investing in, 213–219

leading companies in, 217–219

legalization of cannabis in, 216

U.S. market compared with, 214–217

Canada.ca (website), 215

Canadian Marijuana Index, 162

Canadian Securities Administrators (CSA), 78

Canadian Securities Exchange (CSE), 65, 87, 108–109, 166

candlestick charts, 137, 138

Canna Newswire, 97

cannabis
  adult-use, 24, 25, 48
  investing in, 81–82

Cannabis Act (2018), 216

Cannabis Business Executive newsletters, 97

Cannabis Capital Inc., 101

Cannabis ETF (THCS), 85

Cannabis Industry Journal, 97

Cannabis Product News, 97

Cannabis Stock Trades (website), 16, 91, 105

Cannabis Trade Federation, 51

Cannabis Weekly, 97

Cannabis-Related Legitimate Businesses (CRLBs), 33

Canopy Growth Corporation (NYSE: CGC), 83, 84–85, 213, 217–218, 241

capital
  how companies raise, 74–76
  requirements for, 257

Carey, Christopher, 119

Casa Verde Capital, 101

cash balance, checking for companies, 111

cash flow, 264

cash management services, 32–33

caveat emptor, 166

Central Registration Depository number, 59

Central Registration Depository (CRD) number, 157

change, drivers of, 47–48

Charles Schwab, 150, 159

charts
  about, 130
  identifying patterns in, 138–143

Cheat Sheet (website), 4

Chile, 224–225

choosing
  brokers, 149–159
  exit strategy, 183
  financial advisors, 149–159
  investments, 261–266

Chronos Group Inc. (CRON), 198

clientele, evaluating of cultivators, 123

Clinton, Bill, 52

Cole, James M., 41

Cole Memorandum, 41, 63

Collins, Avery, 53

Colombia, 225

Colorado Leads, 51

column charts, 136–137

commissions, broker, 156

commoditization, risks of potential, 62–63

Company News Releases (Marijuana Business Daily), 97

competitive position, evaluating for companies, 115–116

complexity, extraction and, 29

compliance costs, 53–54, 257

con artists, 58–60

concentrates, 28

conference calls, 119–120

Controlled Substances Act (1970), 41, 51

convergence, 144–145

convertible securities, 118–119

corrupt law enforcement, 10

cost per gram
  checking, 122
  comparing, 123
  defined, 18

costs
  comparing for brokers, 156
  of doing business, 53–56
  extraction and, 29

covered call options, 253

credentials, checking for brokers, 157–158

Cresco Labs, 242

Cronos Group Inc. (NASDAQ: CRON), 83, 213, 218

cultivation
about, 12
as a business type, 27
evaluating business in, 121–123

cultivation tax, 55

cultural landscape. *See also* political landscape; regulatory landscape
about, 39–40, 46–47
activism, 50–51
factors affecting, 47–49
misconceptions of cannabis, 49–50
perception of, 52–53

cup and handle pattern, 140

Curaleaf, 242

customer acquisition and retention, checking for companies, 111

CV EM, 166

Czech Republic, 226

D

Daily Marijuana Observer
Cannabis ETFs databases, 100
over-the-counter (OTC) stocks, 165–167, 167–168

danger, extraction and, 29

data, 130

Data Charts (Marijuana Business Daily), 96

Day timeframe, 187–188

DCM, 101

debt
as an option for raising capital, 20
financing, 75
managing, 266

debt ratios, 110

Decriminalized category, 44

delivery services, 34–35

demand, unpredictability of, 260

Dentons US Cannabis Newsletter, 98

descending triangle pattern, 141

device makers, as a business type, 31

'digging up dirt,' 120

dilution, 61–62, 260

discount brokers, 150–154

dispensaries
about, 23
as a business type, 30–31

dispensary owner, 13

divergence, 145

diversification, 20, 241–242, 267–268

dollar-cost averaging, 20

domestic investing, 79–81

double bottom pattern, 140–141

double top pattern, 140–141

Doventi, 101

downtrend, 132

downward momentum, 207

drivers of change, 47–48

Drug Enforcement Agency (DEA), 36, 51

due diligence, 77, 104, 239–240, 268–269

Dun & Bradstreet, 109, 120

Dusaniwsky, Ihor, 199

E

Ecuador, 226–227

Electronic Data Gathering, Analysis, and Retrieval (EDGAR), 110, 116

Entourage Effect Capital, 101

Epidiolex, 61

equity
as an option for raising capital, 20
financing, 75

ETF Country Exposure Tool (ETFdb.com), 93

ETF Performance Visualizer (ETFdb.com), 93

ETF Screener (ETFdb.com), 93

ETF Stock Exposure Tool (ETFdb.com), 93

ETFdb.com
Marijuana ETF List, 100
website, 84–85, 93

ETFMG Alternative Harvest ETF (MJ), 85, 198

E*TRADE, 83, 87, 100, 150, 159

European Union Good Manufacturing Practices (EU GMP), 241

evaluating
  brokers, 155–159
  company business strategy, 112–114
  company's financial health, 109–111
  competitive position of companies, 115–116
  cultivation businesses, 121–123
  length of trends, 134
  management team, 106–109
  startups, 111–112
exchange, searching stocks by, 163, 164
exchange traded notes (ETNs), buying and selling, 86
exchange-traded funds (ETFs)
  about, 15
  buying and selling, 84–86
  finding opportunities in, 100–101
  monitoring, 243–244
  screening, 170–171
  websites for finding investment opportunities, 17
exercise price, 117
exit strategy, 183
expenses, checking for companies, 110
experience
  of grow master, 121
  for team, 262
expiry date, 117
extraction, 28–29

F

fear of missing out (FOMO), 203
Federal income tax, 54
Federal Insurance Contributions Act (FICA) taxes, 54
Federal regulation, 40–43, 63, 256, 269
Federal Reserve Economic Data (FRED), 93–94
fees
  application, 257
  broker, 156
FeeX, 93
Fidelity, 83, 100, 159, 170
Fill or Kill (FOK) timeframe, 22, 188
filters, for screening, 173–175

financial advisors. *See* brokers
Financial Crimes Enforcement Network (FinCEN), 42
financial health, evaluating for companies, 109–111
Financial Highlights (Yahoo! Finance), 175
Financial Industry Regulatory Authority (FINRA), 151
financial services, risks associated with, 65
finding
  brokers, 155
  investment opportunities, 16–17
FINVIZ, 92
flag pattern, 142
flat fee, 156
Food and Drug Administration (FDA), 36
foreign securities, online brokers and, 158
Form 5, 117
Form 144, 117
4Front Ventures, 242
420 Investor, 105
full-service brokers, 150–154
Fully Illegal category, 44
Fully Legal category, 44
fund managers, 100
fundamental analysis
  about, 103–104
  assessing management team, 106–109
  basics of, 104–106
  combined with technical analysis, 129–130
  company business strategy, 112–114
  company competitive position, 115–116
  company financial health, 109–111
  compared with technical analysis, 126–131
  conference calls, 119–120
  convertible securities, 118–119
  'digging up dirt,' 120
  evaluating cultivation businesses, 121–123
  evaluating startups, 111–112
  following analyst coverage, 119–120
  insider buying/selling, 116–117
  licenses, 111–112
  warrants, 117–118

G

gains, maximizing, 237–246

Ganjapreneur newsletter, 98

gap pattern, 142–143

Gardner, Cory, 63

Germany, 227

global investing, 79–81, 221–235, 264–265

global regulation, 46

Global X Cannabis ETF (POTX), 85

goals, 113

Golden Leaf, 242

Goldman Sachs, 151

Good-till-canceled (GTC) timeframe, 22, 188

Gordon, Josh, 52

Grassroots, 242

Grays, 166

Grays Peak Capital, 101

Greece, 227–228

greed, avoiding, 246

Green Growth Investments, 101

Green Thumb Industries, 242

GreenScreens blog, 98

Greenspan, Alan, 1

grow equipment manufacturers/suppliers, 35

grow master, 18, 121–122

growers, 23

growth investing, 19

GW Pharmaceuticals PLC ADR (NASDAQ: GWPH), 83

H

Harvest Health & Recreation Inc., 242

head and shoulders pattern, 139

Head-to-Head ETF Comparison Tool (ETFdb. com), 93

Hemp Industry Daily, 98

herd mentality, 203

High Times magazine, 98

historical sales data, 60

Horizons Marijuana Life Science Index ETF (HMMI), 198

horizontal trend, 132

Hypur Ventures, 101

I

iAnthus, 242

icons, explained, 3

identifying chart patterns, 138–143

Illan, Ivan
Success as a Financial Advisor For Dummies, 157

illegal operations, 258

immediate or cancel, 22

Immediate or cancel (IOC) timeframe, 188

income investing, 19

income statements, 110

industry
competition in, 271
fragmentation of, 258
keeping up with the, 238–239
reputation in, 266
screening by, 172–173

industry bubbles, 211

industry magazines, 97–99

industry news
for finding investment opportunities, 17
resources for, 96–99

Indxx MicroSectors Cannabis 2X Leveraged ETN (MJO), 86

Indxx MicroSectors Cannabis ETN (MJJ), 85

information ratio, 100–101

initial public offering (IPO), 74

innovative companies, investing in, 244

insider buying/selling, 116–117

institutional investors, 76

Interactive Brokers, 159

interpreting technical indicators, 143–146

investing
in adult-use marijuana, 25
in ancillary businesses, 81–82
in Canadian cannabis companies, 213–219
in cannabis, 81–82
in cannabis businesses, 20–22
in cannabis real estate, 13–14
choosing investments, 261–266

cons of, 9–10
defined, 22
domestically, 79–81
finding opportunities for, 16–17
finding opportunities in, 89–102
globally, 79–81, 221–235
goals for, 68–69
in innovative companies, 244
in large markets, 241
in medical marijuana, 24–25
momentum (*See* momentum investing)
in multi-state operators (MSOs), 242–243
options for, 12–16, 73–88
in overvalued companies, 60–61
in people, 239
planning a strategy, 19–20
private options for, 74–79
pros of, 8–9
public options for, 74–79
reasons not to invest, 255–260
researching opportunities, 17–18
rewards of, 57, 67–69
risks of, 57–67
types of, 11
as a venture capitalist, 88
in what you know, 19
Investing in Weed Stocks app, 17
investment fraud, 59
Investor Intelligence Business Resources (Marijuana Business Daily), 96
Investor Intelligence Virtual Briefings (Marijuana Business Daily), 96
InvestorsHub, 105
Ireland, 228
Israel, 228–229
Italy, 229

J

Jaffray, Piper, 119
Jamaica, 230

K

kitchen operations, 29

L

lagging indicators, 143
LaMarch Capital, LLC, 102
Lavery, Michael, 119
law enforcement, corrupt, 10
laws. *See* regulatory landscape
lawsuits, checking for, 120
leading indicators, 143
Leafly, 98, 107, 115, 244
Lerer Hippeau, 102
leverage, 192
LexisNexis, 120
licensing, 43, 53–54, 111–112, 121, 257
limit, 21
limit orders, 184–185
line charts, 136
liquidity, 76, 178
listed securities, 83
Lizada Capital, LLC, 102
local regulation, 45–46, 64
losses, cutting your, 250
low-priced stocks, 271

M

management team, 106–109, 262
manufacturer of infused products (MIP), 12, 28
manufacturers, 23
manufacturing, as a business type, 28–30
margin, buying on, 191–192
margin call, 192
marginal outcomes, 193
Marihuana Medical Access Regulations Act (MMAR, 2001), 216
Marihuana Tax Act (1937), 40–41
Marijuana Business Daily (website), 17, 96
Marijuana Handbook app, 17, 95

Marijuana Moment, 98

Marijuana Retail Report, 98

Marijuana Stock Universe

  about, 162–165

  over-the-counter (OTC) stocks, 165–167

Marijuana Stocks (website), 16, 94

The Marijuana Index (website), 16, 94

market capitalization, 163, 172

market manipulation, 59–60

Market on close (MOC) timeframe, 189

Market on open (MOO) timeframe, 189

market orders, 184

market share, increasing, 265

Market Watch app, 95–96

marketing firms, 35–36

markets

  defined, 21

  growing, 265

  investing in large, 241

MarketWatch Virtual Stock Exchange, 209

maximizing gains, 237–246

McDonald's, 13

McGovern Capital, LLC, 102

media coverage, as a driver of change, 48

Medical and Decriminalized category, 44

medical cannabis, 24–25, 48

Medical Only category, 44

MedMen, 65, 242

Member-Only Newsletter tool (Cannabis Stock Trades), 91

Merida Capital Partners, 102

mezzanine investing, 16, 76

minimizing risks, 237–246

misconceptions, debunking, 49–50

mistakes, to avoid, 267–271

MJ sector, searching stocks by, 164, 165

MJBizCon, 97

Model Portfolio tool (Cannabis Stock Trades), 91

momentum investing

  about, 19, 203–204

  downward momentum, 207

  risks in, 209–212

smart money, 208–209

  upward momentum, 204–206

monetary impact, as a driver of change, 47

Money Flow Index (MFI), 144, 264

money laundering, 65

monitoring

  exchange-traded funds (ETFs), 243–244

  trends, 131–136

Montreal Exchange, 87

Morgan Stanley, 151

Morningstar, 16, 92

moving average convergence divergence (MACD), 144–145

moving averages, 144

multi-state operators (MSOs), investing in, 242–243

municipal sales tax, 55

mutual fund fees, 156

mutual funds, 15, 86–87

N

NASDAQ, 78, 83, 87, 166

negative profit margin, 263

NEO Exchange, 87

The Netherlands, 230–231

New Cannabis Ventures, 98

New Frontier Data analyst reports, 99

New York Stock Exchange (NYSE), 78, 83, 87, 166

New Zealand, 231–232

News by Topic (Marijuana Business Daily), 96

newsletters, 97–99

Next Green Wave, 105

non-dilutive offering, 74

North American Marijuana Index, 94

Norway, 232

NSD, 166

O

objectives, 113

objectives and key results (OKRs), 114

on close, 22

on open, 22

one percent rule exit strategy, 183

online brokers, 158–159

online information, 268

online resources

  for finding investment opportunities, 16

  investment tools/apps, 90–96

online searches, 17

orders

  placing to buy/sell shares, 179–181

  types of, 183–187, 245

Organigram Holdings Inc. (OGI), 198

OTC Pink (ORCPK), 165

OTCQX, 166

oversupply, 258–259

over-the-counter (OTC) stocks

  about, 78–79

  buying and selling, 84

  Daily Marijuana Observer, 165–167, 167–168

  Marijuana Stock Universe, 165–167

  online brokers and, 158

overvalued companies, investing in, 60–61

P

packaging, 30

Panther Consulting, LLC, 102

patience, 250

patterns, technical analysis and, 127

payroll services, 32–33

peaks, 133

pennant pattern, 142

penny stocks, 84

people, investing in, 239

performance-based fees, 156

Peru, 232–233

pharmaceutical companies, 36–37

planning investment strategies, 19–20

plant-touching investing, 11, 81–82

point-and-figure charts, 137–138

Poland, 233

policies, 113

political landscape. *See also* cultural landscape; regulatory landscape

  about, 39–40, 46–47

  factors affecting, 47–49

portfolio review, 250

Portugal, 233

positive cash flow, 264

preferred stock, 16

price

  screening by, 172

  searching stocks by, 163, 164

  supply and demand and, 127

  in technical analysis, 131

  technical analysis and, 127

price/book value (P/B) ratio, 175

price/earnings to growth (P/E/G) ratio, 174

price-to-earnings (P/E) ratio, 111, 211, 263–264

price-to-sales ratio (PSR), 174

private companies, investing in, 76–78

private equity (PE)

  about, 16

  finding funds/firms, 101–102

  screening funds, 170–171

private investment groups, 17

private investments, 15–16

private markets, 240

private placement memorandum (PPM), 77–78

Privateer, 102

pro forma projections, 110

processed product brand, 12, 30

professional employer organizations (PEOs), 36

profit

  consistent growth in, 263

  earning, 257

  when a market drops, 249–253

profit and loss (P&L) statements, 110

profit margin, checking for companies, 111

public companies, 78–79

public relations firms, 35–36

publicly traded companies, 14

pump-and-dump scams, 210

Q

quality, comparing for brokers, 156–157

R

real estate, 13–14, 37

region, screening by, 172

registered representative. *See* brokers

registering, to buy on margin, 192

regulatory costs, 53–54

regulatory landscape. *See also* cultural landscape; political landscape

  about, 39–40

  changes in, 259

  costs of doing business, 53–56

  failing to account for, 269

  federal, 40–43

  global, 46

  impact of laws on industry, 40–46

  local, 45–46

  state, 44–45

Relative Strength Index (RSI), 143–144

Remember icon, 3

reputation

  of grow master, 121

  in industry, 266

researching. *See* fundamental analysis

resistance, in technical analysis, 135–136

restricted stock, 117

retailers

  about, 13

  as a business type, 30–31

return on investment (ROI), checking for companies, 111

revenue

  checking for companies, 110

  steady growth in, 262–263

reverse head and shoulders pattern, 139–140

reverse merger, 79

reverse takeover (RTO), 79

rewards, of investing, 57, 67–69

risk tolerance, assessing, 69

risks

  of investing, 57–67

  minimizing, 237–246

  in momentum investing, 209–212

Roosevelt, Franklin D., 40–41

S

scams, 256–257

Schedule 1 substance, 51

Schedule 2 substance, 51

Schedule 3 substance, 51

Schedule 4 substance, 51

Schedule 5 substance, 51

The Scotts Company, 11

screening tools

  about, 161–162, 170, 176

  Barchart, 169

  categories for, 172–176

  Daily Marijuana Observer, 170–171

  Daily Marijuana Observer's OTC database, 165–168

  exchange-traded funds (ETFs), 170–171

  filters for, 173–175

  investment funds, 170–171

  Marijuana Stock Universe, 162–167

  private equity (PE) funds, 170–171

  Trade Ideas, 168–169

  venture capitalist (VC) funds, 170–171

  Yahoo! Finance Stock Screener, 169

Scutify app, 17, 95

secondary offerings, 74

sectors

  rotating, 252

  screening by, 172–173

Secure and Fair Enforcement (SAFE) Banking Act (2019), 33

securities, convertible, 118–119

Securities and Exchange Commission (SEC), 59, 78, 108, 116, 120

security costs, 55–56

security equipment suppliers, 38

security services, 38

Sell action, 182

Sell All Shares action, 183

selling. *See also* trading

  cannabis stocks, 83–87

  exchange traded notes (ETNs), 86

  exchange-traded funds (ETFs), 84–86

  insider, 116–117

  mutual funds, 86–87

  over-the-counter (OTC)stocks, 84

  shares of Canadian cannabis companies, 87

  stocks, 14

  too late/early, 270

service, comparing for brokers, 156–157

Sessions, Jeff, 41, 63

share price, 178

Share Statistics (Yahoo! Finance), 173–174

Shelton, Jenn, 53

Shevin, Eric, 107

short squeeze, 209–210

shorting stocks, 195–199, 251

sideways trend, 132

simple moving average (SMA), 205–206, 211

Skytree Capital Partners, 102

smart money, 208–209

software companies, 38

speculating, 22. *See also* momentum investing

Sperber, Avery, 53

standard deviation, 211

Standard & Poor's (S&P), 90

starting your own business, 82

startups, evaluating, 111–112

state regulation, 44–45, 64

state taxes, 55

The State of Legal Cannabis Markets report, 104–105, 216, 241

stereotypes, 52

stigma, reduction in, as a driver of change, 48

Stock Analysis tool (Cannabis Stock Trades), 91

stock bubbles, 211

Stock Market Game, 209

stock warrants, 117–118

stocks

  buying and selling, 14, 83–87

  competition with, 271

  low-priced, 271

  preferred, 16

  shorting, 195–199, 251

  trading on private markets, 240

  value, 251

stop limit, 21, 186

stop loss, 21, 185–186

stop orders, 185–186

Strengthening the Tenth Amendment Through Entrusting States (STATES) Act, 43

strike price, 117

Success as a Financial Advisor For Dummies (Illan), 157

supply and demand

  defined, 178

  imbalances in, 65–67

  technical analysis and, 127

support, in technical analysis, 135–136

support and resistance exit strategy, 183

Switzerland, 233–234

symmetrical triangle pattern, 141

systematic/organized nature, of grow master, 122

T

tactics, 113

taxes, 54–55, 257

TD Ameritrade, 150, 159, 170

technical analysis

  about, 125–126

  combined with fundamental analysis, 129–130

  compared with fundamental analysis, 126–131

  interpreting technical indicators, 143–146

  monitoring trends, 131–136

  pros and cons of, 128–129

  referencing technical charts, 136–143

technical charts, referencing, 136–143

technical indicators, interpreting, 143–146

10K report, 110

TerraTech, 242

Thailand, 234

Tilray, 84–85, 241

time, in technical analysis, 131

time exit strategy, 183

timeframes, specifying, 187–189

Tip icon, 3

tools, online investment, 90–96

Toronto Stock Exchange (TSX), 83, 87, 166

Trade Alerts tool (Cannabis Stock Trades), 91

Trade Ideas, 168–169

trading

  about, 177–178

  advanced techniques for, 191–199

  bid-ask spread, 178–179

  choosing actions, 182–183

  choosing an exit strategy, 183

  order types, 183–187, 245

  placing orders to buy/sell, 179–181

  specifying timeframes, 187–189

  stocks on private markets, 240

trailing stop, 21

trailing stop orders, 186–187

transaction cost, 178–179

trendline, 132, 134–135

trends

  monitoring, 131–136

  technical analysis and, 127

Tress Capital, LLC, 102

triangle patterns, 141

triple bottom pattern, 141

triple top pattern, 141

troughs, 133

Trudeau, Justin, 216

Trulieve, 242

Trump, Donald, 63

TSX, 78

TSX Venture Exchange (TSXV), 166

Tuatara Capital, L.P., 102

Tusk Ventures, 102

U

undervalued companies, 19

United Kingdom, 234–235

uptick rule, 197

uptrend, 131

upward momentum, 204–206

Uruguay, 81

U.S. Marijuana Index, 162

U.S. market, compared with Canadian market, 214–217

U.S. Securities and Exchange Commission (SEC), 59, 78, 108, 116, 120

V

Valuation Measures (Yahoo! Finance), 174–175

valuation risks, 61

value investing, 19

value stocks, 251

vaping, 26, 31

venture capital funds/firms, 101–102

venture capital investing, 15, 76

venture capitalist (VC)

  investing as a, 88

  screening funds, 170–171

The Venture Market (OTCQB), 166

vertical integration, 27, 66

vertically integrated company, 11

vigilance, 250

volatility, 178

volume

  searching stocks by, 163

  in technical analysis, 131

W

Wall Street Journal, 90

Warning icon, 3

warrants, 117–118

websites

  Ancient Strains, 101

  Aphria Inc. (APHA), 219

  Aurora Cannabis Inc. (NYSE: ACB), 218

  Baker (blog), 97

  Barchart, 94, 169

  BDSA, 97

  BrokerCheck, 157

  Canada.ca, 215

  Canada's cannabis industry, 215

Canadian Securities Exchange (CSE), 108–109

Canna Newswire, 97

Cannabis Business Executive newsletters, 97

cannabis Capital Inc., 101

Cannabis Industry Journal, 97

Cannabis Product News, 97

Cannabis Stock Trades, 16, 91

Cannabis Stock Trades (website), 105

Cannabis Weekly, 97

Canopy Growth Corporation (NYSE: CGC), 217

Casa Verde Capital, 101

Charles Schwab, 159

Cheat Sheet, 4

Cronos Group Inc. (NASDAQ: CRON), 218

Daily Marijuana Observer over-the-counter (OTC) stocks database, 167

Daily Marijuana Observer's Cannabis ETFs databases, 100

DCM, 101

Dentons US Cannabis Newsletter, 98

Doventi, 101

Dun & Bradstreet, 109, 120

Electronic Data Gathering, Analysis, and Retrieval (EDGAR), 110

Entourage Effect Capital, 101

ETFdb.com, 84–85, 93

ETFdb.com's Marijuana ETF List, 100

E*TRADE, 159

FeeX, 93

Fidelity, 159

FINVIZ, 92

420 Investor, 105

Ganjapreneur newsletter, 98

Grays Peak Capital, 101

Green Growth Investments, 101

GreenScreens blog, 98

Hemp Industry Daily, 98

High Times magazine, 98

Hypur Ventures, 101

Interactive Brokers, 159

InvestorsHub, 105

LaMarch Capital, LLC, 102

Leafly, 107, 115, 244

Leafly's cannabis news, 98

Lerer Hippeau, 102

LexisNexis, 120

Lizada Capital, LLC, 102

Marijuana Business Daily, 17, 96

Marijuana Handbook app, 95

Marijuana Index, 94

Marijuana Moment, 98

Marijuana Retail Report, 98

Marijuana Stock Universe, 162

Marijuana Stocks, 16, 94

The Marijuana Index, 16

Market Watch app, 96

MarketWatch Virtual Stock Exchange, 209

McGovern Capital, LLC, 102

Merida Capital Partners, 102

MJBizCon, 97

Morningstar, 16, 92

New Cannabis Ventures, 98

New Frontier Data analyst reports, 99

Next Green Wave, 105

North American Marijuana Index, 94

Panther Consulting, LLC, 102

Privateer, 102

Scutify app, 95

Securities and Exchange Commission (SEC), 120

Shevin, Eric, 107

Skytree Capital Partners, 102

The State of Legal Cannabis Markets report, 104–105

Stock Market Game, 209

TD Ameritrade, 159

Trade Ideas, 168

Tress Capital, LLC, 102

Tuatara Capital, L.P., 102

Tusk Ventures, 102

U.S. Securities and Exchange Commission (SEC), 59

WeedMaps, 107, 115

Winklevoss Capital Management, LLC, 102

Yahoo! Finance, 16, 91, 105, 172

Yahoo! Finance app, 95

Yahoo! Finance Stock Screener, 169

wedge pattern, 142

WeedMaps, 107, 115

width, in technical analysis, 131

Wilde, Oscar, 271

Winklevoss Capital Management, LLC, 102

word of mouth, for finding investment
opportunities, 16

Y

Yahoo! Finance, 16, 91, 105, 172

Yahoo! Finance app, 95

Yahoo! Finance Stock Screener, 169

Z

Zambia, 235

About the Author

Steve Gormley is a renowned expert in the legal marijuana sector, with nearly 30 years experience developing, branding, marketing, launching, managing, and operating businesses in the U.S. and international markets. He is widely considered a pioneer in the cannabis industry, with nearly a decade of professional experience in the sector. His analysis is featured prominently in outlets including Forbes, The Wall Street Journal, CBS News, U.S. News and World Report, Chicago Tribune, and MarketWatch, and he is a regular fixture on the speaking circuit.

Steve currently serves as CEO and director for Radiko Holdings (CES: RDKO), a publicly traded Canadian cannabis and CBD company, domiciled in Calgary with operations in California and Nevada. Radiko Holdings is a vertically integrated company that owns and operates cultivation capabilities to provide quality, best-of-breed products that naturally complement today's consumer lifestyles and generate higher profits for its CBD and brand portfolio.

Steve also serves as COO of Silverback Investments, Inc., a management services company providing business solutions to licensed, lawfully operating medical marijuana cultivation and distribution businesses. Silverback is focused on the Michigan market. Steve served in C-level roles in a U.S.-based, publicly traded cannabis company and ran a private equity venture focused on rolling up lawfully operating dispensaries in the Los Angeles market. He operated a hydroponics retail gardening supply enterprise in Los Angeles, as well as licensed cultivation facilities in California. He has worked in cannabis retail, cultivation, manufacturing, distribution, lobbying, and finance.

Dedication

To my four brilliant and beautiful children — Zachary, Amanda, Elizabeth, and Anna Renee. You are the sum total of all that is good in me and are the inspiration behind all my achievements. I am the luckiest dad in the world.

Author's Acknowledgments

Special thanks to all the cannabis industry pioneers, activists, and advocates who came before me in their drive for common-sense marijuana laws and transformational business opportunities, and to all those who have fought for safe and legal access to medical cannabis products. This book, and my continued work in the industry, would not be possible without the efforts of these unsung heroes.

Thanks to Mark Scott, one of the best CFOs in cannabis, for his tireless and ongoing efforts to legitimize the marijuana business. Thanks also to Ariane Young and Scott Reeves, two of the best securities attorneys specializing in the cannabis industry. Ariane and Scott are pioneers in the field, and I am proud to count them as esteemed colleagues and friends. Thanks to Bob Yosaitis, a skilled and successful entrepreneur who has brought his considerable talents and his success in other industries to the cannabis industry. Also, thanks to Graham Saunders of Canaccord Genuity, whose expertise, support, and guidance have served me well in my career in cannabis. I also want to thank and acknowledge Dave Gorcyca, my partner in the Michigan cannabis industry. Dave is a brilliant legal mind and an ethical entrepreneur whom I am proud to call my friend. I would also like to thank Renee Gagnon and Erica Sharf, two women whom I consider to be pioneers in the cannabis industry. Renee and Erica inspire me and are blazing a trail for women in the business. Last, but certainly not least, I would like to thank Jeff Malinovitz, founder of Nameless Genetics. Jeff is a cannabis industry pioneer. His friendship and professional partnership have helped shape my career in cannabis.

Every book is a team project, and this book is no exception. Thanks to Wiley acquisitions editor Tracy Boggier for kick-starting this project and choosing me to write this book, to wordsmith Joe Kraynak for assisting in its composition, to development editor Chrissy Guthrie for her editorial and organizational expertise and her infinite patience, and to copy editor Marylouise Wiack for her keen eye. Special thanks to Paul Mladjenovic, author of *Stock Investing For Dummies,* for his valuable contributions and for stepping in at the last minute to serve as tech editor.

Publisher's Acknowledgments

Senior Acquisitions Editor: Tracy Boggier

Managing Editor: Kristie Rees

Editorial Project Manager and Development Editor: Christina N. Guthrie

Copy Editor: Marylouise Wiack

Technical Editor: Paul Mladjenovic

Production Editor: Siddique Shaik

Cover Photos: © panida wijitpanya/Getty Images

Take dummies with you everywhere you go!

Whether you are excited about e-books, want more from the web, must have your mobile apps, or are swept up in social media, dummies makes everything easier.

Find us online!

Dummies is the global leader in the reference category and one of the most trusted and highly regarded brands in the world. No longer just focused on books, customers now have access to the dummies content they need in the format they want. Together we'll craft a solution that engages your customers, stands out from the competition, and helps you meet your goals.

Advertising & Sponsorships

Connect with an engaged audience on a powerful multimedia site, and position your message alongside expert how-to content. Dummies.com is a one-stop shop for free, online information and know-how curated by a team of experts.

- Targeted ads
- Video
- Email Marketing
- Microsites
- Sweepstakes sponsorship

20 MILLION PAGE VIEWS EVERY SINGLE MONTH

15 MILLION UNIQUE VISITORS PER MONTH

43% OF ALL VISITORS ACCESS THE SITE VIA THEIR MOBILE DEVICES

700,000 NEWSLETTER SUBSCRIPTIONS TO THE INBOXES OF

300,000 UNIQUE INDIVIDUALS EVERY WEEK

Custom Publishing

Reach a global audience in any language by creating a solution that will differentiate you from competitors, amplify your message, and encourage customers to make a buying decision.

- Apps
- Books
- eBooks
- Video
- Audio
- Webinars

Brand Licensing & Content

Leverage the strength of the world's most popular reference brand to reach new audiences and channels of distribution.

For more information, visit **dummies.com/biz**

PERSONAL ENRICHMENT

9781119187790
USA $26.00
CAN $31.99
UK £19.99

9781119179030
USA $21.99
CAN $25.99
UK £16.99

9781119293354
USA $24.99
CAN $29.99
UK £17.99

9781119293347
USA $22.99
CAN $27.99
UK £16.99

9781119310068
USA $22.99
CAN $27.99
UK £16.99

9781119235606
USA $24.99
CAN $29.99
UK £17.99

9781119251163
USA $24.99
CAN $29.99
UK £17.99

9781119235491
USA $26.99
CAN $31.99
UK £19.99

9781119279952
USA $24.99
CAN $29.99
UK £17.99

9781119283133
USA $24.99
CAN $29.99
UK £17.99

9781119287117
USA $24.99
CAN $29.99
UK £16.99

9781119130246
USA $22.99
CAN $27.99
UK £16.99

PROFESSIONAL DEVELOPMENT

9781119311041
USA $24.99
CAN $29.99
UK £17.99

9781119255796
USA $39.99
CAN $47.99
UK £27.99

9781119293439
USA $26.99
CAN $31.99
UK £19.99

9781119281467
USA $26.99
CAN $31.99
UK £19.99

9781119280651
USA $29.99
CAN $35.99
UK £21.99

9781119251132
USA $24.99
CAN $29.99
UK £17.99

9781119310563
USA $34.00
CAN $41.99
UK £24.99

9781119181705
USA $29.99
CAN $35.99
UK £21.99

9781119263593
USA $26.99
CAN $31.99
UK £19.99

9781119257769
USA $29.99
CAN $35.99
UK £21.99

9781119293477
USA $26.99
CAN $31.99
UK £19.99

9781119265313
USA $24.99
CAN $29.99
UK £17.99

9781119239314
USA $29.99
CAN $35.99
UK £21.99

9781119293323
USA $29.99
CAN $35.99
UK £21.99

dummies.com

dummies
A Wiley Brand